Rebecca Harding Davis

Twayne's United States Authors Series

Nancy Walker, Editor
Vanderbilt University

TUSAS 623

Rebecca Harding Davis, about 30 years old. From the collection of Mrs. Hope Davis Kehrig. Reprinted by permission of Henry Holt and Company, Inc.

Rebecca Harding Davis

Jane Atteridge Rose

Georgia College

Twayne Publishers ■ New York

Maxwell Macmillan Canada ■ Toronto

Maxwell Macmillan International ■ New York Oxford Singapore Sydney

Rebecca Harding Davis
Jane Atteridge Rose

Twayne Publishers
Macmillan Publishing Company
866 Third Avenue
New York, New York 10022

Maxwell Macmillan Canada, Inc.
1200 Eglinton Avenue East
Suite 200
Don Mills, Ontario M3C 3N1

Library of Congress Cataloging-in-Publication Data

Rose, Jane Atteridge.
Rebecca Harding Davis / Jane Atteridge Rose
p. cm. – (Twayne's United States authors series; TUSAS 623)
Includes bibliographical references and index.
ISBN 0-8057-3958-0
1. Davis, Rebecca Harding, 1831-1910 – Criticism and interpretation. I. Title. II. Series.
PS1517.Z5R67. 1993
813 .4 – dc20 93-16153
CIP
AC

The paper used in this publication meets the minimum requirements of American National Standard for Information Sciences – Permanence of Paper for Printed Library Materials, ANSI Z39.48-1984.

10 9 8 7 6 5 4 3 2 1

Printed in the United States of America.

For Jennifer and Matthew

with love

Contents

Preface

Rebecca Harding Davis (1831-1910) holds an important place in American literary history. Her significance as a pioneering realist whose story "Life in the Iron-Mills" (1861) anticipated the work of Emile Zola by six years is undisputed. That story is the first to have recognized the industrial workplace, ghettoized poverty, and an immigrant subculture as the matter of America. Readers of Davis's fiction recognize that she was also an innovator in her development of factory operatives ("Life in the Iron-Mills" and *Margret Howth*) as well as slaves and illiterate freed blacks ("John Lamar" and *Waiting for the Verdict*) as protagonists. She was one of the first to deal with the experience of the Civil War nonpolemically ("Lamar," "David Gaunt," and "Paul Blecker"). Throughout much of her career, Davis was in the vanguard of writers who pursued fiction as exposé. After the war, she exposed racism in America's northern cities (*Waiting*). And later in the century, her fiction treated such topics as the political corruption of the Whiskey Ring (*John Andross*), inhumane insanity laws ("Put Out of the Way"), and the injustice of legal restrictions on women (*A Law unto Herself*). She also led the way in developing psychologically complex female characters, from *Margret Howth* to *Frances Waldeaux*.

Yet Davis, whose career spanned 50 years, remains unfamiliar to many students of American literature. Like numerous nineteenth-century writers, she wrote for periodical publication. Between 1861 and 1909 she published at least 292 stories and serials in more than 25 different journals – primarily in the more prestigious ones, such as the *Atlantic*, *Harper's*, and *Scribner's*, but also in popular magazines of lesser quality, like the nation's largest circulator, *Peterson's*. She also published another 124 juvenile pieces in children's magazines like *Riverside* and *St. Nicholas*. In addition to being a writer of magazine fiction, she was an essayist for many of those same journals. Furthermore, from 1869 through 1908 she was associated consecutively with the *New York Tribune*, the *New York*

Independent, and the *Saturday Evening Post* as a contributing editor. Finally, 12 of her serialized pieces were published as books.[1]

To encapsulate a career so large in scope is, of course, impossible, but certain generalizations can be helpful in introducing Davis to readers. The usual description of Davis as an early realist, while basically correct, is vague and somewhat inaccurate. Davis's early writing more closely exemplifies naturalism's kinship to romanticism. Most of her fiction, however, can best be described as critical realism – nonobjective, with the intent to inform and reform. In the middle of her career, Davis wrote a great many local-color sketches of character and place. Her late writing, with its satiric tone and psychological focus, reflects the development of realism toward the end of the century. From first to last, though, Davis melds two perspectives: a satirist's cynical view of the present and a meliorist's optimistic vision of the future.

If Davis's long career also reveals certain choices that seem to have compromised her potential, these too are instructive. They show what it was like to be a female writer in the nineteenth century. As a young woman beginning her career, Davis was influenced by her publisher to lighten her somber vision and by her husband, a crusading journalist, to become more didactic. While these men did not change her direction entirely, they do seem to have altered it slightly, as did several decisions of her own. As a new wife trying to help her struggling husband financially, she chose quantity over quality in her work. Her desire for sure and lucrative publication led her to write increasingly for high-paying popular journals. Later, as a busy mother of three, she chose to write less demanding children's fiction and journalistic essays. But Davis never stopped writing, and as a mature woman with fewer demands on her time, she returned to more ambitious forms. She was a female writer who managed successfully to have a family and a career in an age when doing so was almost unheard of. A writer of talent and vision, she created numerous texts of lasting interest.

The most distinctive feature of Rebecca Harding Davis's writing is its juxtaposition of antithetical values: vocation and family, egoism and self-denial, faith and cynicism, the material and the spiritual. Her plots negotiate between the opposites that compose America: North-South, East-West, agriculture-industry, black-white, male-female, owners-workers, educated-illiterate. This mediation was conscious, but Rebecca Harding Davis also reveals a less deliberate tension in her writing. A middle-class, Protestant, white woman reared within the context of nineteenth-century ideology, Davis naturally accepted many received values – as a daughter, wife, and mother. Often these values seem to conflict with her chosen authorial stance. As a writer, for instance, she tried to disassociate herself from popular sentimentality to produce serious, honest fiction; as a woman, however, she had no desire to disavow her female perspective. This perspective is always detectable in the resolution of her fiction. The result of Davis's constant mediation is a body of work that is highly idiosyncratic, complex, and paradoxical.

It is not surprising that Davis's inclination to see both sides of every situation and her ambivalence about her own place in society sometimes blurs her images, diffusing their impact. Equally understandable, though regrettable, is the little scholarly attention that Davis, whose work fits no neat critical category, has attracted over the years. Thanks to Tillie Olsen's recovery of "Life in the Iron-Mills" for the Feminist Press in 1972, Davis has received increased attention. But as yet, relatively few of her texts have been reprinted or discussed. Other than this Twayne volume on Davis, Sharon M. Harris's *Rebecca Harding Davis and Literary Realism* (University of Pennsylvania Press, 1991) offers the only comprehensive analysis of Davis's entire canon. Interest in Davis is growing, however; as Davis is studied and taught, more and more students of American literature are recognizing her as an important writer who helped shape the development of American literary realism and whose texts are valuable artifacts of nineteenth-century culture.[2]

Although the body of Davis scholarship is not large, my research has been aided by five previous studies of her, each making a significant contribution. Two are unpublished dissertations. Helen Woodward Shaeffer's "Rebecca Harding Davis: Pioneer Realist" (University of Pennsylvania, 1947) represents the earliest full-length scholarly attention given Davis. Providing the first effort at a complete bibliography of Davis's work, Shaeffer's study is invaluable also for its interviews with surviving friends and family. William Frazer Grayburn's "The Major Fiction of Rebecca Harding Davis" (Pennsylvania State University, 1965) has proven very helpful because of its extensive use of Davis's correspondence, much of which is illegible in manuscript. Grayburn's study provides many letters in their entirety and dates previously undated pieces through internal evidence. His study also documents Davis's late writing for the *Saturday Evening Post*.

The other three studies are more accessible. Gerald Langford devotes the first four chapters of his *The Richard Harding Davis Years* (Holt, 1961) to biographical information about Rebecca, his mother. In addition to Rebecca Harding Davis's correspondence, Langford's study benefits from private family papers that are now lost. Tillie Olsen's biographical interpretation of "Life in the Iron-Mills" in the Feminist Press collection *Life in the Iron Mills and Other Stories* remains noteworthy as an insightful reading that breathed new literary life into a text that had laid dormant for a century. Most recently, Sharon M. Harris's enlightening and authoritative critical reassessment of Davis's writing demonstrates Davis's relevance to the American literary tradition. Harris's exhaustive primary research also contributes new information on Davis's life.

Davis, whose sense of privacy was extreme and whose humility was sincere, destroyed most of her personal correspondence. Most of her letters that have survived in various collections are professionally related. Fortunately, we do have the letters from her 40-year correspondence with Annie Fields, the wife of Davis's editor at the *Atlantic*. Regrettably, a family history written by the elderly Rebecca Harding Davis for her descendants and the only two photographs of her, which were privately owned by Davis's granddaughter, now seem to be lost. Perhaps the most important source for biographical information, however, is Davis's published reminiscence, *Bits of Gossip* (1904).

I wish to acknowledge those institutions that made Davis's papers available to me: The Richard Harding Davis Collection (#6109), Clifton Waller Barrett Library, Manuscripts Division, Special Collections Department, University of Virginia Library, and The Huntington Library, San Marino, California. I would also like to thank the following universities for access to unpublished dissertations on Davis: the University of Pennsylvania (Shaeffer, 1947) and Pennsylvania State University (Grayburn, 1965). And, for use of materials no longer extant, I wish to recognize *The Richard Harding Davis Years* by Gerald Langford (Copyright 1961, 1981, Gerald Langford).

I appreciate the support I have received from Faculty Research and Development funds at Georgia College to cover certain research expenses. I would also like to thank the Georgia College librarians and the Interlibrary Loan staff at the University of Georgia.

Several individuals have assisted my study in ways perhaps unknown to them. To Professor Rosemary F. Franklin, my mentor, I will always be grateful; she showed me the way. I also thank previous scholars of Davis, William F. Grayburn and Gerald Langford, for their encouragement during the early stages of my research. I am particularly indebted to Tillie Olsen for her inspiring words and her example. Finally, I thank Nancy Walker, TUSAS editor, for her prompt and astute guidance in the final stages of publication.

Friends and family have fortified me in untold ways throughout this project. My dear friend Donna Maddock-Cowart has seen me through this venture from its beginning, contributing her wisdom and enthusiasm. David Muschell, my friend and colleague, has helped me with his good advice and the courage to give it. Finally, I wish to thank my family. My children, Jennifer and Matthew, have spent many a summer patiently being ignored while I wrote. I am indebted most of all to Rick Rose, my helpmate for 23 years, who has supported and encouraged me not just in the writing of this book but in everything, always. Thank you, all, for caring.

Chronology

1830 Rachel Leets of Locust Hill, Washington, Pennsylvania, elopes with English immigrant Richard Harding; they move to Big Spring, Alabama.

1831 Rebecca Blaine Harding, the first of five children, is born June 24 at Bradford House, the home of her mother's sister, Rebecca Blaine, in Washington. Shortly after, mother and baby return to Big Spring.

c. 1836 The Harding family moves to newly chartered Wheeling, then Virginia, where Richard becomes a substantial businessman and city official.

1844 September, previously tutored by her mother, Rebecca enters Washington Female Seminary.

1848 June, Rebecca graduates as valedictorian; she then returns home to Wheeling.

1860 December, Rebecca sends "Life in the Iron-Mills" to the *Atlantic Monthly*.

1861 January, she receives letter of acceptance, with $50 payment and the offer of a $100 for a second contribution. April, South Carolina secedes from the Union, and "Life in the Iron-Mills" is published in *Atlantic*. May, *Atlantic* editor James T. Fields rejects first "gloomy" version of "A Story of To-day" (*Margret Howth*). August, northwest portion of Virginia secedes from the Confederacy, becoming New [soon-to-be West] Virginia. October, revised, "A Story of To-day" begins run as serial in *Atlantic*. L. Clarke Davis, an admirer of her writing, begins correspondence with Rebecca Harding.

1862 *Margret Howth: A Story of To-day*, a realistic novel, is published by Ticknor and Fields of Boston. Spring, L. Clarke Davis comes to Wheeling to meet her; their courtship begins. July, Rebecca makes her long-postponed visit to the Fields home in Boston and also the Hawthornes in Concord; she then spends a week with Clarke Davis in Philadelphia, where they become engaged.

1863 On 5 March Rebecca Harding and Clarke Davis marry in Wheeling and move to his sister's home in Philadelphia. Summer, Rebecca's pregnancy and depression begin.

1864 On 20 March Rebecca's father dies. On 18 April Rebecca and Clarke's first child is born and named after her father, Richard Harding Davis. Summer, the Davises spend their first annual family vacation at Point Pleasant, New Jersey. Fall, the family of three move into the first home of their own. Rebecca's depression ceases.

1866 On 24 January the Davises' second child is born and named after Clarke's brother, Charles Belmont Davis. Davis begins publishing in *Galaxy*, a new monthly, under her own name.

1868 *Dallas Galbraith*, a novel, is published by Lippincott of Philadelphia. *Waiting for the Verdict*, a realistic novel about the Civil War, is published by Sheldon of New York.

1869 Davis begins 20-year affiliation with the *New York Tribune* as a regular contributing editor; Clarke becomes managing editor of the *Philadelphia Inquirer*. Harriet Beecher Stowe solicits Davis's work for her new monthly, *Hearth and Home.*

1870 The Davises buy their lifelong home at 230 S. Twenty-first Street.

1871 Davis begins writing for children's presses; she continues to write for them for the rest of her life.

1872 The Davises third child, a daughter named Nora, is born.

1873 *Kitty's Choice, or Berrytown and Other Stories*, a novella and two stories, is published by Lippincott.

1874 *John Andross*, a novel about political corruption, is published by Orange Judd of New York.

1875 Davis begins writing editorials and fiction regularly for the weekly *New York Independent*; her relationship with this paper will continue for the rest of her life.

1876 Centennial Exposition in Philadelphia.

1878 *A Law unto Herself*, a novel about female independence, is published by Lippincott.

1886 *Natasqua*, a satiric novel of manners, is published by Cassell of New York in its Rainbow Series for young readers.

1889 Davis resigns from the *Tribune* in protest over editorial censorship of her articles. She becomes a regular weekly contributor to the *Independent*. Clarke leaves the *Inquirer* to become associate editor of the *Philadelphia Public Ledger*.

1890 August, publication of Richard's story "Gallegher" in *Scribner's Magazine* propels him to fame.

1891 Rebecca, Clarke, and Nora spend summer in England.

1892 *Kent Hampden*, a novel for young people, is published by Scribner's of New York. *Silhouettes of American Life*, a collection of 13 stories, is published by Scribners.

Family vacations move to Marion, Massachusetts.

1893 Clarke is promoted to the editorship of the *Public Ledger*; Charles becomes the American Consul in Florence, Italy.

1895 Rebecca and Nora summer in Europe.

1896 *Doctor Warrick's Daughters*, a novel of manners, is published by Harper of New York.

1898 *Frances Waldeaux*, a novel of manners, is published by Harper.

1899 On 4 May Richard marries Cecil Clark. Fall, first mention of Nora's suffering from a recurring nervous illness.

1902 Davis becomes a regular contributor to the *Saturday Evening Post* and continues as one for several years.

1904 *Bits of Gossip*, a memoir, is published by Houghton Mifflin of Boston. On 14 December Clarke Davis dies at home of heart disease.

1906 Nora and Rebecca travel to Italy for Nora's health.

1910 While visiting Richard at his estate in Mt. Kisco, New York, Davis suffers a stroke. She dies there, at 79, on 29 September 1910.

Chapter One

Beginnings (1831-1860)

Family Background

Much of Rebecca Harding Davis's work reflects what she once described as "a perverse inclination to the other side of the question, especially if there was little to be said for it."[1] This tendency to admit legitimacy on both sides of any question was a natural result of her personal background. As the eldest child of Rachel Leet Wilson and Richard Harding, she was herself a product of cultural mediation. Her mother was a genteel young woman, whose family estate, Locust Hill, had been established in Washington, Pennsylvania, during colonial times.[2] According to family legend, Rachel's grandfather, "Panther Jim" Wilson, had fought at Valley Forge and her grandmother had danced with Lafayette.[3] Rebecca's father, on the other hand, was a brash young Englishman whose parents had colonized in Ireland. He had immigrated to America to make his fortune. Although the couple had fallen in love when Rachel was a girl of 13 and Richard, newly arrived, was 25, they did not marry until August 1830, nine years after they met. Then the two eloped because Rachel's father was opposed to a "foreigner" who had "gone into business" in far-off Alabama (Langford, 4).

Rebecca Blaine Harding was born at Bradford House, the Washington home of her mother's older sister, for whom she was named, on 24 June 1831. As soon as mother and baby were able, they returned home to Big Spring, Alabama, which was soon to be renamed Huntsville. Rebecca's first five years were spent in this hamlet in the deep South – composed of a general store that traded pelts with Indians, a forge, and a tavern kept by one Ody Peay, in whose "dirty, dark chamber," it was said, "no decent traveler had ever been known to stay overnight" (*Bits*, 65).

Having been just a young child when her family lived in Alabama, Davis did not remember much from those years. But her account in

Bits of Gossip shows that the experience entered family lore and the consciousness of all its members, chiefly through anecdotes retold by her mother. Rachel Harding's penchant for noting iconographic images and incidents was her greatest influence on Davis's narrative style. Davis remembers, for example, her mother's description of "the mixed magnificence and squalor of the life on the plantations among which we lived; the great one-storied wooden houses built on piles; the pits of mud below them in which pigs wallowed." For the entire Harding family, it seems, their "sojourn in the far South was remembered as an uneasy dream," a dream "of roses through which crawled rattlesnakes," of "the extravagant slovenliness of both nature and man" (*Bits*, 68-69).

Home

In 1837 the Hardings moved to the recently chartered steel-manufacturing town of Wheeling, at that time still a part of Virginia. Unlike sleepy Big Spring, Wheeling, situated on both the Ohio River and the National Road, was a bustling thoroughfare of western migration. Although as she matured the town would impress Davis with its satanic mills, it seems to have provided her with a stable childhood. The Wheeling of her youth was a place where, "if you were born into a good family and were 'converted,' you were considered safe for this world and the next." It was a protected world where "both men and women were then busy with farming or other manual labor," and "among gentlefolk it was considered vulgar to talk of money at all" (*Bits*, 2-3).

Even in quiet Wheeling, however, stock speculation, that first germ of what Davis would later describe in an essay as the nineteenth-century "Disease of Money-Getting," was present. The Harding children were taken regularly by their mother to "pay their respects" to two of its victims: the aging Colonel Richard and Mistress Stuart. These two, once the town's models of genteel splendor, were now, as impoverished toll-gate keepers on the turnpike, models of genteel honor. The Colonel, who had sold everything to pay his debts after losing all in a bad investment, was offered as an exemplar by Rebecca's mother: " 'You *must* understand,' she said, the tears in her eyes, 'The Colonel is penniless and homeless. But he has kept his honor!' " (*Bits*, 18).

Even as she enjoyed the town's agrarian stability, Rebecca Harding was exposed to the reality of flux and difference as she watched the European immigrants trundling through town in their Conestoga wagons. She and her friends, she remembered, "used to look after the children peeping out at us with bitter envy; for, naturally, as we never left home, the world outside of our encircling hills was a vast secret to us" (*Bits,* 4-5). As a young girl, she was confronted with another memorable instance of cultural difference when her family received three Indian chiefs in full state dress: "their faces painted in scarlet streaks; they wore crowns of eagle feathers and robes embroidered with beads and quills." The chiefs, on their way to Washington, D.C., had stopped to speak to Mr. Harding. Mrs. Harding, seeing an educational opportunity, arranged for her children to have tea with the Indians (*Bits,* 10).

At a very early age, Rebecca was exposed to people on the fringes of society. One, a little old woman named Cathy Warren, whom everyone called "Knocky-luft," had come from County Cork with her son, Jim, years before the Hardings arrived in Wheeling. When the two got to the shores of the Ohio, Jim left his mother to proceed West, promising to return with a fortune. As years went by, Knocky-luft lived from hand to mouth, increasingly within her own fantasies. She never doubted her son's return; and generations, including Rebecca's, grew up learning to indulge the old woman's proud delusions. Rebecca was there to witness the wonderful day when a "stout, oldish man," saying he was James Warren, arrived in town, and told her father "that he had grown rich in the West and had come to take his mother home" (*Bits,* 24). Rebecca was never to know why he had not come before, nor was she ever to get over the tragedy she witnessed upon his delinquent arrival. The intensity of the old woman's joy was apparently too great for her age; she collapsed at a reunion celebration and died soon after. The rest of her life, Davis was haunted by the image of the delinquent son holding his dying mother as he realized, "I came too late" (*Bits,* 27).

Rebecca Harding's world was a simple one. But, seen with the symbolic vision of her mother, which Rebecca had evidently mastered herself at an early age, it was a world rich with human drama. It provided prototypes for characters and plots that recur, slightly altered, in her fiction. But the real world of human experience was not the only one she inhabited. She also dwelled in a world of literary fiction. The portal to this imaginary world was in the boughs of an old backyard cherry tree, where her nurse, Barbara, constructed for her a private realm away from the younger children. There she would enter the few literary worlds open to a young girl in the 1830s: "only Bunyan, and Miss Edgeworth and Sir Walter."[4]

One book that was to affect the rest of her life was simply bound in two volumes of yellow paper, the first "cheap book" she had ever seen. *Moral Tales* was a collection of anonymous pieces, probably pirated from annual gift books, deemed acceptable for young readers. Although most of the tales "were as thin and cheap as the paper," several impressed this young reader as nothing had before. She sensed immediately a certain power of vision in three stories – "Little Annie's Rambles," "A Rill from the Town Pump," and "Sunday at Home": "There was no talk of enchantment in them. But in these papers the commonplace folk and things which I saw every day took on a sudden mystery and charm, and, for the first time, I found that they, too, belonged to the magic world of knights and pilgrims and fiends" (*Bits,* 30). It was not until 1861, after she had written "Iron-Mills," that she read Nathaniel Hawthorne's *Twice-Told Tales*. Discovering there the stories that had so affected her, she realized the debt she owed Hawthorne for shaping her vision and sensibility.

Until Rebecca Harding was 14, she was educated at home by her mother, whom Davis later described as "the most accurate historian and grammarian I ever have known," one who "had enough knowledge to fit out half a dozen modern college bred women" (Langford, 4). Under the protection of this capable teacher and moral guide, whom the children referred to as "our good Angel," Rebecca's home life seems to have been happy and secure (*Bits,* 9). Although Davis would later describe her father as "a man of stern integrity," he seems to have taken an active part in the loving nurture of his five children (Langford, 4). It was he who shaped for them worlds of fantasy. Like many families, the Davises spent evenings around a glowing coal fire with their father reading romances such as *Ivanhoe*. But Richard Harding did more than read romance; he created it. He invented fantastic personalities such as Monsieur Jean Crapeaud, a magical Tom Thumb-sized French nobleman who sallied forth every day to battle worthy causes, returning each night to his quarters in the dark top shelf of the chimney cabinet. Looking back, Davis remembered a home filled with magic as well as love (*Bits,* 11-13).

Years later, Louisa May Alcott was to record her first impression of Davis in her diary: "Met Miss Rebecca Harding, author of "Margret Howth," which has made a stir and is very good. A handsome, quiet woman, who says she never had any troubles, through she writes of woes. I told her I had had lots of troubles; so I write jolly tales; and we wondered why we each did so."[5] One is struck now, as the two young women were then, with the truth of this statement, particularly in regard to Rebecca's claim. She grew up with comfort and security. The facts of her later married life read the same way. Although there were some instances when she voiced frustration with the restrictions placed on her as a woman, these were rare. Her own life never presented her with much cause for personal complaint.

School

At fourteen, Rebecca left home to go to Washington Female Seminary. Her sparse references to these years suggest that they also were full and happy. She lived in the home of her Aunt Rebecca Blaine in Washington, Pennsylvania, where Washington College was also located. There she was able to enjoy the comfort and support of a family circle – which included her cousin James G. Blaine, who would later be a Presidential candidate – while thriving on the intellectual atmosphere of a college town.

At the seminary she studied Paley's *Evidences of Christianity* and Butler's *Analogy of Religion*, as well as French, English literature, philosophy, geometry, music, and drawing. Davis's education, shaped by the combined perspectives of Joseph Butler's rational defense of miracles and William Paley's defense of design as apparent in natural phenomena, probably helped shape the paradoxes in her thought.[6] In addition to the stimulation of academic courses, she was also able to attend lectures by nationally known figures. One such occasion was an abolition speech by Horace Greeley, about which Davis later wrote. She seems to be describing her own response to Greeley's "high and fine" earnestness when she remembers, "something choked in your throat, and hot tears stood in your eyes" (*Bits,* 182). In Washington, which was just over the Mason-Dixon line, Rebecca Harding was exposed to even more abolitionist opinion than she had been in her hometown of Wheeling, which was just below the line until the Civil War. At her aunt's she met Dr. Francis

Julius LeMoyne, a friend of the family who had been the Abolitionist Party vice-presidential candidate in 1840. From this radical reformer she first heard the extreme attitude that is echoed by a number of her obsessed-zealot characters: "Cut out the cancer, and cut it *now*, though the patient die" (*Bits*, 168).

In June 1848, Rebecca Harding graduated valedictorian of her class at the Washington Female Seminary. It was the year of revolution in Europe and reform in England. It was the summer that American feminists convened in Seneca Falls, New York, to draft their demands for Constitutional recognition of women's rights. The 18-year-old Rebecca Harding, however, did not belong to that world. For her it was not a summer of new beginnings and growth; it was an end and a return.

She went home after completing her three years of formal education. Although she stood out from her peers as a superior student, she was typical in that her scholastic performance and inclination in no way altered the fact that her education, unlike that of her brother Wilson, had ended. Like all the young women of her class, she returned from school to domestic life. And like all the members of her class who were not becoming wives, she returned to the same home in Wheeling where she had grown up. No longer a child, she remained in her parent's house, assisting her mother in the care of the younger children and in the maintenance of the home. In this way, she matured into womanhood, bearing a marked resemblance to the description of her first female protagonist, Margret Howth: "a quiet, dark girl, coarsely dressed in brown."[7]

Adulthood

Very little is known about Davis's life during those next 12 years, which included that dynamic decade of the 1850s. She left no records of social activities or suitors. If one is to accept the view of midcentury middle America that Davis herself presents in her 1904 memoir, one must assume that she found satisfactory outlets for intellectual stimulation. "Before the birth of the New Woman," she tells us, "the country was not an intellectual desert." If a girl "had the capacity or desire for further development in any direction, she easily obtained it" (*Bits*, 101). She could not, however, obtain it directly, as young men could.

Although Wheeling was not on the college lecture circuit as Washington had been, Davis had access to books. She read widely from the library of her father, who, though a prosperous businessman and public official, according to Davis, really had "no energy or business ability." He pursued with much more sincerity his lifelong avocation of reading "Shakespeare or some other English dramatist" (Langford, 6). While her brother Wilson attended Washington College, she used his texts to study those subjects which she had not had in her own curriculum, particularly French and German literature. Although she never makes any reference as to how her own literary pursuits were received at home, they do not appear to have been discouraged. Her writing, like her studying, was probably viewed by her family in much the same recreational light as her father's reading.

Davis seems to have spent much of this period honing her writing skills and discovering her voice. In the late 1850s Davis began writing reviews, poems, stories, and editorials for the *Wheeling Intelligencer*, the largest newspaper in western Virginia. She even filled in briefly as its editor in 1859, and discovered what she described as "a most insane ambition that way."[8] This experience certainly must have increased Davis's confidence even as it sharpened her powers of observation and expression. While journalistic work caused Davis to realize new ambitions, it does not seem to have satisfied her. When the aspiring author burst onto the national literary scene two years later, she was asked by her editor James T. Fields about previous writing. Responding, she dismissed her work for the *Intelligencer* as insignificant "verses and stories, impelled by the necessity or whim of the moment."[9]

Of equal significance to Davis's development as a writer during these years was the education she received on what she would often later refer to as her "vagabond tramps." Rebecca Harding, like many young woman of her day, took long walks – not just for decorous exercise but for decorous experience. Some critics have faulted Davis's realism, as Gordon S. Haight does in reference to "Iron-Mills," pointing out that "Mrs. Davis violates her own ruling of the commonplace. Few mill workers are hunchbacks, and except in a reformer's tract no consumptive could long be an iron puddler."[10] Such criticism, however, misses the greater wonder that a young woman reared within the conventional mores of the midnineteenth century not only had the inclination to know that demimonde but also was able to get close enough to know it. Her walks must have ranged wider than anyone knew – wide enough to expose her to thieves, convicts, prostitutes, drunks, addicts, and suicides.

Davis's silent years of obedient domesticity while reading, watching, listening, and quietly writing continued until the end of 1860. Then, at 29, she apparently decided that she had written something worth publishing. Evidently without consulting anyone, she sent "Life in the Iron-Mills" to the editors of the *Atlantic Monthly* and waited. She waited only one month. In January she received a response from the *Atlantic*. Years later, in a letter to her son Richard on the occasion of his first acceptance, she could still recall how she timorously "carried the letter half a day before opening it, being so sure it was a refusal."[11] She discovered, instead, eager acceptance and a check for $50.

The bold authority with which Davis, a demure young woman, first asserted her voice in fiction is as amazing today as it was in 1861. Fortunately, she has left a valuable glimpse of herself as she took her first bold steps into the public world of authorship. Davis's own analysis of Margret Howth, the female protagonist of her first novel, who is in many ways a projection of Rebecca Harding, provides critical insight into the young author at this time:

> The writing here is curious: concise, square, not flowing, – very legible, however, exactly suited to its purpose. People who profess to read character in chirography would decipher but little from these cramped, quiet lines. Only this, probably: that the woman, whoever she was, had not the usual fancy of her sex for dramatizing her soul in her writing, her dress, her face, – kept it locked up instead, intact; that her words and looks, like her writing, were most likely simple, mere absorbents by which she drew what she needed of the outer world to her, not flaunting helps to fling herself, or the tragedy or comedy that lay within, before careless passers-by. . . . I am sure the woman's hand trembled a little when she took up the pen; but there is no sign of it here; for it was a new, desperate adventure to her, and she was young, with no faith in herself. (*Margret Howth*, 8-9)

Here, Davis raises critical issues of gender and genre. Her heroine is a "trembling" young woman "with no faith in herself," but she has "not the usual fancy of her sex." Her writing – characterized as simple, practical, and nonegotistical – is atypical of popular "woman's" fiction of the period.[12] Appreciation of Davis's unique handling of these issues requires an understanding of the often conflicting ideological and aesthetic values that she mediated. Davis was a woman of her age. The values shaping the nineteenth-century worldview naturally affected her sense of herself as a woman and as a writer. While she criticized numerous aspects of her society, she also maintained many of its traditional values. From "Iron-Mills" to *Frances Waldeaux*, her writing demonstrates an effort to integrate new aesthetic principles with certain received nineteenth-century beliefs. In her narrative posture and in the matter of her fiction, she also repeatedly reveals a desire to reconcile ambivalence toward ideas about womanhood. While all her efforts at synthesis are not equally successful, they are always instructive. Davis's distinctive, original style, resulting from her commitment to see every side and her impulse to heal through reconciliation, is often successful and frequently fascinating.

Cultural Contexts of the Nineteenth Century

Ideology

Understanding the values that shaped Rebecca Harding Davis's world begins with the doctrine of spheres: the belief that men and women possessed gender-determined attributes. The masculine sphere, governed by reason, was the world of ideas, politics, and commerce. The feminine sphere, governed by the heart, was the home and family. Historically, the industrial revolution helped entrench the separation of spheres. Women remaining at home to care for children lost their economic roles. And as the relativity and materialism of the marketplace became the world of men, the perpetuation of morality fell to women.

Associated with the doctrine of gender spheres were idealism, sentimentalism, and evangelicalism. Idealism led fiction writers to use fact as an inductive approach to spiritual mystery and caused women to perceive their role and their sphere symbolically. Like Christ's, their self-sacrifice was redemptive; like heaven, their home was a haven of loving peace. Related to idealism was sentimentalism, with its vision of a benevolent God. The supremacy of love as the definition of the Godhead was a primary force behind the elevation of woman in the nineteenth century; hers was the affective domain of loving. Sentimentalism provided a way to view female self-abnegation as messianic. With its stress on the demonstration of love through self-sacrifice and on the social benefits of altruistic cooperation, sentimentalism was the antithesis of romanticism's defiant egoism.

Idealism and sentimentalism, which confirmed the affinity between Christian and feminine values, also led to an optimistic faith in the eventual success of both. This millennial vision of social reform through spiritual transformation was evident in evangelicalism. Like the other values discussed here, evangelicalism, while it pervaded the culture, was experienced primarily by women. The only way that women writing within the context of these values could combine their multiple vocations as authors, women, and reformers was by writing moral fiction. As realism developed an aesthetic of objectivity, the genre became problematic for female writers who, with identities shaped in the nineteenth century, saw themselves as preachers through fiction. Though narrow, this ideology infused women with a sense of power. It provided the impetus behind both the temperance movement and the suffrage movement. Ironically, while requiring that women accept their preordained place in society, it also provided them with a mandate to reform it. While Davis was often critical of fiction serving these ideologies, we see evidence of their influence in her own writing.

Aesthetics

Although Davis spoke as a proponent of the new realistic literature, evaluation of her work in terms of genre is complicated for many reasons. As a Christian and a woman in the nineteenth century, she assumed certain perspectives that twentieth-century readers find inconsistent with realism. Furthermore, though Davis called herself a realist, it is important to remember that she was a transition writer, in the vanguard of change. Her writing demonstrates important facets of all four nineteenth-century aesthetic movements: sentimentalism, romanticism, naturalism, and realism. While Davis's synthesis is extreme, it is not unusual in midnineteenth-century writers. In 1861 *realism* was a plastic, reactive term, defining opposition to popular romantic fiction with its escapism and heroics and also to popular sentimental fiction with its espousal of institutional norms and formulas. From the start realism celebrated the commonplace, the ordinary, and the immediate. For many devout Chistians like Davis, however, focus on the material world did not disallow idealism, nor did an awareness of environmental determinism prohibit meliorism. Also, although early realists aspired to objectivity and dramatic presentation, they and their readers accepted authorial moralizing in moderation. The strain of realism that Davis initiated has been called critical realism.[13] Critical realists, far from detached, were impelled by the motive to reform. They found realistic principles consistent with their desire to examine social issues, to raise consciousness, to effect change in each individual reader.

Davis's avant-garde realism naturally retains elements of the earlier romanticism and sentimentalism. In fiction written by, for, or about women – particularly in the journals for which Davis wrote – sentimentalism was the dominant aesthetic. Highly conventional, it upheld traditional Christian values. Premised on idealism, its narratives were often allegorical and typological, linking the known material world with the unknown spiritual one. Believing in a benign God and the essential goodness of humanity, most sentimentalists valued nature and the natural. Writers like Davis demonstrate how, by offering a Christian critique of society, sentimentalism was closely aligned with critical realism during its formative stage. Harriet Beecher Stowe's sentimental novel *Uncle Tom's Cabin*, for example, was praised by British novelist George Eliot for its realistic "pictures of religious life among the negroes."[14]

Romanticism diverged from sentimentalism, rejecting certain perspectives but retaining others. Like sentimentalism, romanticism was an idealistic sensibility; symbolism was integral to both. Transcendental romantics, however, influenced by Oriental thought, abandoned conventional theology, reverencing nature and individual creativity as evidence of benign and imminent Divine Unity. Most nineteenth-century readers equated romanticism with the dark passions and brooding heroes of Lord Byron or the chivalric past of Sir Walter Scott. These Davis disavowed. But frequently present in her realism is a tension created by a romantic attraction to individual genius, moral ambiguity, and the unknown.

In her early writing, Davis's sensibility seems more naturalistic than realistic, but her naturalism evidences a romantic vision. Here, once again, semantics confuses the issue. *Naturalism* has been defined in a variety of contradictory ways over the years. Today, naturalism is most often understood as uncompromisingly realistic, focusing on sordid life, and also as scientific – totally materialistic and deterministic. Its first practitioners, such as Davis and Emile Zola, had a different perspective, even though they themselves confused the issue by describing their own writing as realistic and scientific. The most accurate view of Davis's naturalism is provided by later naturalist Frank Norris, who observed of Zola's work that "naturalism is a form of romanticism, not an inner circle of realism."[15] The brutal experiences and squalid conditions of grotesque characters in naturalistic writing are as remote from the ordinary bourgeois lives of average readers as are those of romance. For Norris, the difference lies in milieu, but clearly the difference is also one of tone. While romanticism is essentially escapist, this strain of naturalism, like critical realism, is confrontational.

When read with an understanding of nineteenth-century ideology and aesthetics, Rebecca Harding Davis's writing gains a new, rewarding dimension. Her impulse to mediate difference, to reconcile opposition, to negotiate limitations – both in society and in herself – strongly affected her writing, though not always in a positive way. Passages that seem to show inconsistencies in Davis's realism or compromises of her feminism, however, also reveal her complex imaginative response to the ideas and mores that shaped her world. Davis's writing offers insight into a dynamic period of intellectual history, in which many thinkers and artists found themselves struggling in a whirlpool created by the confluence of many new ideas. Her writing also awakens sympathy for early female writers who frequently found themselves enmeshed in a web of beliefs that restricted even as they sustained.

Chapter Two

Entering the World (1861-1862)

A Published Author

When readers of the *Atlantic Monthly* opened the April 1861 issue, they encountered an exciting new voice asking them, "A cloudy day: do you know what that is in a town of iron-works?" Most of them did not. Reading on, they encountered a scene unfamiliar to most Americans then, an industrially polluted city: "The idiosyncrasy of this town is smoke. It rolls sullenly in slow folds from the great chimneys of the iron-foundries, and settles down in black, slimy pools on the muddy streets."[1]

Like the attack on Fort Sumter, which occurred the same month, "Life in the Iron-Mills" exploded with a force that shook America's Eastern intellectual community to its foundation. Like the Civil War, Davis's story was revolutionary. Her radical experiment in realism confronted readers with their own ignorance and challenged their complacency as she told them, "I want you to hide your disgust, take no heed to your clean clothes, and come right down with me, – here, into the thickest of the fog and mud and foul effluvia" (13). Like her protagonist's own artistic creation, a statue with "not one line of beauty or grace in it: a nude woman's form, muscular, grown coarse with labor, the powerful limbs instinct with some one poignant longing" (32), her uncompromising treatment of unpleasant subjects also defied social expectations about the woman's sphere in writing. The boldness with which this story forces its readers to face reality is startling, but that this daring voice belonged to a young woman at a time when femininity was defined as innocent, passive, decorative, and domestic is even more remarkable.

In 1910, the year Davis died, author Elizabeth Stuart Phelps spoke for many when she recalled the impact that "Iron-Mills" had made on her.[2] Phelps touched on the two issues that have always fascinated its readers: the new aesthetic of realism that it portends and the insight into a female literary imagination that it reveals. Phelps explains its impact on her: "That story was a distinct crisis for one young writer at the point where the intellect and the moral nature meet. It was never possible after reading to ignore. One could never say again that one did not understand" (120). A female writer who was strongly influenced by Davis, Phelps also notes that Davis's writing transcends the gender-specific limitations of the nineteenth century. While Davis does not deny her femininity, neither is she restricted by it. "Her intensity was essentially feminine," says Phelps, "but her grip was like that of a masculine hand" (120).

Unlike realism as it was later codified by William Dean Howells and Henry James, the realism of "Iron-Mills" affirms the symbolism and idealism of romance as well as the Christianity and moral efficacy of sentimental fiction. As an imaginative creation, "Iron-Mills" also reveals the concerns and values of a young female artist in nineteenth-century America. These qualities continue to be the two central issues that stimulate critical discussion of "Iron-Mills."[3] Insight into these concerns also provides a good introduction to Davis's lesser-known writings, which reiterate the same themes.

Both in her own time and in ours, Davis's literary reputation has been based on "Life in the Iron-Mills." Because it is such a dense compression of disturbing images and ideas that make such a great impression on the reader's consciousness, Davis's first story has frequently created the impression of being a much longer piece than it is. Phelps, for instance, begins her essay, "Stories that Stay," with the unnecessary disclaimer that she was not "sure that this could strictly be called a short story. It may have run through several numbers." Apparently, her memory of "Iron-Mills" was of its being much longer than it is. More recently, Tillie Olsen, in her recovery of the text, defends her decision to italicize the title as one would a novel, explaining that she considers "it to be of that weight" ("Iron-Mills," 159). Its complexity and significance warrant close attention.

"Life in the Iron-Mills"

Although "Life in the Iron-Mills" is most often described as realism, it anticipates the naturalism that Norris appreciated in Zola. Davis shares a naturalistic perspective that focuses on the "dregs" of society, as Zola does, and recognizes the power of a hostile industrialized world to crush human potential. She also demonstrates an aesthetic more akin to romance than realism. The concerns of this story are spiritual and its structure is mythic.

The impassioned narrator declares to the reader, "I want you to hear this story" about "the reality of soul starvation" in "a world gone wrong" (13, 23, 30). It is a story of people whose desperate lives lead them to desperate acts, like thievery and suicide. "There is a secret down here, in this nightmare fog, that has lain dumb for centuries," the narrator explains, "I want to make it a real thing to you" (14). The secret is that all human beings, having souls, suffer under degradation and oppression. Crimes, as acts of desperation, prove the failure of society to provide an environment for soul fulfillment.

The focus of this story is split between Hugh Wolfe and his cousin, Deborah, both immigrant laborers. Operatives in "the machinery of system by which the bodies of workmen are governed" (19), they exist insufficiently inured to deprivation and pain in a crowded and filthy slum. Human beings "full of thwarted energy and unused power," they have been reduced by socioeconomic circumstance to lives of desperate survival, like the wolves their name alludes to. The physically deformed Deborah is a cotton-mill picker whose soul is starved for love; the artistically sensitive Hugh is an iron-mill puddler whose soul is starved for freedom.[4] As dual protagonists Hugh and Deborah also carry the two sides of Davis's vision. Destroyed by brutal reality, Hugh enacts her pessimism about the present; healed by loving spirituality, Deborah asserts her optimism about the future.

Aside from Hugh and Deborah, the other main character is the narrator, who frames the story and intercedes among Davis, her characters, and the reader. This character, whose indeterminate sex would most likely be assumed to be masculine, is nevertheless closely aligned with Davis.[5] From the outset this narrator reveals a perspective that mediates realism and romance. Explaining, "I open the window, and looking out, can scarcely see through the rain the grocer's shop opposite, where a crowd of drunken Irishmen are puffing Lynchburg tobacco," he creates a mood of immediacy and a scene that is palpably oppressive: "The idiosyncrasy of this town is smoke. It rolls sullenly in slow folds from the great chimneys of the iron-foundries, and settles down in black, slimy pools on the muddy streets. Smoke on the wharves, smoke on the dingy boats, on the yellow river, – clinging in a coating of greasy soot to the house-front, the two faded poplars, the faces of the passers-by" (11).

Davis's social critique becomes imbued with the symbolic resonance of romance, however, as the narrator describes, "inside, is a little broken figure of an angel pointing upward from the mantel-shelf; but even its wings are covered with smoke, clotted and black." In this passage she combines the impacts of realism and symbolism in the image of "a dirty canary chirp[ing] desolately in a cage" (12). The well-documented fact of caged birds being kept in mines to indicate toxic air by their death is horrific. The image of fragile beauty and potential freedom being sullied and imprisoned by a hostile environment is equally powerful. Drawing from both realism and romance, Davis's critique of industrial America places "Iron-Mills" squarely in the American literary tradition as the narrator concludes that the "dream of green fields and sunshine is a very old dream, – almost worn out." (12)

"Iron-Mills" is structured on three concentric rings, each inhabited by one of the focal characters. The narrative proceeds from the narrator in the outer ring through Deborah Wolfe to Hugh Wolfe, with his creation, the korl woman, at the core. Then it moves back out again to the narrator, who is in possession of the korl woman.

The Narrator

In her framing narrator, Davis demonstrates her debt to Nathaniel Hawthorne, America's greatest romancer, as her character relates "fragments of an old story . . . a story of this old house" (13). By occupying a common space, the narrator links the reader in the present to the Wolfes in the not-so-distant past. The narrator has come to the old house, which had been rented "to half a dozen families" 30 years before. While distancing the story slightly in the past, he emphasizes its relevance to the present. The residents were employed by Kirby & John's mills – "You know the mills? They took the great order for the lower Virginia railroads there last winter" (14) – making railroad iron. The Wolfes occupied two cellar rooms: "Their lives were like those of their class: incessant labor, sleeping in kennel-like rooms, eating rank pork and molasses, drinking." Though they are gone now, the Wolfes' existence was just like that of "their duplicates swarming the streets today" (15). Several times throughout the story the narrator admonishes the reader to receive this story on two levels: "A reality of soul-starvation, of living death, that meets you every day under the besotted faces on the street, – I can paint nothing of this, only give you the outside outlines of a night, a crisis in the life of one man: Whatever muddy depth of soul-history lies beneath you can read according to the eyes God has given you" (23).

Deborah

The story itself opens on Deborah coming home from her shift at the cotton mill at 11 o'clock on a rainy night. In this section, which carries the reader into the demimonde, Davis uses dialect speech as the mill girls converse:

> "Dah's a ball to Miss Potts' to-night. Ye'd best come."
> "Inteet, Deb, if her'll come, hur'll hef fun." (16)

Later in Hugh's section Davis drops dialect, bringing the reader into greater linguistic intimacy with her characters. When Hugh converses with members of the upper class, however, his dialect returns. This strategy creates a tension in the reader, who is emotionally aligned with Hugh and Deb, but linguistically aligned with the outsiders.

"Iron-Mills" ponders the secret of destiny, both in this world and the next. One of the social mysteries considered in this story is privilege in an ostensibly classless society. Deborah is of the lowest caste possible. She is not only an illiterate immigrant laborer; she is an ugly woman. An albino with blue lips and watery eyes, "she was deformed, almost hunchback" (17). Noting "her thwarted woman's form, her colorless life, her waking stupor that smothered pain and hunger," the narrator objectifies her as "not an unfitting figure to crown the scene of hopeless discomfort and veiled crime" (21).

The "unused power" that fills the soul of this unattractive woman is love. Hugh, the object of her affection, cares instead for blue-eyed, lithe-bodied Janey. Though exhausted, Deb demonstrates her selfless love for Hugh, as she does every night, by going back out into the drizzling night to take him some dinner, though "she knew she would receive small word of thanks" (19).

Another mystery is environmental determinism. Deborah first guides the reader into the slum dwelling, which was "low, damp, – the earthen floor covered with a green, slimy moss, – a fetid air smothering the breath." She then leads him into the iron works in which the new Bessemer steel-smelting process keeps the factory working day and night. There Davis paints the horrific new world of the industrial laborer: "the unsleeping engines groan and shriek, the fiery pools of metal boil and surge" (19).

Hugh

At the mill Hugh Wolfe becomes the focus. Since it is rainy, cold, and late when Deborah brings his dinner, Hugh makes her a place to sleep on the warm ashes of burnt iron until his shift ends. As Deborah silently watches Hugh work, the reader's attention shifts to him also. He is a slight man. Though only 19, "he had already lost the strength and instinct vigor of a man, his muscles were thin, his nerves weak." Not unusual in his profession, he is consumptive. Hugh is not just a frail man, though; he is sensitive, quiet, responsive to beauty. Davis depicts him as an effeminate man. He is known as one of the "girl-men": "Molly Wolfe" was his nickname at the mill. His spare moments are spent "chipping and moulding [*sic*] figures, – hideous, fantastic enough, but strangely beautiful" out of a refuse material called korl: "a light, porous substance, of a delicate, waxen, flesh-colored tinge" (24).

Creativity brings Hugh Wolfe little solace. Born into poverty and ignorance, his natural appetites have been frustrated and undermined. "Think," the narrator directs the reader, "that God put into this man's soul a fierce thirst for beauty, – to know it, to create it; to *be* – something, he knows not what, – other than he is" (25). As Tillie Olsen first demonstrated, Hugh Wolfe's frustration offers an illuminating parallel to what Davis must have experienced as a young woman wanting to write.

For Davis, however, the mystery of "the world gone wrong" is not simple. Nor is the answer to be found in ways of thinking that created the problem. To develop and discredit prevalent attitudes toward industrial reform, Davis introduces three men. On the evening of the story, several visitors tour the mill. Among them are Kirby, the owner's son; Dr. May, a local reformer; and Mitchell, a Northern intellectual. Hugh is drawn to them, sensing their genteel world and longing to be part of it. The men are surprised by the figure of "a woman, white, of gigantic proportions, crouching on the ground, her arms flung out in some wild gesture of warning," and become interested in Hugh, its creator (31).

The korl woman, a symbolic expression of Hugh's soul, starving for freedom and self-realization, is the core of this story. Her whole body expresses "some one poignant longing . . . in the tense, rigid muscles, the clutching hands, the wild, eager face, like that of a starving wolf's" (32). Troubled, the visitors interrogate Hugh. His inability to express himself shows Davis's awareness of the role language plays as a tool of power. In his stumbling explanation he also reveals Davis's awareness of alcohol abuse as a self-destructive but understandable attempt to alleviate pain and despair, a social problem that first reached epidemic proportions with the industrial revolution. When Dr. May asks, "But what did you mean by it?" Wolfe's only reply is "She be hungry." In response, he receives an inane lecture about his statue's inappropriate musculature. Finally, he can only stammer, "Not hungry for meat." Here, Kirby, feeling he knows his laborers, jeers, "What then? Whiskey?":

> Wolfe was silent a moment, thinking.
>
> "I dunno," he said, with a bewildered look. "It mebbe. Summat to make her live, I think, – like you. Whiskey ull do it, in a way" (33).

Waiting for the rain to cease, the "pocket," the "heart," and the "head" of the world, as the narrator refers to the three men, debate the social and moral dilemma that Hugh and his creation represent. Each rationalizes his own inaction. Kirby, the owner's son, forswears any responsibility for Hugh, saying, "My duty to my operatives has a narrow limit, – the pay-hour on Saturday night" (35). Dr. Mays prompts Hugh, "God has given you stronger powers than many men," urging him, "make yourself what you will. It is your right." Hugh's simple response, "I know. Will you help me?" silences the doctor, whose sympathy lacks commitment (37). Mitchell, the intellectual, best comprehends Wolfe's creation. "It asks questions of God," he realizes, "and says, 'I have a right to know.' Good God, how hungry it is!" (34). But ultimately he rationalizes his detachment as he lectures May, "Reform is born of need, not pity" (39).

Both Dr. May, the sentimental altruist, and Mitchell, the romantic egoist, profess popular nineteenth-century dogma. Davis's story points out that the Wolfes' tragedy results not just from their own desperate longing but also from their own acceptance of capitalistic ideology. Deborah demonstrates the erroneous lesson communicated by this debate: that money is the only solution and that the downtrodden must lift themselves. Realizing that she can help Hugh, she picks Mitchell's pocket.

When proudly presented with a monetary solution to his agony, Hugh first rejects it, demonstrating that even the most lowly born can be righteous. Davis's purpose, however, is not simply to assert human potential; it is to demonstrate the very real power of circumstance to subvert that potential. On his way to return the money, he too goes through a crisis of temptation. Contemplating the money, he sees himself "as he might be. . . . A consciousness of power stir[s] within him. . . . free to work, to live, to love! Free! His right!" (47).

When Hugh is caught, Davis continues to emphasize the ethic that motivates her naturalism. Seeing clearly the lives of others leads first to understanding and then to sympathy. While the reader understands Deborah and Hugh's thievery, no one in the story does. Found holding the money, Hugh is sentenced to 19 years in prison; Deborah gets 3 as his accomplice. Dr. May, abandoning all sympathy for what he sees as ingratitude, turns his back on Hugh, saying, "Serves him right! After all our kindness that night!" (50). Mitchell visits him in jail, but only to satisfy his curiosity; then he leaves.

A life behind bars in chains is the ultimate constraint for Hugh Wolfe, who reacts to jail like a desperate, caged animal. He realizes that only death will give his soul the freedom he craves. In Hugh's death Davis combines the immediacy of realism with the resonance of symbolism. Alone in his cell, "he bare[s] his arms, looking intently at their corded veins and sinews," and quietly slits his wrists with a sharpened piece of tin. In the next cell Deborah, realizing what Hugh has done and understanding why, commits her final act of selfless love as she shuts "her lips tightly, that she might not scream" (59). As he lies "quite still, his arms outstretched," with only "the black nauseous stream of blood dripping slowly from the pallet to the floor" (61), allusions to Christ's crucifixion imbue the scene.

Deborah

After Hugh's sacrificial death, Deborah's redemption completes the story's mythic structure. Of the people who crowd the jail the next day, one woman, "a homely body, coarsely dressed in gray and white" is different (61). She, not the men with their secure positions in the establishment, offers real help. A recurring figure in Davis's fiction, this Quaker woman embodies the author's vision of social reform arising out of moral reform. Empowered by her own integrity, she defies social norms. She refutes the popular belief that purity requires innocence, the assumption that kept women within the protected limits of the domestic sphere. The Quaker woman enacts the mystery of love and the power of individuals to make a difference. Though a stranger to the Wolfes and their sordid world of poverty, crime, and death, she comforts Deborah. To Deborah, who has hungered for love, she offers the hope of a new life after prison in her community of Friends. Though Hugh has been lost to the system, Deborah can still be saved.

The Quaker community envisioned at the end, affirming the reality of environmental determinism, asserts society's ability to create for itself a positive environment in which the individual spirit can thrive. The last scene, focusing on Deborah, carries the story into the present where "a woman, old, deformed" takes "her humble place" in a "Friends' meeting-house" (63). This scene asserts a reformative plan implicit in much of Davis's fiction, in which society is restructured on feminine principles: sentimental theology, spiritual integrity, and agrarian familial communities.

The Narrator

The closing frame entwines Hugh Wolfe and his female projection of self, the korl woman, with Rebecca Harding Davis and her masculine projection, the narrator. Doing so, it illuminates another important strain in Davis's fiction: her projection of ambivalence toward her own artistic desires in stories of failed artists. As a young woman in the nineteenth century, Davis was torn between her frustrated desire to be a serious writer and her guilt over having this egoistic desire. In many later stories she projects her frustration and guilt into female artist characters. In this first expression, she acts out her ambivalent feelings in male guise. As the narrator concludes his story, the laden images reveal a number of psychological issues, such as insecurity, frustration, guilt, and repressed desire:

> Nothing remains to tell that the poor Welch puddler once lived, but this figure of the mill-woman cut in korl. I have it here in a corner of my library. I keep it hid behind a curtain, – it is such a rough, ungainly thing. Yet there are about

> it touches, grand sweeps of outline, that show a master's hand. Sometimes, – to-night, for instance, the curtain is accidentally drawn back, and I see a bare arm stretched out imploringly in the darkness, and an eager, wolfish face watching mine: a wan, woful [*sic*] face, through which the spirit of the dead korl-cutter looks out, with its thwarted life, its mighty hunger, its unfinished work. (64)

Evident in this passage is Davis's anxiety that compromised artists produce compromised art. Her concern turned out to be prophetic in many ways. In the course of her career, Davis made a number of decisions that were right for her personally as a wife and mother, but that sometimes compromised her fulfilling the promise of this first story.

This first flowering, though, was astonishing by all estimation. Editor James T. Fields's praise of the manuscript was unqualified, as evidenced by his advance offer of $100 for another story, which she declined. His only suggestion was the consideration of a different title, to which she was amenable. The titles that she offered for consideration are illustrative of Davis's mediation of realism and idealism. The alternatives to her bluntly prosaic first choice were a metaphysically pondering "Beyond?" or a symbolic image "The Korl-Woman."[6] The *Atlantic* kept her original title.

New Horizons

The Civil War

In April 1861, the same month of her first publication in the *Atlantic*, South Carolina seceded from the Union. By August, the northwestern portion of Virginia had seceded from the Confederacy to rejoin the Union as New Virginia. The capital of this new state, which was soon renamed West Virginia, was Wheeling. Again accidents of circumstance had placed Rebecca Harding in a position to experience the drama of differing values. New archetypal patterns and personalities presented themselves to her consciousness. Foremost of these was the split family, a reality in West Virginia, where some were in favor of abolition yet also in favor of states' rights, while others accepted slavery but could not accept dissolution of the Union. Among Rebecca's friends and relatives were young men who chose to fight for the South, and others, for the North. She also knew those who chose to be outcast, hiding in the mountains and refusing to fight against their nation or neighbors: "The war was never broached in your home, where opinions differed; but, one morning, the boys were missing" (*Bits,* 117). She hated war for the way it was reductive to the individual and destructive to the community; she also hated the lie that war "uplifts a nation" as it "develops patriotism and courage" (*Bits,* 124). What Davis referred to as the "general wretchedness and the squalid misery of war" is a theme in all her Civil War stories (*Bits,* 116).

Friendships

About the time of her first publication, Davis first read *Twice-Told Tales* and discovered that Hawthorne, when he had been what he called "the obscurest man in letters," was the author of the favorite stories of her childhood. Perhaps buoyed by her own success, she found the courage to write Hawthorne, telling him all about her tree house "and of what he had done for the child who used to hide there" (*Bits,* 31). One assumes that her recent connection with the *Atlantic* made writing this fan letter easier, but from the account in her memoirs there is no hint of realization that as the author of "Iron-Mills" she was someone Hawthorne was eager to meet. She explains his responding letter, in which Hawthorne, the recluse of the early 1860s, asked to come "see the cherry tree and me," by saying that "the little story [of her childhood], coming from the back woods, touched his fancy" (*Bits,* 31). The Civil War broke out, though, and Hawthorne's plans to visit Rebecca while on his trip to Harper's Ferry had to be cancelled. A year later, they did meet when he invited her to stay several days with his family at the The Wayside, their home in Concord. No other event in her life as a writer meant as much to Rebecca Harding Davis. Through the rest of her life, she cherished his farewell – "I am sorry you are going away. It seems as if we had known you always" – as a testimony to their kindred spirits (*Bits,* 64).

Her eventual trip north in the summer of 1862 had been put off for over a year from the time of her first hesitant acceptance of James T. and Annie Fields's repeated invitation. In his desire to encourage this young woman writer from Virginia who wrote like no one in New England or even in America, Fields did the wisest thing he could have done. Shortly after his discouraging rejection of her first version of *Margret Howth* because its excessive "gloom," he had his wife, Annie, the woman behind the man and the magazine during the Fields years, begin a correspondence with her, urging her to continue to write for the *Atlantic.* Rebecca was pleased with Annie Fields's "courteous and womanly" encouragement, and she immediately wrote back, promising to "try to meet [Fields's] wishes of being more cheerful" (UVA, 20 May [1861]).

The friendship between Annie and Rebecca deepened as their correspondence continued and became personal. By October 1861, when the first installment of the revised *Margret Howth* appeared, she had been invited to visit the couple in Boston. At first she declined, "until the war is over," saying, "I cannot tell when I can leave home now" (UVA, 28 September [1861]). But, even after the war seemed less of a deterrent, there were other considerations. Her father became ill, and she, as the eldest daughter, was needed to nurse him. By 14 April 1862, she finally wrote Annie to "expect a very determined looking female" for a summer visit, as she had only a single impediment to overcome: she needed an escort. Nineteenth-century propriety dictated that, as a single woman, she could not travel alone, regardless of the fact that she was a published author in her thirties. Because of this final impediment, she was still unable to set her date after weeks of frustration. "How good it must be," she complained, "to be a man when you want to travel" (UVA, 24 May [1862]).

Margret Howth: A Story of To-day

Rebecca Harding Davis could not have asked for a better champion than James T. Fields, co-owner of Ticknor and Fields publishing house as well as editor of the *Atlantic.* Yet their early correspondence concerning her next piece suggests that, though a proponent of the new realism, he was responsible to some extent for her movement away from the dark vision of "Iron-Mills" toward the conventional happy endings of sentimental fiction. Ironically, his apparent concern for her salability adversely affected her lasting appeal.

In April 1861 Davis responded to Fields's request for another piece, reporting the she had begun a story called "The Deaf and the Dumb."[7] This story, which grew into novel length by the time it was submitted, was the original version of what would become first the serial "A Story of To-day" and then the novel *Margret Howth*.

Fields accepted Davis's revised version with its new title, "A Story of To-day," and published it in six installments, beginning October 1861. Again the difference in tone between her original title and her final one demonstrates Davis's mediation of the material and the symbolic. "The Deaf and the Dumb" does not refer to literal handicaps; the failed senses function as a metaphor for the human experience. The deaf are those whose ears are attuned only to superficiality; the dumb are those who comprehend profundity but lack the power to express it. The new title stresses the immediate and mundane; yet it still alludes to spiritual connection. For Davis, "today" has significance for those who can comprehend its relation to the unknown tomorrow. In the first chapter Davis explains her vision to the reader: "You want something, in fact, to lift you out of this crowded, tobacco-stained commonplace, to kindle and chafe and glow in you. I want you to dig into this commonplace, this vulgar American life, and see what is in it. Sometimes I think it has a new and awful significance that we do not see" (6).

While still retaining some sentimental and romantic elements, "A Story of To-day" demonstrates the new realistic principles more than "Iron-Mills" does. Here, Davis objectively presents mundane and immediate subject matter featuring complicated individuals. The "today" of which she speaks is 2 October through 25 December 1860. The story takes place in an unnamed manufacturing city on the Wabash River in Indiana, at a remove from the heroic glare of Civil War issues. Writing during the first year of conflict, Davis admonishes readers thirsty for fiction that glorifies war as a heroic test of one's "manlier nature." It is an error, she explains, to trivialize that ongoing quest for "the poor daily necessity for bread and butter." She tells them, "I want you to go down into this common, every-day drudgery, and consider if there might not be in it also a great warfare" (6).

While more realistic, "To-day" further amplifies some of the same spiritual and social concerns as "Iron-Mills." Davis's characters inhabit an intimidating industrial environment where "overhead the ceiling look[s] like a heavy maze of iron cylinders and black swinging bars and wheels, all in swift, ponderous motion." Their brains are made dizzy "with the clanging thunder of the engines, the whizzing spindles" (116). Rather than focusing on labor, this story turns its attention to the bourgeois and their desire to ignore "the under-life of America . . . where all men are born free and equal" (152). Like her first, this story is a forerunner of proletarian fiction in its critique of American capitalism. Davis, however, never validates Karl Marx's economic theory of dialectical materialism, just as she never validates scientific determinism.

In a letter to James Fields, Davis presents her theme as "the development in common vulgar life of the Fichtean philosophy and its effect upon a self-made man."[8] For Davis, the barbarisms of American economic, social, and political policy all receive their sanction from the romantic celebration of ego and individual development, which she credited to Fichte. While these theories may seem attractive when espoused abstractly by transcendentalists such as Emerson or Carlyle, they become pernicious when applied by men of more limited vision. Therefore, the "great warfare" of today, which she discusses in her introduction, is the same one celebrated in more heroic times; we all must fight against the "enemy, Self" (7).

Early in the story Mr. Howth, an aristocratic classics scholar who resembles Davis's father, and Dr. Knowles, a radical socialist reformer patterned after Dr. Francis LeMoyne of Washington, Pennsylvania, engage in a debate that aligns this theme with Davis's realism. To Mr. Howth's appeal for uplifting, purifying epic and chivalric romances, Dr. Knowles barks, "Dead days for dead men: The world hears a bugle call to-day more noble than any of your piping troubadours." Listening to them both, Margret, and the author, wonder whether "pain, and martyrdom, and victory lie back in the days of Galahad and Arthur alone?" (31-33). Davis's story of today shows that they do not. It tells of four people "and how they conquered or were worsted in the fight" against "Self" (7). Each has dreams that are stifled by situations out of his or her control. The three realistic characters – Margret Howth, Stephen Holmes, and Dr. Knowles – learn the Christian lessons of humility and love from Lois Yare, the one idealized character.

Margret Howth

Margret Howth, with "no gloss to her skin, no glitter to her eyes," is typical of Davis's females in her lack of conventional beauty. A young bookkeeper working to support her parents, she has had her life's dream of marriage and family shattered by the betrayal of her lover, Stephen Holmes. The story opens as Margret begins her first day at Knowles & Co. Wool Manufacturers in a cramped, dark office on the seventh floor. Margret has taken the job out of a sense of duty to her parents, who became impoverished when her father, blinded by illness, lost his livelihood as a schoolmaster. Although she seems to accept her dull existence stoically, inside she rankles at the prospect of a joyless future and aches for the life she has lost now that Stephen Holmes is betrothed to another. She knows the job will not fulfill her as only being a wife and mother could.

Margret is sympathetic, but not heroic. She has survived a trial of the soul in an act of selfless love by releasing Stephen from his betrothal to her so he can achieve his ambitions. But she is desolate, loathing herself as "unworthy of every woman's right, – to love and be loved" (60). She is also self-centered in her pain. At first consumed with her own "starved and thwarted" life, she closes herself off from others in need – in particular Lois, a handicapped black woman, and the unfortuantes at Dr. Knowles's House of Refuge. Eventually, through Dr. Knowles's appeals and Lois's example, Margret realizes "the blood of these her brothers call[s] against *her* from the ground." Admitting her complicity in the world's "gulf of pain and wrong," she commits her life to helping the less fortunate (71).

Margret's character is not satisfactorily delineated. Davis seems to have muddied Margret's motivations in the revised conclusion. In all likelihood, the realistic portrayal of Margret Howth was the most difficult task Davis had attempted so far as a writer. The character is much like Davis at the time. Although there is no record of a failed romance like Margret's, Davis, at 30, was probably accepting her own spinsterhood. Some biographers have speculated that Davis probably gained her insights into the "underside of America" by doing some sort of charity work like Margret Howth's efforts at the House of Refuge. As Margret is influenced by Dr. Knowles, Davis had been influenced by the radical Dr. Francis LeMoyne, whose views contrasted with the elitist ideas of her scholarly British father.

Dr. Knowles

The deistic physician and philanthropist Dr. Knowles is at once the most realistic and haunting character in the novel. Part Indian, he is gruff and uncouth in appearance, carrying "the blood of a despised race." But he is a true humanitarian; having come "out of the mire," he carries "their pain and hunger with him" (50). Though wise and sympathetic, Dr. Knowles is misguided in two ways. First, he wrongly perceives social work as grander than domestic work, thinking that Margret has "been planned and kept by God for higher uses than daughter or wife or mother" (20). Davis exposes this error repeatedly in fiction and essays throughout her life. Next, even his noble plan has been perverted by ego. Lacking faith, he wants to witness the success of his labor to reform society.

Knowles undergoes his soul's trial when fate destroys his great plan for a communal farm. By selling his factory, he plans to achieve his life-long dream of establishing a socialist commune for the destitute. He also hopes to solicit Margret to help him in his great work. When his mill burns before the sale, his dreams go up in smoke as well. At first, "sore and bitter against God, because He did not know how much His universe needed" the project, Knowles seems to be failing his trial. Gradually, though, Knowles learns humility and the value of little private acts of kindness. He also learns to have faith that good deeds will bear fruit, though perhaps not in one's lifetime. Instead of carrying out his great social experiment, he ministers at his House of Refuge by the railroad tracks.

Besides learning his own lessons of humility, Knowles teaches Margret. Taking her to his House of Refuge, he forces her out of her own petty world: "You sit by the road-side, with help in your hands, and Christ in your heart, and call your life lost, quarrel with your God, because that mass of selfishness [Holmes] has left you, – because you are balked in your puny hope! Look at these women. What is their loss, do you think? Go back, will you, and drone out your life whimpering over your lost dream, and go to Shakespeare for tragedy when you want it? Tragedy! Come here, – let me hear what you call this" (152). Regrettably, in revision Dr. Knowles's role also seems to have become ambiguous. The lessons he learns and the ones he teaches, though integral to the story's theme, are diminished by Stephen Holmes's reformation.

Stephen Holmes

Stephen Holmes, a man blessed with talent and intelligence, demonstrates thematic antithesis. Lois's loyalty to him for his past kindness when he set her up as a huckster, as well as Margret's love for him, suggests he is redeemable. But Davis tells us that by exemplifying the "American motto, Go ahead," Holmes shows that "self-salvation, self-elevation . . . give birth to, and destroy half of our Christianity, half of our philanthropy" (121). In his denigration of love, Holmes aligns the opposition between sentimental Christianity and romantic egoism as a female-male opposition. Told that "God was love," Holmes responds, "Was He? No wonder, then, He was the God of women, and children and unsuccessful men" (138).

The soul of Stephen Holmes is tested when his dreams, too, are destroyed by a fire. A self-made man, he stands at the threshold of realizing his aspirations by marrying wealth and buying a factory. A man of ambition, he sincerely believes that nothing is nobler than developing one's potential. Realizing early that such development needs the assistance of money and power, he has abandoned any idea of a life with Margret, who has neither. Instead, he has become engaged to a wealthy heiress whom he admits he does not love. His plan to buy Dr. Knowles's factory has been made possible by his future father-in-law's willingness to be a partner. When he is on the verge of achieving success, his aspirations are crushed by fire, which destroys the mill and almost kills him.

His change of heart occurs as he is nursed back to health in the hospital. There, in Lois and the female nurses, he discovers a different kind of heroism, one defined by selfless service instead of self-development. Realizing that he has wasted his life on false values, his soul sickens as his body heals. Determined to ask Margret's forgiveness, he goes to her on Christmas Eve. There, as the hope of a new day dawns, the two declare their love for each other. In the end, Stephen Holmes forsakes egoistic romanticism, "the faith of Fichte," to be "led by a woman's hand" (244).

Lois Yare

In contrast to the characters of Margret, Knowles, and Stephen is Lois Yare, who comprehends the joy of living, even in pain and poverty. Born to an alcoholic mother and a criminal father, she is stunted and deformed from rickets. She is also a victim of industrial brutality. References to Lois's "misshapen forehead" allude to a factory accident that has left her brain damaged. Though she left the mill at 16, she is still haunted by memories of the noxious air, the deafening noise, and the unbearable heat.

At the start of the story Lois's father, Joe Yare, has just returned from prison. Lois's happy plans to set up house with her father are soon dashed. Stephen Holmes, who upholds justice above mercy, knows of Joe's having committed another crime, for which he would be sent back to prison. To save himself, Joe Yare sets fire to the mill one night, knowing that Holmes is inside. Lois, seeing the fire, realizes what has happened. Although she has sworn never to enter the mill again, she does so and saves Stephen's life. Later it is discovered that her supreme act of courage will cost her her life; she has inhaled the toxic fumes released from the dye vats in the burning mill.

The novel's nexus, Lois, whose nickname is simply Lo, is an archetypal figure: the redemptive suffering servant. Her life, which reifies the Beatitudes, teaches the three protagonists vital lessons in humility, love, sympathy, and – in the original version of the story – resignation. Her faith that "things allus do come right, some time" and that everyone will "have a chance – somewhere" (67, 71) is unwavering, even in death.

Synthesis

Margret, Stephen, and Dr. Knowles are all bettered by learning from Lois. No single character, however, not even Lois, carries Davis's vision; each is needed to balance the others. Davis has shown enough of the "seething caldron" – where "the blood of uncounted races was fused, but not mingled," where "creeds, philosophies, centuries old, grappled," where "smothered rights and triumphant wrongs warred together" – for the reader to realize that the world needs both Lois's faith and Dr. Knowles's works (89-90). People helping each other can make "things come right" a little faster. The union of Margret and Stephen also demonstrates an important aspect of Davis's vision of social reform. As social institutions, marriage and family replicate God's plan of loving interconnectedness and self-sacrifice. Whether in the story's original tragic ending or its final happy one, marriage as a celebration of loving commitment is the antithesis of egoism.

Revision

James Fields first rejected "The Deaf and the Dumb," apparently dissatisfied with its narrative tone, which he described as an unrelieved "pathetic minor." Davis's response portends the direction she would take during the rest of her career:

> When I began the story, I meant to make it end in full sunshine – to show how even "Lois" was not dumb, how even the meanest of things in life were "voices in the World, and none of them without its signification." Her life and death were to be the only dark thread, But "Stephen Holmes" was drawn from life and in my eagerness to show the effects of a creed like his, I "assembled the gloom" you complain of. I tell you this in order to ask you if you think I could alter the story so as to make it acceptable by returning to my original idea. (Huntington, FI 1167)

This letter records Davis's natural inclination toward realistic plot development through character motivation and her sacrificing that instinctive desire to fulfill audience expectation. The changes that she made to resolve "To-day" "more cheerfully" mar the story's integrity. The problem, however, is not the happy ending or the employment of a conventional device, but that the formula was inconsistent with Davis's vision, which in the early years was definitely the "pathetic minor" of which Fields complains.[9] Regrettably, similarly contrived happy endings compromise many of Davis's later works as well.

At the beginning of chapter 5, the third installment of "To-day," Davis again addresses the reader to discuss her realistic character portrayal. Explaining that she "never saw a full-blooded saint or sinner," she excuses her "half and half" characters:

> How can I help it, if the people in my story seem coarse to you, – if the hero, unlike all other heroes, stopped to count the cost before he fell in love. . . . Of course, if I could, I would have blotted out every meanness before I showed him to you; I would have told you Margret was an impetuous, whole-souled woman, glad to throw her life down for her father, without one bitter thought of the wife and mother she might have been. . . . but what can I do? I must show you men and woman as they are. (104-5)

Many of the story's original readers probably needed this explanation to understand a heroine who is miserable caring for her parents, an egocentric, superficial hero, and an antagonist who expresses the moral attitudes of the author.

Today, readers well used to complex characters have greater trouble accepting the unmotivated actions and inconsistent attitudes that result from Davis's rewriting for a happy ending. Although it is impossible to know exactly what Davis's original intentions were, careful reading of "To-day" in light of her other fiction at this time clearly indicates a different scenario. Evidence in the text suggests that in the earlier version, after surviving the fire, Stephen Holmes commits suicide. A vestige of this plot remains in the revised version, in which he resolves to "end it all" on Christmas Eve (200). Perhaps in the original version he realized that he had lost everything after seeing Margret in her new life at Dr. Knowles's House of Refuge or perhaps she rejected his love as being offered too late. Either scenario would be consistent in character, theme, and time. But the ending love scene, in which all is forgiven and consequences are nullified, is not. Textual evidence also suggests that with Holmes's death, Margret's life too would have been much bleaker. Humbled like Knowles, she would find some, but not complete, solace in her life of service. Most likely, Lois's death scene originally played a vital role in Margret's acceptance of her fate. Though Davis attempts to explain the optimism of the novel's resolution, its inconsistencies indicate a forced alteration of her original conception.

The *Atlantic* accepted the rewritten story, with its happy ending in which the ambitious and egoistic male becomes domesticated and the self-sacrificing female is fulfilled through marriage. The new version disappointed Davis, though; she felt that "it was so much like giving people broken bits of apple-rind to chew" (UVA, 9 August [1861]). In the acceptance letter Fields urged Davis to change the title to "Margret Howth." Davis refused this change at first, explaining, "I don't like 'Margret Howth' at all, because she is the completest failure in the story, besides *not* being the nucleus of it" (UVA, 17 August [1861]). By the time plans for book publication were under way, however, Davis's faith in Fields – as a man of letters, a businessman, and a friend – was absolute; she acquiesced to the title change.

Margret Howth has been cited as the earliest realistic depiction of an American woman as an individual and as ordinary.[10] Perhaps Fields saw this innovation when he insisted on the title. Perhaps he anticipated better sales with the new title, considering the fact that most nineteenth-century novel readers were women. Davis was conscious of neither; she intended to write "A Story of To-day," which began as a story of "The Deaf and the Dumb." The original intent of her first novel becomes more accessible in light of its two early titles.

Travel

In June, since her brother Wilson had to go north on business, Rebecca was finally able to make her long-awaited trip, which in addition to Boston included a visit with family friends General John C. Frémont and his wife, Jessie, in New York and a very important stop in Philadelphia. Her two-week stay in Boston and Concord was one of the significant events of her life. Fifteen months before, she had been unpublished and unknown. Now, however, she was received as the amazing young female author who had appeared in 8 of the last 12 numbers of the *Atlantic* and who had published a novel with Ticknor and Fields. It was a heady experience. Except for the deceased Margaret Fuller, all the significant minds that had shaped her thinking were there, eager to meet her. Of personal importance was the fact that as a guest of the Fieldses, her long-distance friendship with Annie deepened into a real and lasting affection. More important, however, her new experiences tested some of her untried beliefs and matured her into a woman with a greater confidence in her own individuality.

The "Areopagites"

The pleasure of her visit was discolored by only one discovery, but this had a profound effect. She was horrified to learn that the "Areopagites," as she referred to the famed Boston literary coterie, who "thought they were guiding the real world," in fact "stood quite outside of it, and never would see it as it was."[11] She was repelled by Bronson Alcott, whom she met at Hawthorne's home, as "he chanted paeans to the war, the 'armed angel.' " She confronted the group with her experience:

> I had just come up from the border where I had seen the actual war; the filthy spewings of it; the political jobbery in Union and Confederate camps; the malignant personal hatreds wearing patriotic masks, and glutted by burning homes and outraged women; the chances in it, well improved on both sides, for brutish men to grow more brutish, and for honorable gentlemen to degenerate into thieves and sots. War may be an armed angel with a mission, but

> she has the personal habits of the slums. This would-be seer who was talking of it, and the real seer who listened, knew no more of war as it was, than I had done in my cherry-tree when I dreamed of bannered legions of crusaders debouching [*sic*] in the misty fields. (*Bits,* 34)

Still, Alcott, whom she considered a sham, disturbed her less than Emerson, the seer, who idolized the sham, and even Hawthorne, who indulged the sham.

Running through Davis's work for the rest of her life is a strain of bitterness toward the cerebral detachment she was shocked to find in Emerson, whom she had idolized as "the modern Moses who had talked with God" (*Bits,* 42). She continued to praise the prophet, but she was impelled to criticize the man for lack of human sympathy. Although flattered by the interest he paid her during her visit at The Wayside and at the Fields home in Boston, she was left with the impression that for him she had been merely a human specimen for his study. Her impression that Emerson "took from each man his drop of honey, and after that the man counted for no more than any robbed bee" was reinforced when he said to her, "I wish Thoreau had not died before you came. He was an interesting study" (*Bits,* 44-45).

Her scorn for Alcott was not confused by any ambivalence. As far as she was concerned, his popularity in Concord was a testimony to the clouded vision of the place. Noting his family's home as "bleak and bitter cold with poverty," she observed that in "any other town he would have been more respected if he had tried to put his poor carpentering skill to use to support" his family, concluding sardonically that "the homelier virtues were not, apparently, in vogue in Concord" (*Bits,* 38).

Rebecca was terrifically impressed with one young woman her own age, whom she saw as a victim of Alcott's criminal irresponsibility and Concord's error. Louisa May Alcott, his daughter, was "plainly dressed, and had that watchful, defiant air with which the woman whose youth is slipping away is apt to face the world which has offered no place to her" (*Bits,* 38-39). Davis was haunted by the thwarted energy, the unused power that she saw in Alcott. Later, after returning home, she would write to Annie Fields, "Tell me about Miss Alcott, if ever she does any thing, or finds rest – poor girl – how many hungry women with empty hands I know!" (UVA, 22 August 1862). This first meeting of the future author of *Little*

Women during a reception at the Fields home was also recorded by Alcott in her diary. Both women had a deep respect for each other throughout their lives. Years later, when Davis was recording her own first impressions in her memoir, she observed that although she "had known many women and girls who were fighting with poverty and loneliness, wondering why God had sent them in to a life where apparently there was no place for them," she had never met one like Alcott. "Amid her grim surroundings, she had the gracious instincts of a queen," Davis remembered. Alcott remained for Davis the embodiment of heroic, nurturing womanhood: "it was her delight to give, to feed living creatures, to make them happy in body and soul" (*Bits,* 40).

Besides Hawthorne, Rebecca was most pleased with her personal acquaintance of the Fieldses' neighbor, Oliver Wendell Holmes, "the little doctor." Holmes, who possessed that human sympathy Emerson lacked, impressed her with his honest interest in everything. Her descriptions of him also indicate another quality deemed attractive by Davis, whose male protagonists are always markedly feminine: "He had the fervor, the irritability, the tenderness of a woman, and her whimsical fancies, too" (*Bits,* 50). Although she never praised Hawthorne specifically for his femininity, it is a trait well documented by others. Coincidentally, both these men shared with Davis a fascination for graveyards as storehouses of untold stories of ordinary people with which the imagination could play. Holmes took her on a tour of Cambridge's Mount Auburn Cemetery, and Hawthorne introduced her to Concord's Sleepy Hollow. The other trait Davis shared with these men she admired was the ability to look with a satiric eye at the world they were part of while still maintaining a sympathy for their fellow inhabitants.

Love

When Davis left Boston, she spent a short time in Philadelphia, visiting and falling in love with Clarke Davis. Unlike her New England sojourn, this visit was never described by Davis in any account for public or private posterity. What is known is gathered from contingent facts. One assumes that the real reason Rebecca suddenly became "a determined young woman" about taking this trip, which had so often been postponed, actually had more to do with the prospects awaiting her in Philadelphia than with those in Boston. Of this brief visit during which she became engaged to Clarke, she said in a letter to Annie Fields only that she had "a happy week in Philadelphia" (Huntington, FI 1168).

Davis guarded the progress of their entire courtship as an intensely personal concern at the time and throughout her life. Details of their storybook romance have been pieced together by interviews with family members (Shaeffer, 88). Lemuel Clarke Davis was a young apprentice-lawyer in Philadelphia who had literary interests. He was also passionately concerned with abolition and social reform. Like a number of *Atlantic* readers across the country, he sent a letter of admiration to the unknown author of "Iron-Mills" via the journal editor, who forwarded the mail to Davis. Apparently finding the earnest young Clarke Davis admirable also, Davis responded. Discovering the subject of his admiration to be a single woman about his age (actually three years older), Clarke began a friendlier correspondence. After exchanging several letters, Clarke travelled to Wheeling to meet Rebecca personally. By the end of his visit, they had begun their courtship. Following his stay with her in late 1861 or early 1862, Clarke invited Rebecca to visit him Philadelphia.

When she finally did announce her marriage plans to Annie, the joy was strangely mixed with a painful embarrassment, as she explained, "It is'nt [*sic*] easy for me to tell you this I don't know why. I would rather tell other women's stories than my own." In closing, she even urged her friend "not to speak of this to anyone. No one here knows it except ourselves." The letter's final line offers perhaps a hint at the cause of Rebecca's bittersweet anxiety. As one reads that Davis, whose life had so far been one of acknowledged comfort, calm, and success, perceives that at last her "summer days are coming now," one begins to sense the significance invested in this particular event and the weight of anxiety that must have accompanied any doubt of its eventual occurrence (UVA, 10 January [1863]).

The marriage, which was planned for that December, probably surprised most of Rebecca's acquaintances. Having shown no interest in romantic involvement by the age of 31, she already qualified as an old maid. Furthermore, reticence concerning her courtship kept even close friends such as Annie Fields uninformed. But Rebecca never seems to have doubted the rightness of Clarke Davis, a man who had been attracted first to her mind, as her husband.

Chapter Three

New Directions, New Tensions (1862-1867)

Literary Tensions

On a personal level L. Clarke Davis appears to have been an ideal spouse for Rebecca Harding. Although for most of his life he was an influential liberal editor, first of the *Philadelphia Inquirer* and then of the *Public Ledger*, he was as family focused as she. At his death his obituary would describe him as a private man whose "sphere was that of the sanctum and the home" (Langford, 24). His greatest flaw as a husband seems to have been a fondness for cigars. His influence on Rebecca's writing, however, may not have been so positive. As her life-long counselor and confidant, Clarke hampered her artistic development because, while upholding her ideals of critical realism, he also urged her in the direction of journalistic speed and reformist didacticism. Davis's movement away from the "earnest" writing she did for the *Atlantic* began a long time before their marriage, though.

Very soon after her first publications, Davis began being courted by other publishers. In May 1862 she reported to Fields, "I had a letter from a publisher the other day saying if I would write a novel on 'The rebellion' & have it ready by fall he would make 'liberal offers' " (UVA, 14 May [1862]). The offer probably came from Charles Godfrey Leland, editor of *Knickerbocker* and vocal advocate of the new realism, who solicited her for his new *Continental* magazine. Although she declined out of loyalty to the *Atlantic*, he continued to champion her career. In the April 1862 issue of *Knickerbocker* Leland inadvertently exposed Davis's anonymity, praising "that noble book 'Margret Howth,' by the great-hearted REBECCA HARDING."[1]

Davis's loyalty was not as steadfast as she led Fields to believe, however. Some requests were apparently more difficult to turn down than others. Clarke Davis had solicited her work for his friend,

Philadelphia publisher Charles J. Peterson, early in their relationship, probably while they were first corresponding. Her first story in *Peterson's*, a sensational mystery called "Murder of the Glenn Ross," appeared in November and December of 1861. While "A Story of To-day" was impressing *Atlantic* readers with its scrupulous realism, three of her gothic mysteries ran simultaneously in *Peterson's*.

Added to the pressures of friendship was the attraction of much better pay at *Peterson's*. While the *Atlantic Monthly* appealed to a relatively small audience of America's educated elite, *Peterson's Magazine*, with 140,000 subscribers, boasted "the largest circulation of any ladies' periodical in the United States, or even in the world."[2] It also advertised that it paid "more for original stories than all the other ladies' magazines put together."[3] Faced for the first time with a dilemma between artistic and practical concerns that would haunt her career, she felt forced, as she always would, to be practical. After receiving $300 from *Peterson's* for a two-installment story that she knew was "very inferior" to her *Atlantic* work and had taken her only two weeks to write, she wrote to Fields: "You know I would like to write only for you, partly because we are friends, and partly because I am *in earnest* when I write and I find the audience I like in Atlantic readers. But I'm going to be perfectly honest now. If I wrote stories suitable for other magazines I could make more." Explaining, "as times are, I am not justified in refusing the higher price," she urged Fields to "give as much for future articles as you can legitimately afford so that I can write solely for the A. M." (UVA, 20 October 1862). When Fields responded with an offer of $8 per page, Davis replied "I accept your offer to write for the Atlantic exclusively for this year" (UVA, 3 November 1862). Davis's bibliography proves she reneged on that promise and continued to write potboilers. The coming year saw her in three *Atlantic* numbers and nine *Peterson's*.

Peterson's Magazine

Particularly in the early years Davis's *Peterson's* fiction was markedly different from her *Atlantic* pieces. Here she strove to fulfill audience expectations rather than educate them to appreciate a new aesthetic. Her gothic mysteries are filled with supernatural and grotesque elements, containing conventionally good and evil characters. Interestingly, these stories, though very different from "Iron-Mills," also employ a male narrator to increase credibility and, therefore, horror.

Here, however, her narrating character, John Page, identifies himself in the first lines of her first story, "The Murder of the Glen Ross," by a "New Contributor": "The tragedy I am about to relate occurred many years ago when I practiced law in Virginia, before removing to Philadelphia, where I have lived since I retired from the bar. All the facts, therefore, came within my own personal knowledge."[4] With the assistance of Pine, his clever black office boy, and Flint, his legal apprentice, Page solves a mystery and vindicates his falsely accused client.

The Reverend Geoffrey Hope, who is engaged to Page's cousin Sarah Berkely, is wrongly accused of murdering Gertrude, his first wife. Gertrude, whom Hope believes to be dead, has been living in Louisiana with her lover, Gustav Aix. They have come to Virginia with plans of blackmailing Hope. When Hope answers a summons to tend a sick woman in the desolate and eerie Glen Ross, he does not expect to find Gertrude. When Gertrude is later found dead and her connection to Geoffrey Hope discovered, he is accused of the murder. At the last minute, Pine discovers proof that Gustav Aix killed her, finding a fragment of wadding from Aix's gun in the dead woman's heart.

While perhaps not of historic significance, as is Davis's early *Atlantic* work, "Murder" is a well-crafted mystery – suspenseful and imaginative. Furthermore, it represents a large, overlooked portion of Davis's writing during the early years.

John Page, Pine, and Flint reappear in Davis's next five *Peterson's* stories: "The Locked Chamber," a story of forgery and framing; "The Asbestos Box," about a stolen will; "A Story of Life Insurance," telling of mixed blood and illegitimacy; "My First Case," anticipating later sentimental character sketches; and "The Egyptian Beetle," a supernatural tale. Page's stories all recount weird cases that he has worked on. Davis's repeated use of the same narrator created an aura of authenticity for her fictional voice and her sensational tales. This was a technique she would use again later, writing local color character sketches for *Scribner's Monthly*.

After "A Story of To-day" finished its run, Davis wrote to Fields, "I'll write only short articles for the A. M. in future, and if ever a book 'grows' publish it at once. People do *not* like serial tales" (UVA, 14 May [1862]. While she kept that resolve with the *Atlantic*, she wrote a novel-length serial for *Peterson's* every year for the next six years. The first to appear was "The Second Life" in 1863.[5] Like "Murder," this Gothic mystery-romance is well-written for a suspense story; still, it also includes highly conventional elements such as villainy, insanity, unlikely coincidences, and total resolution.

The story begins one day in 1858, when John Lashley, a hardened California broker, hears and sees the ghost of his old love, Esther, calling him for help. Years earlier, John had left the family home in Virginia when Esther married his evil brother Clayton. This supernatural communication prompts him to packs up immediately and leave for the East.

On a boat trip up the Ohio River, he meets an admirable young man whom he discovers to be his nephew Pressley, son of Clayton and Esther. Pressley Lashley is traveling with a mysterious companion, whom he keeps locked in his stateroom. Going to Pressley's room one night, John explains their relationship. Pressley informs him that Esther is dead, that he has been raised by John's other brother Robert, and that he is in love with Robert's daughter, his cousin Emmy. While loving Pressley like a son, Robert has refused his consent to their marriage. When the ship accidentally runs aground, John and the readers get a glimpse of the secret that Pressley hides, as "a bony arm – whether of an ape or a human being, I know not, but whose claws even were overgrown with hair – was thrust out. Groping in the darkness, clutching – like one who drowns, sinks in depths of death – and again – the low, awful cry" (129).

With Pressley's mysterious companion still unexplained, the two relations part in Pittsburgh as John continues on. Reunited with his brother Robert in Virginia, he finally learns the whole story of Clayton and Esther. During the first 10 years of marriage Clayton had tormented his wife, first into a morbid depression and finally into madness. After moving her to a remote village of Pennsylvania, Clayton disappeared, and Esther was accused of his murder. At that time Robert brought Pressley to live with him. Acquitted only because of lack of evidence, Esther abandoned her former life and disappeared. The unresolved suspicions about Esther led Robert to withhold his blessings from Pressley and Emmy.

Refusing to accept Esther's guilt, John resolves to find her, prove her innocence, and give her a second life. With the help of Emmy he finally finds her in the spring and brings her home to a new house built just for her, hoping new life can "bloom for human hearts also"

(350). With his mother found, Pressley also returns with his mysterious companion, his father. After finding his father, destitute, degenerate, and senile in Missouri, he has been caring for this man who had abandoned him and his mother.

Clayton's presence clears Esther, so Pressley and Emmy are able to marry in the summer. That autumn Clayton attempts to kill Esther, but kills himself instead. With his death, the entire Lashley family seems to bloom into a second life. As Christmas ushers in the new year, John and Esther begin their new life together.

The other novel-length serials Davis wrote for *Peterson's* during the 1860s – "The Lost Estate," "The Missing Diamond," "The Stolen Bond," "The Long Journey," and "The Tragedy of Fauquier" – are all similar in tone and subject matter. All of these serials, plus more than 50 other sensational or sentimental potboilers, appeared with the byline "By the Author of 'The Second Life' " for *Peterson's* over the next 25 years.

For several years Davis resisted Charles Peterson's desire to associate her work for his magazine with her published novel. Eventually she consented for more money, and in April 1865 *Peterson's* proudly announced as the author of "The Haunted Manor House" a new contributor: "the Author of MARGRET HOWTH." Thus Davis began a second, less anonymous identity in that magazine. She continued to publish most of her work for *Peterson's* as the author of "A Second Life," sometimes publishing under both identities in the same issue. With the serialization of "Waiting for the Verdict" in *Galaxy* in 1867, Davis began signing her own name. By 1869 she began to connect *Margret Howth* with Rebecca Harding Davis. In all, she wrote 28 more stories for *Peterson's* that were linked to her name during the same 25-year period.

While Davis's private papers confirm for modern scholars her authorship of anonymous *Peterson's* work, her double identity might have remained a secret among her contemporaries if it had not been for one incident. Apparently ignorant of the professional impropriety, as well as careless about her anonymity, she published essentially the same weird-but-true story in two journals. "Ellen" first appeared in *Peterson's* in 1863 by the author of "The Second Life." Two years later, when the *Atlantic* solicited a true story about the war, she sent them the same story. "Ellen" appeared in the *Atlantic* in 1865, by the author of "Life in the Iron-Mills." When some observant reader brought the irregularity to the attention of Ticknor and Fields, they naturally sought an explanation. Apparently, however, they accepted Davis's explanation that she used the "incident of Ellen Carroll's search for her brother as groundwork for a story" in *Peterson's* and presented "the bald facts of her history" in the *Atlantic* (Shaeffer, 117). The fact remains that the two versions are almost identical, however, and irrefutably link all of Davis's publishing identities.

Atlantic Monthly

Between 1862 and 1867 Davis wrote 14 more stories for the *Atlantic Monthly*. In some of these she further developed her naturalistic and realistic technique. In others she began to anticipate elements of her later journalistic and satiric realism. In a few she also began to incorporate more conventional sentimental motifs.

"The Promise of the Dawn," with its title alluding to a line from "Iron-Mills," echoes many of the naturalistic themes of that earlier story.[6] Its protagonist, Lot Tyndal, is a child prostitute. Although the story tends toward sentimentality in its conclusion, it depicts many aspects of Lot's life with uncompromising honesty. Lot is a victim, but not a sentimental one. At one point a kind man, shocked at her youth, voices his pity, saying, "I'm sorry for you." Her response to this is both jaded and blunt: "Why? There's more like me" (18). Later she explains the simple facts: "I always was what you see. My mother drank herself to death in the Bowery dens. I learned my trade there, slow and sure. . . . I had to live!" (19). Her world-weariness castigates a culture that could create her and then dismiss her as anomalous.

The story reveals that Lot's tough exterior hides not just shame, but also a fervent desire to make her life respectable before Benny, the little brother she is raising, realizes how she supports them. She thinks she will have a chance when a theater manager takes an interest in her voice. But she soon becomes sadly wiser. To her request for legitimate work, he only offers money and facts:

> "There's no place for such as you. Those that have made you what you are hold good stations among us, but when a woman's once down, there's no raising her up."

> "Never?"
> "Never." (19)

The only answer that Lot finds is suicide. Assured that Benny will be cared for, she finally takes her own life as Hugh Wolfe had. Like his, her death is redemptive for other characters, but her life as an outcast has wasted a soul's potential.

Like "Iron-Mills," this story, which is subtitled "A Christmas Story," urges social reformation. It promotes a sentimental theology led by Christian mothers instead of by Christian soldiers. Women in it are recognized as having a redemptive power on earth. The mission of women is to bring the comfort of home into the community; the mission of society is to recognize its need. "Promise" argues that Lot's misery is caused by her homelessness. For if home is heaven on earth, then the homeless are damned. The goal of domestic reformation is that someday no one like Lot will stand on a threshold knowing "within was a home, a chance for heaven; out yonder in the night – what?" (22).

Ironically, Davis's ability to create realistic characters seems to undermine the intended spiritual consolation of the conclusion. Lot Tyndal, an opium eater as well as a prostitute, with a "strange fierceness under her dead, gray eyes," pursues her survival with a pathetic bravado that engages the reader as she vainly solicits legitimate work, asking, "Do you mean to employ me?" while "biting her finger-ends until they bled" (17). Her characterization makes believable the narrator's assertion that "if this girl's soul were let loose, it would utter a madder cry than any fiend in hell" (17). Therefore, when Lot finally gives up her struggle for survival and commits suicide, the reader finds little comfort in knowing that, although too late, she has taught the story's other characters the true meaning of Christmas: the regenerative power of love.

The problems that Davis's critical realism exposes in stories like "Iron-mills" and "Promise" are often so global that her individualized remedies seem inadequate. Inadequate or not, for Davis, welfare reform must start at the kitchen door, between one human being and another. In "Promise" she remonstrates against organized, impersonal reform: "There's not one of those Christian women up in the town yonder 'ud take Lot into their kitchens to give her a chance to save herself from hell. . . . So near at hand, you know. Lot was neither a Sioux nor a Rebel" (21).

Although Davis wrote no more novel-length pieces for the *Atlantic*, she did write a few short serials. One, "Paul Blecker," contains the realistic spirit of "To-day."[7] Like *Margret Howth*, this story's title is misleading because it does not focus on Paul Blecker. A love story set during the Civil War, it focuses on four people, each with individual temperaments shaped by their environment.

On their way to Harper's Ferry two Union soldiers meet and fall in love with the Gurney sisters of Washington, Pennsylvania. One, Dr. Paul Blecker, an army surgeon, is a free-thinking Yankee who shocks his comrades by announcing that "the great discovery of this age is woman . . . It did well enough for the crusading times to hold them as angels in theory, and in practice as idiots; but in these rough-and-tumble days we'd better give 'em their places as flesh and blood, with exactly such wants and passions as men" (582-83).

Blecker immediately sees the worth of Grey Gurney, the plain and practical eldest daughter of an impoverished scholar. "Neither an angel nor an idiot," Grey has been trapped in an unfulfilling life (588). First "sold to a man in marriage" – her cousin John Gurney – by well-meaning parents with too many mouths to feed (592), she was then abandoned when her husband turned adventurer and went off to Cuba. At news of her husband's death, she returned home to help raise her father's nine younger children. Grey is the most sympathetic character in the story; she also initiates important action. Seeing in Blecker the "chance that comes to some few women, once in their lives, to escape into the full development of their natures by contact with the one soul made in the same mould [*sic*] as their own" (594), she defies civil and religious law by following him to a hospital on the front lines.

The possibility of Grey and Paul's finding happiness in their love is challenged early in their relationship when Paul discovers Grey's husband still alive and in the army. When he meets John Gurney, who is hospitalized for battle wounds, Blecker struggles with the temptation to kill him by simple medical neglect. Conveniently, Gurney dies, allowing Paul and Grey to begin their lives together. Ironically, a casualty of war enables them to live happily ever after.

The love story of Grey Gurney and Paul Blecker is balanced by that of her sister Lizzie, a delicate artist, and her lover, Captain

Daniel McKinstry of Virginia. This marriage of a woman who demands pampering and a chivalrous man who loves to pamper her is an equally perfect match. The war is not kind to Lizzie, who is widowed by it. When challenged by hard times, however, Lizzie discovers her own strength. Renouncing social respectability, she goes on the stage to support herself as well as her sisters and brothers. Both love stories demonstrate the need to understand difference and to foster individuality. They also advocate female independence.

In "Blecker," Davis once again strives to illuminate complex social problems, in this case focusing on the narrowness of women's lives. Both Grey and Lizzie demonstrate problems of social proscription. From the beginning Grey, like Hugh Wolfe, declares that "the world's all wrong, somehow" (593). Sympathetic, yet ignorant of socioeconomic realities, Blecker makes an ideal sounding board. As he registers indignation at her arranged loveless marriage, Grey explains:

> "It is so in most families like ours. . . . I am very dull about books, – stupid, they say. I could not teach; and they would not let me sew for money, because of the disgrace. These are the only ways a woman has. If I had been a boy" –
>
> "I understand." [Blecker]
>
> "No man can understand," – her voice growing shrill with pain. "It's not easy to eat the bread needed for other mouths day after day, with your hands tied, idle and helpless. A boy can go out and work, in a hundred ways: a girl must marry; it's her only chance for a livelihood, or a home, or anything to fill her heart with."

With dawning insight Blecker comments that Grey is "coming to political economy by a woman's road." But Grey goes further: "I was only a child, but when that man came and held out his hand to take me, I was willing when they gave me to him, – when they sold me, Doctor Blecker. It was like leaving some choking pit, where air was given to me from other lungs, to go out and find it for my own." To this Blecker responds idealistically, that a life of compromise "should not touch a true woman, Grey. Any young girl can find work and honourable place for herself in the world, without the defilement of a false marriage." Grey, however, counters with unpleasant realism: "I know that now. But young girls are not taught that. . . . If [a girl] marries the first man who says he loves her, out of that first instinct of escape from dependence, and hunger for love, she does not know she is selling herself, until it's too late" (592-93).

After McKinstry's death, Lizzie discovers her own potential and renounces respectable uselessness. She chooses social and religious ostracism as an actress for the simple reason that her ability to perform is a way she can contribute to the family welfare, saying, "I never was of any use before" (66). Her decision to go on the stage as an opera singer requires that she renounce much more than social acceptability. As Blecker explains to her: "When [McKinstry] was dying, he said, 'Tell my wife to be true and pure.' There is a bare possibility that you can be both as an opera-singer, but he never would believe it. If you met him in heaven, he would turn his back on you, if you should do this thing" (66). With the belief that "had she stayed at home, selfish and useless, there might have been a chance for her yonder" (69), she goes on the stage, sacrificing social and, according to popular belief, heavenly acceptability.

For at least one future author, "Paul Blecker" had a power similar to that of "Iron-Mills" to awaken and inspire. Elizabeth Stuart Phelps begins "At Bay," one of her first published stories (1867), with a lengthy tribute to Davis:

> I read a story once – it was a good while ago – called "Paul Blecker." I saw in a paper that it was written by a lady who had written something called "Life in the Iron Mills." I never saw that nor any thing more of hers, and I don't know who she is. I wish I could find her out and thank her for having written that story. It made you feel as if she knew all about you, and were sorry for you; and as if she thought nobody was too poor or too uneducated, or too worn-out with washing day, all the things that do not sound a bit grand in books, to be writing about. I think of it often now, since I have had the care and worry of the children here at home. It makes me love her, and it makes me respect her – stranger as she is.[8]

In 1862 James T. Fields and Charles Dickens began an arrangement by which they would occasionally publish the same story simultaneously in the *Atlantic* and in *All the Year Round*, the English monthly Dickens edited. The first piece they published was Davis's "Blind Tom."[9] Basically a true account, this story anticipates Davis's journalism. A blind slave owned by a Columbus, Georgia, plantation owner named Cauthen, Tom was a musical prodigy of such unexplainable dimension that he was exhibited as an idiot-savant, performing in packed concert halls throughout the slave states and even at the White House. Davis's account apparently results from her having seen his performance at one of these concerts. Although she had no insight into what Tom's soul longed to play, she was most pained by those moments in his concert when it became clear that Tom could not play what he wanted: "the moments when Tom was left to himself, – when a weary despair seemed to settle down on the distorted face, and the stubby little black fingers, wandering over the keys, spoke for Tom's own caged soul within" (585).

In Tom's story Davis found an absolutely realistic articulation of her "Iron-Mills" themes. Both Hugh Wolfe and Tom are frustrated artists who are handicapped in some way. "Blind Tom," the story of an enslaved genius, confronts the evil of sanctioned control of individual talent rather than the repression of it. Perhaps because she was a female writer who frequently felt limited by social expectation of women's fiction, she seems to have been keenly sensitive to the fact that he was not even free to use his gift as he chose. The real music of Tom the slave, like the fictional statue of Hugh Wolfe, offers proof that the divine spark of talent can appear in socially unacceptable, disenfranchised individuals. It also reminds the reader that, for the artist who must serve the two masters of self and society, this spark can bring as much pain as joy.

As she would in scores of narrative essays for the *New York Tribune*, the *New York Independent*, and the *Saturday Evening Post*, Davis concludes her tale of "Blind Tom," the slave prodigy, with a direct appeal: "You cannot help Tom, either; . . . But (do you hate the moral to a story?) in your own kitchen, in your own back-alley, there are spirits as beautiful, caged in forms as bestial, that you *could* set free, if you pleased" (585).

Another piece based on a true story that Davis wrote for the *Atlantic* during these early years is "Ellen," the story she had run two years earlier in *Peterson's*.[10] In both versions she recounts the true story of a young woman named Ellen Carrol, the youngest in a family of Irish immigrants who settled in Michigan. She, "like most children coming in the advanced age of their parents, was peculiar"; everyone "thought of her as 'natural' or 'innocent' " (23). After a sequence of tragedies – three siblings die of fever, the father dies in a factory accident, finally the invalid mother dies – only Ellen and her brother

Joe are left. Joe, we are told, "absorbed all the world which her weak mind knew" (25). When he enlists in the army, it never occurs to Ellen to wait patiently. Her simple mind knows only that "she was going to Joe. . . . He would expect her" (25).

Through the years of the Civil War, Ellen travels all over the country without money, following the trail of her brother, always a few steps behind. Sometimes her innocence makes her easy prey, like the time when the camp sutler turns her in as a spy to a regiment "made up of the offal of a large city; the men both brutal and idle, eager for excitement." This one experience – in which she is handled by the bully of the regiment, pelted with mud by the other men, and strip-searched by the camp follower – shows that Ellen has known humiliation (32). But the story reports much more of the kindnesses that she knew. For Davis, the life of Ellen Carrol is truly symbolic: "I like to remember Him as going step by step with this half-crazed child in her long and solitary journey. When I hear how her danger was warded back, how every rough face turned at last towards her with a strange kindness and tenderness. . . . I see again the face of Him who took little children in His arms and blessed them" (31-32).

The tribulations of Ellen's odyssey are not the crux of the story, nor is the melodrama of her repeated failures to find Joe. The story is really about the redemptive effect of her presence on people. Davis had been impressed by this when she met the real Ellen Carrol in Wheeling: "She was not pretty, – with an awkward, ungainly build, and homely face; but there hung about her a great innocence and purity; and she had a certain trustful manner that went home to the roughest and gained their best feeling from them. . . . I used to think Ellen was sent into the world to show how near one of the very least of these, His brethren, came to Him" (33). Like the slave-genius Tom, Ellen Carrol demonstrated for Davis the truth of her fictional characters, such as Deborah Wolfe and Lois Yare.

Later in her career Davis would develop a more satirical attitude. Although this tone is not frequently found in her early work, the tendency is detectable in some of her social criticism. The most obvious example occurs in "The Harmonists," a story also based in fact.[11] For this story she resurrects Dr. Knowles from *Margret Howth*, now a widowed war veteran with a small boy to care for. Rejecting the capitalistic vision of the world as "a great property-exchanging machine, where everything has its weight and value," he joins George Rapp's communist community of Harmonists in their town of Economy. There he gradually discovers that Rapp has substituted one patriarchal form for another, holding office "not by election of the people," but assuming it "as by Divine commission, as Moses and Aaron held theirs" (532). Knowles is seeking a brave new world in this celibate community, unpolluted by any bonds but "lofty human brotherhood." Instead, he finds only old "dried, withered" women, who hunger for the love and motherhood they've been denied. But his most crushing discovery occurs in the men's house, where he meets the society's directors. There he learns that since Father Rapp's death the communist society has become a "successful corporation," which he will have to buy stock in if he wishes to join (537). Criticism of the communitarian movement for being ill-conceived social reform, as destructive to home and family as the world of trade and production, is a recurring theme for Davis.

Though Davis's plea for anonymity in the early years reflects her feminine modesty and a sense of decorum, it also seems motivated by a desire for freedom. Nameless, she was able to be two different writers for two different magazines. In the *Atlantic*, for instance, "A Story of To-day" had been signed "By the Author of 'Life in the Iron-Mills' "; all subsequent stories were signed as "By the Author of" either *Margret Howth* or "Iron-Mills." In *Peterson's* her stories were first signed "By the Author of 'Murder of the Glenn Ross,' " and then "By the Author of 'The Second Life.' " Except for the one instance when she published essentially the same story – "Ellen" – in both magazines, she managed to sustain her separate identities. When she finally consented to linking her non-anonymous *Atlantic* identity as the author of *Margret Howth* to some *Peterson's* stories, she began to maintain two separate identities within that one magazine. Although after 1869 she allowed her name to be associated with everything else she wrote, she continued to maintain one anonymous identity in *Peterson's* until 1890.

In the beginning of her career Davis wrote intentionally experimental fiction for the *Atlantic* and intentionally conventional fiction for *Peterson's*. As the years went by, however, concern for genre seemed to lessen. Her first *Peterson's* signing as "the author of *Margret Howth*," for instance, was "The Haunted Manor-House," a sensational mystery. Yet she signed her first version of "Ellen," a totally realistic narrative, as "the author of 'The Second Life.' " The major factor in journal selection seems to have been quality, with the better crafted stories going to the *Atlantic*. Four stories that illustrate this standard are "The Great Air-Engine," "Steven Yarrow," "The Luck of Abel Steadman," and "George Bedillion, Knight." All of these stories contain interesting characters and evocative settings. While well told and particularized, however, they rely on sentimental elements, such as formulaic exemplars and happy resolutions. All reify the truths of familial love and faith in God.

Dual Vision

Davis's simultaneous writing for the *Atlantic* and *Peterson's* attests to the tension that was pulling her at this time between artistic and commercial desires. It was not just in her writing that she felt pulled in opposing directions. She continued to be torn by her sympathetic understanding of both sides in the Civil War, and to despise the war itself. Her first year as a young wife and mother were also stressful, as she learned to compromise her individual artistic needs. Davis's awareness of both sides of any issue affected all these arenas, sometimes intensifying the tension, other times providing an equilibrium. Several incidents occurring at this time demonstrate once again how thoroughly this dual vision shaped her perspective.

Hoping to introduce Rebecca to some women with whom she might feel comfortable in Philadelphia, where Rebecca moved after her marriage, Annie Fields requested that her friend, the venerable Philadelphian Lucretia Mott, pay her respects to the newcomer. For Davis, Mott was the epitome of her ideal Quaker woman; she was female power incarnate: "No man in the Abolition party had a more vigorous brain or ready eloquence than this famous Quaker preacher, but much of her power came from the fact that she was one of the most womanly of women. She had pity and tenderness enough in her heart for the mother of mankind, and that keen sense of humor without which the tenderest of women is but a dull clod" (*Bits,* 193). Davis, however, an individualist who never involved herself in any organized cause, was not persuaded to join Mott's abolitionist or suffragist army. In real life she seems to have been repelled as well as awed by the "dove-colored" women who never doubted "that they had come into the world for any other purpose than to reform it" (*Bits*, 192).

As the war continued, Rebecca naturally became concerned that her husband might have to fight. Having been a long-time abolitionist, he was active in the party during the war years. But, as Davis told Annie Fields, it was not until Gettysburg that "the pain of the present hour" struck home, causing her to fear that "Mr. Davis might feel he ought to and *must go*." Even in the stress of this concern, though, Davis demonstrates her dual vision. As much as she dreaded the prospect of Clarke's being drafted and as deeply as she hated the war, she also despised hypocrisy. After describing her anguish, she goes on to tell Annie that the "trouble is all over now," because, when Clarke was drafted, he bought himself out of military service. It is in the voice of a cynic that she reports Clarke's own masked guilt as he informed her "very heroically that $300 is very little service for him to offer his country" (UVA, 27 July [1863]).

Even regarding her husband, she could be a cynic; even with women she admired, like Mott, Davis remained a loner. The double vision that compelled her to "see the other side enough to see the wrong[,] the tyranny of both" (UVA, 22 August [1862]) made her unfit to join any coordinated effort. As she once told Annie, "When our sex get into corporate bodies I have an instinct that warns me off" (UVA, 6 November [1876]. She chose to associate with neither the "philanthropists, litterateurs, people with missions and cotton umbrellas" nor the matrons "whose bulk and black velvet and hook nose and turrets of white hair atop symbolize a sort of social Gibraltar" (UVA, 27 July [1863]).

Civil War Tensions

In addition to Davis's 1904 remembrance of her disgust with war and those who glorified it (*Bits*) we also have her letters written during the Civil War. In her frequent correspondence with Annie Fields in Boston, Davis repeatedly shared her vision of the war from her vantage point in West Virginia, where it was "surging up close about" them. Venting her "inexpressible loathing," she wrote her friend, "I could tell you things *I know* that would make your heart sick" (UVA, 22 August 1862). During the first years of the war, Davis wrote several stories that draw their power from her regional perspective.

"John Lamar"

While "A Story of To-day" was running in the *Atlantic*, Davis sent in a new story about the Civil War, urging, "won't you publish John Lamar as soon as you can? I have a fancy of writing for *today* you see" (UVA, 26 November 1861). Appearing in the April 1862 issue, "John Lamar" is perhaps the first fictional treatment of the Civil War in American literature. Though second only to "Iron-Mills" for its disturbing power, this story has never received the attention it deserves.[12]

Set in the mountainous "Rebel Cheat" counties of western Virginia, this story of the Civil War takes place in the aftermath of a border-state guerilla skirmish between northern "Snake-hunters" and "Secession Bush-whackers." Davis dramatizes the tragedy of divided families as Union Captain Charley Dorr, must hold as prisoner his cousin, Confederate Captain John Lamar of Georgia. The story takes place on the Dorr farm, where his regiment is camped. Ironically, Lamar's prison holds many happy memories of childhood, when he had visited his Virginia cousins. Typically for Davis, even the scenes of carnage are not battlefields, but homesteads. Before being captured, Lamar discovers in the remains of a plundered home "the small face [of a slaughtered child] in its woollen hood, dimpled yet, though dead for days" (413). In this setting Davis unfolds a story of destruction. She exposes the distrust and ignorance destroying the nation, and she exposes the white guilt and fear inherent in slavery.

Titled ambiguously, like so many of Davis's pieces, this story is not solely about John Lamar, the southern aristocrat and soldier. As a matter of fact, this story is credited as being the earliest in which a black character appears as a protagonist.[13] Davis again splits her focus, developing a story about the relationship between Lamar and Ben, his personal slave, who kills him. Both men are presented sympathetically as victims of forces beyond their comprehension.

Lamar carries the burden of white, masculine guilt and fear; Ben, the burden of repression and oppression. Davis subtly scrutinizes Lamar's paternalistic anxieties over both Floy, his unprotected sister, and his undisciplined slaves, all of whom he has left at home: "It angered Lamar, remembering how the creamy whiteness of the full-blown flower exhaled passion of which the crimsonest rose knew nothing, – a content, ecstasy, in animal life. Would Floy – Well, God help them both! They needed help. Three hundred souls was a heavy weight for those thin little hands to hold sway over, – to lead to hell or heaven" (413). A good man, Lamar's mind is nevertheless "shut in the worst of mud-moulds, – belief in caste" (414).

Ben, on the other hand, is trapped in ignorance; he is the result of generations of oppression. When Lamar is taken as a prisoner, Ben is exposed for the first time to the highly emotional rhetoric of a Methodist preaching Union soldier, who urges Old Testament justice: "As he hath done unto My people, be it done unto him!" (422). Ben is stirred to rebellion; in his mind are "some old thoughts creeping out of their hiding-places through the torpor, like rats to the sunshine" (415). Given a knife, he kills his master. In confused ecstasy, he runs off, not North but South, back to the plantation; "it was his turn to be master now!" (422).

When the silence of the night is "shattered by a wild, revengeful laugh," Lamar, dying, realizes, "It was Ben" (422). The moment of his death, Davis guesses, was probably one of epiphany: "In that dying flash of comprehension, it may be, the wrongs of the white man and the black stood clearer to his eyes than ours: the two lives trampled down" (422). Lamar, we are led to believe, realizes the depravity inherent in slavery for both slave and master. Pondering the dead man, Dave Hall, the preaching soldier responsible for Ben's act and Lamar's death, also undergoes a transformation. In his realization that God has "uttered no cry of vengeance against the doomed city," he begins to comprehend the value of divine love and mercy over justice (422).

"John Lamar" retains much of its original impact even today. Rather than compromising the story's realism, the tardy epiphanies of "John Lamar" seem to intensify the horror of Lamar's and Ben's "two trampled lives." This first story of the Civil War questions the so-called honorable motivations of both North and South, abolitionist and slaveholder. Noting that judgment is near, it asks "who can abide it?" (423). After the war, Davis would further explore the responsibility of all of white Americans toward black Americans as the theme of *Waiting for the Verdict* (1868).

"David Gaunt"

Davis followed "Lamar" with a longer Civil War story, the two-part "David Gaunt."[14] In this story she confronts polarities grounded in region, gender, and religion. Placing the war on her characters' doorsteps, she exposes the political as personal and questions the war's nobility, no matter how noble the cause. Apparently impressed with this story's powerful portrayal of the war at close range, Fields opened the September 1862 issue of the *Atlantic* with "David Gaunt."

Set in the Virginia Alleghenies, most of the action takes place during one night in January 1862. Federal troops holding the town of Rodney prepare for and execute the ambush of a Confederate stronghold in Blue's Gap. This story negotiates between the conflicting perspectives of four people whose lives have been swept into the war that surrounds them. Old Joe Scofield, whose life was tied up in "the farm, and the dead and live Scofields, and the Democratic party, with an ideal reverence for 'Firginya' under all," defends the right of secession (259). Having recently lost his son, Geordy, who was fighting for the Confederacy at Manassas, he is left with only his daughter Theadora, whom he calls Dode. His friend David Gaunt, the local Methodist minister, preaches a narrow and hard Christianity for himself and others. He loves Dode Scofield, "as well as so holy a man could love anything carnal" (260). After great soulsearching, Gaunt abandons his pacifism to enlist in the Federal army – "It was God's cause, holy" (261). Geordy's best friend and Dode's sweetheart, Douglas Palmer, is a Virginia loyalist, fighting for the Union. But, more troubling to Dode, having been raised in Gaunt's faith, he is also "a doubter, an infidel." Unlike the men in her life, Dode, with her "odd habit of trying to pick the good lesson out of everybody," takes no side (260).

David Gaunt is not the central character; as Davis tells the reader on the third page, "My story is of Dode." Never leaving her home, Dode is the physical and emotional center of several tensions in the story. As her father says, "She don't take sides sharp in this war. . . . allays got somethin' till say fur t' other side" (260). Perhaps even more than she had in *Margret Howth*, Davis put herself into this character. Writing this story prior to her own engagement, she explains Dode's restlessness: "women, before their life-work is given them, pass through such hunger, – seasons of dull, hot inaction, fierce struggles to tame and bind to some unfitting work the power within" (259). Dode's faith, as the author explains it, echoes the theology implicit in Davis's fiction: "she cried hot, wet tears, for instance, over the wrongs of the slaves about her, her old father's ignorance, her own cramped life, but she never said for these things, 'Does God still live' " (267).

The story begins as evening falls. Joe Scofield, a Rebel sympathizer, attends a rally of Federal troops to gain information about the planned attack on the Confederate encampment in the mountains. Suspicious of David Gaunt's sympathies, he has not confided in the minister, who accompanies him. Unknown to Joe is the fact that Gaunt too has a secret; having enlisted, he will be part of the planned raid. On their way they meet Douglas Palmer, the Federal officer who will lead the raid. After the meeting, Joe travels as fast as he can to inform the Rebels, but is just a little ahead of the troops. When Gaunt and another soldier spy Scofield, Gaunt is required to shoot his friend. After a hesitation that almost kills his partner, Gaunt pulls the trigger: "there was a blinding flash. The old man stood a moment on the ridge, the wind blowing his gray hair back, then staggered, and fell" (410). The Rebels, having been warned by the shot, are prepared, and the battle ensues. One of the many wounded is Palmer, who falls in a ditch and is covered with snow.

The next morning, after learning first of her father's death, Dode hears of Palmer's. Refusing to believe he has died, she goes in search of his body. Eventually she finds him alive in an empty shed being nursed by a remorseful Gaunt. The story closes with Dode and Douglas Palmer finding happiness in marriage amid the horrors of war. Nothing has been achieved by the battle. The Rebel forces have successfully defended their position.

The closing lines of the story focus on David Gaunt. Burdened with guilt, he has gone West to nurse in an army hospital. But still "there is blood on his hands. He sees the old man's gray hairs blown again by the wind, sees him stagger and fall. Gaunt covers his bony face with his hands, but he cannot shut it out" (421).

"David Gaunt" shows that, for those trying to live in its midst, war holds no glory: "women had seen their door-posts slopped with blood, – that made a difference" (404). People often decide their loyalties not on principle; rather " 't depends on who burned their barns fust" (403). The armies of both sides are filled with soldiers who have "quit the hog-killing for the man-killing business, with no other motive than the percentage" (403).

Davis wrote Civil War stories for other journals as well, such as "Captain Jean," a story of bushwackers and border warfare that appeared in *Peterson's* in 1869. It was only for the *Atlantic*, however, that she wrote them as "stories of to-day," while the war was raging.

Domestic Tensions

A New Life – Wife, Mother, Home

After one postponement because of family illness, the marriage of Rebecca Harding and L. Clarke Davis was performed in a blizzard on 5 March 1863. Though all evidence of their long and happy marriage proves theirs to have been an idyllic match, the scenario of this marriage's beginning was as ominous as the weather. Their relationship, after all, had developed through correspondence. Other than Clarke's introductory visit to her home and her "happy week in Philadelphia," there is no record of any time spent together. Furthermore, as mature adults they were both probably fairly set in their ways. Rebecca's family, for instance, had long made allowances for her idiosyncratic need for privacy. Also, as a legal apprentice, Clarke had no real profession as yet, so there would be financial insecurity. The lack of money, in fact, precluded any honeymoon.

As Rebecca informed Annie Fields, there would not be the usual " 'wedding trip' ordained by rule." But money was not the reason she gave Annie; rather, she explained, "I have new relatives to meet whom I scarcely know, and I wish to know them soon and feel at home with them" (UVA, 18 February [1863]). After the wedding, the couple lived with Clarke's sister, Carrie Cooper, and her family. Rebecca's privacy suffered terribly in her new home. Her dissatisfaction was probably aggravated by the awareness both that she could hardly resent the presence of others when she and Clarke were the intruders and that the family seems by all accounts to have been pleasant and eager to welcome her. One wonders if all the happy composite families in her fiction are not the exorcising of some guilt, some sense of weakness in her dissatisfaction with this living arrangement.

She clearly was not happy. Though married now and in her 30s, she still had no domestic sphere of her own to care for. The primary connubial duty that befell her as a young wife was making social acquaintances by returning bridal calls. This aspect of a woman's domestic life held as little appeal for Davis as it would have for one of her characters. But, while Davis's characters would have somehow created an ideal home by reforming social expectations, Davis herself escaped demands, seeking refuge in the Philadelphia Public Library. There she was flattered to find the librarian eager to provide the author of *Margret Howth* with her own desk (Langford, 34). Rebecca was also thrilled to find that her reputation gave her license to ignore certain proprieties: "Only write for a magazine Annie, and come live in the west and you can wear feathers in July or pin your shawl behind, with impunity if you like" (UVA, 1 May [1863]). This was all just as well, too, because her writing was needed to supplement the small income Clarke received as a law clerk and as a part-time postal clerk.

So Rebecca, with a new husband, a new family, and a new community, busied herself reading – having discovered the library's archive of colonial manuscripts – and writing. She must have been needed to assist in the domestic duties at the Cooper house, though, because her sister-in-law, Carrie, seems to have had the nineteenth-century female propensity for undetermined illnesses. Repeatedly in her letters Rebecca mentions that "Carrie is sick again."

In June, Rebecca also became mysteriously ill. Although morning sickness might account for some of her complaint, since this was approximately the time she became pregnant, the duration and severity of her illness suggests something more in the order of severe depression, then called neurasthenia. For several months she was unable to do or write anything. Then in September she wrote to Annie that, after having tried allopathy and homeopathy, she had finally turned back to common-sense exercise: "back to my old Western habit of a long, *fatiguing* walk every day, and now I have old healthy cheerful days and dreamless nights" (UVA, 29 September [1863]).

She was not better, however. She was soon so ill that her mother was sent for. Mrs. Harding took her daughter back to Wheeling to be nursed there. Rebecca went home, worked on several stories, improved, and returned happily to Clarke and the Coopers. Getting stronger, contemplating the joyous prospects of a new home and a new baby, she seems to have ended the year in a state of grateful bliss: "I never felt before how hard it was to justify my right to love as since I was sick nor how beyond all hope God has blessed me."[15] Shortly before she left again, a much stronger woman, to spend Christmas in Wheeling, she wrote Annie. The letter includes a tantalizingly cryptic statement of what the year had meant to Davis: "I could tell you a story which I cannot write, sadder and stranger than any fiction, which has made the days and nights very feverish for a long time. Some day I will tell you, but maybe now I ought not to have even said this much. There's a happy ending coming at last, I hope" (UVA [December 1863]).

Both her mental and physical health continued fluctuating all winter, sometimes totally incapacitating her. By spring the undefined illness accompanying her pregnancy seems to have reached the proportion of a nervous breakdown; she was in bed, describing her days as being "like the valley of the shadow of death," and feeling "afraid of the end." Davis also reported that, like Charlotte Perkins Gilman and many other women who suffered from similar symptoms, she was forbidden "the least reading or writing for fear of bringing back the trouble in [her] head." That same letter reveals that Clarke was working on plans of his own to help his wife and himself. Probably as much responsible for her eventual return to health as being nursed by her mother in her old home was Clarke's promise, which she happily reported to Annie: "If I get well we are going directly to live by ourselves – it is all clear now. *You* know all that means to me."[16]

She did enjoy some periods of calm during her last trimester of pregnancy. Much of her comfort at this time seems caused by her discovering, like many other women of the period, the benefits of sedating drugs. She still had moments when she felt that "every faculty had been rasped and handled unbearably and *must* rest." When she did find herself "enough ailing in mind to be nervous and irritable" and unable to satisfy her "stupid desire to be quiet and forgotten," Hoffman's anodyne helped. But even this time of personal weakness seems to have lent further insight into the experiences of others: It "makes one feel mean and paltry and degraded to think how the ailments of the body can so goad and conquer the nobler part" (UVA, 23 March [1864]). But for the most part 1864 began "full of a deep breath of content and waiting" (UVA, 11 January [1864]).

Any calm she might have enjoyed seems to have ended right when she was ready to give birth. When her mother came to help with the birth, she brought the awful news that her father, Richard Harding, had died three weeks earlier. On 18 April 1864 Rebecca gave birth to a healthy son, who was named Richard Harding Davis, in honor of her father. Complications at the birth caused her to be ill and bedridden for a month following the delivery. Furthermore, Carrie also became ill, and then Rebecca's mother succumbed. One can only imagine the chaos of all that illness with a newborn and the other children in the house.

Stronger in body and spirit by summer, Davis was able to look back on the dark days that filled her first year of marriage with new wisdom. As she told Annie, "I never knew before how much 'to be weak is to be miserable' " (UVA, 27 June [1864]). In many ways, though, a story written during the period articulates her extreme anxiety about marriage and motherhood, even better than her letters. Titled simply "The Wife's Story," this tale enacts the conflict between feminine maternal domesticity and egoistic artistic ambition.[17] The story's tension is premised on the nineteenth-century assumption that the roles of wife and mother and the role of artist are mutually exclusive.

"The Wife's Story"

This story represents a change of direction for Davis in several ways. While Davis consistently condemns egoism, in her early stories she withholds her censure of artists like Hugh Wolfe and Blind Tom. "The Wife's Story" is the first in which she denounces artistic egoism. Significantly, in this story the artist is for the first time a woman, more specifically, a wife and a mother. Davis also chose to write this highly autobiographical story from the protagonist's first-person point of view. Hetty Manning, the wife, begins: "I will tell you the story of my life, since you ask it . . . though the meaning of the life of any woman of my character would be the same" (177). In this story, filled with the need to transfer, act out, and punish guilty desire, Davis's protagonist, an unhappy new wife and mother who longs to be a composer of opera, suffers humiliating failure before she renounces her artistic ambition for domesticity.[18]

Hetty, a New England woman who has "an unquiet brain and moderate power" (181), has been strongly influenced by Margaret Fuller.[19] She is a recurring character type in Davis's fiction, suggestive of anxiety. A mature woman of developed sensibility who has recently married a widower with children, Hetty finds it impossible to acclimate herself to her new domestic role. She feels no kinship with her new family of exuberant but insensitive Westerners or with her new baby daughter, "a weazen-faced little mortal, crying night and day" (192). Having been raised on Fuller's motto, "The only object in life is to grow," she finds herself unable to abandon her dream: "There had been a time when I had dreams of attaining Margaret's stature, and as I thought of that, some old sublime flame stirred in me with a keen delight. New to me, almost; for, since my baby was born, my soul as well as my body had been weak and nauseated" (192). In addition to Fuller's influence, the memory of Hetty's previous acquaintance with Rosa Bonheur haunts her.[20] She remembers the Parisian artist saying of her art: "Any woman can be a wife or mother, but this is my work alone" (193).

A new wife and mother, Hetty sits in the hearth-glow of domestic peace, amid "the white bust of Psyche, and a chubby plaster angel" (185), and agonizes over her unrealized "gift" – her "power" – asking, "was I to give it unused back to God? I could sing: not that only; I could compose music, – the highest soul-utterance" (193). She regrets her marriage, realizing, "If I remained with Doctor Manning, my *role* was outlined plain to the end: years of cooking, stitching, scraping together of cents" (194). Hetty's crime is twofold: the rejection of her domestic role and the assertion of artistic egoism. "No poet or artist," she says, "was ever more sincere in the belief that the divine power spoke through him than I" (197).

Hetty does not leave her husband, though; and when events cause the family to move to Newport, near New York City, she eagerly goes. There Hetty meets an impresario who is willing to produce her opera and to feature her in the leading role. One day, after long and troubled deliberation, she finally decides to do her opera, even if doing so meets with the disapproval of her new family. Her decision occurs during a solitary walk on the beach, in contemplation of the sea's affinity with her own soul: "It was no work of God's praising Him continually: it was the eternal protest and outcry against Fate, – chained, helpless, unappealing" (200). According to the story, she proceeds to fulfill her ambition. When produced, her opera fails; the audience's rejection of her composition and of her performance is described in humiliating detail.

This scene illuminates another dimension of the nineteenth-century female artist's anxiety. In addition to fear of the consequences that will befall her rejection of the divinely ordained domestic role, there is the very real fear of failure. Independence is fantasized as a double-edged sword that is both attractive and frightening. Hetty leaves the theater penniless, homeless, hungry, ashamed, and beaten: "If the home I had desolated, the man and child I had abandoned, had chosen their revenge, they could not have asked that the woman's flesh and soul should rise in me with a hunger so mad as this, only to discover that [I would fail]" (213).

But Davis has not yet punished her artist projection enough. Hetty soon discovers that her loving husband has been in the audience and has had a heart attack. Racked with grief and guilt, she wanders the Bowery, hoping to die herself, until she awakes to find that the entire attempt at being an artist has been a dream of her "brain-fever," which hit her while out by the sea. Renouncing art as an enticing false value, she joyfully accepts her regained life as wife and mother.

Davis wrote "The Wife's Story" sometime during her first year of marriage, when she was living with her husband's family in a strange city. She was also suffering a difficult pregnancy, which was accompanied by what she herself referred to as a "brain-fever." Treated with S. Weir Mitchell's popular rest-cure, she was prohibited from reading and writing. Davis never had anything but praise for Mitchell and his treatment, but one is led to wonder how she followed her doctor's orders and still managed to submit her manuscript for publication in the July issue of the *Atlantic*.

The birth of her first son, with whom she was to share a life-long mutual devotion, seems to have reaffirmed for Davis her faith that indeed "all good things lie in the future." As she explained to Annie, "God is keeping them for us – like a mother holding her baby's toys till he is old enough to use them" (UVA [early 1864]). Soon everyone was healthy again, and baby Richard, nicknamed Hardy, was growing fat.

The Davises spent July and August of that summer at Point Pleasant, New Jersey, on the Manasquan River. Point Pleasant summers would become part of the pattern of their lives. The first few years they boarded with several families in an old farmhouse. This seems to have been a comfortable arrangement, but it did not comprise her fictional ideal family. Rebecca liked most that they were nice folks "whom you could avoid if you choose to live alone" (UVA, 15 May [1864]). In later years they would have their own cottage, called Vagabond's Rest, and begin to build a summer colony of their closest friends, most of whom were members of the Philadelphia theatrical community: the Drews, the Barrymores, the Furnesses. The coast of Jersey and Delaware, like the mountains of West Virginia and Pennsylvania, would appear in much of Davis's fiction as the setting of agrarian peace, of real values. Philadelphia, where she was to live out the rest of her life, would be present only as a place to be escaped.

"Out of the Sea"

"Out of the Sea," the first of many stories set on the Jersey coast, was written following their first Point Pleasant vacation.[21] Published when baby Hardy was a year old, this story demonstrates again Davis's attempt to nullify anxieties regarding matrimony and motherhood and to affirm love over art. In it Mary Defourchet, a proud and rebellious young bride-to-be, learns from humble old Phoebe Trull that, though passive, traditional female attributes such as suffering patience and self-sacrifice require great strength.

Mary Defourchet has been sent on a seashore vacation to prepare both physically and mentally for her pending marriage, when she will begin "life in earnest." Mary is an intimidating woman, who has "lectured in public, nursed in the hospitals" and whose blood seems "always at fever heat" (534). She is indignant at her uncle's paternalism in having sent her on this holiday: "She was over thirty, an eager humanitarian, had taught the freedmen at Port Royal, gone to Gettysburg and Antietam with sanitary stores, – surely, she did not need to be told that she had yet to begin life in earnest!" (535). She is, however, also anxious about marrying a man whom she feels she does not know well enough: "Her love for him was, as yet, only a delicate intellectual appreciation" (535). More than love at this point, she feels "keen delight" in the prospect of sharing her life with the famous Dr. Birkenshead, a "surprisingly young man to have gained his reputation" (534). As the story begins, she eagerly awaits the doctor's planned visit to share the retreat with her, hoping that "they could see each other unmasked" (535). While waiting she becomes friends with Phoebe Trull, an old woman of the village who has spent years waiting patiently for her son's return. Not until the story's climax do they realize that they expect the same man, one as son, the other as lover.

As each unknowingly awaits the same man, due to arrive on the same ship one stormy night, they talk. Mary condescends to the old woman, but Phoebe in her wisdom perceives Mary, "in spite of blood and education, to be no truer woman than herself" (549). The influence of love has already begun to change Mary, but after the shipwreck and the old woman's display of maternal devotion that occur later in the story, Mary becomes a convert. By the time everyone discovers that Phoebe's son, Derrick, is Mary's fiancé, Dr. Birkenshead, Mary has also discovered the lasting truth of feminine, domestic values. In obeisance to her new "mother," Phoebe, she professes "true love at home." Kneeling to kiss the old woman, Mary also professes the superiority of humble, self-abnegating love, of which maternal devotion is the purest form, saying, "I never loved him so well as when he came back to you" (549).

Old Phoebe Trull is modeled after the colorful Knocky-luft of Davis's childhood. Phoebe has been waiting "twenty years, come February" for word from her son. As one of her neighbors reports, "she's never heerd a word in that time, an' she never misses a mail-day" (537). One sees "how the long sickness of hope deferred [has] touched the poor creature's brain" (537). Phoebe's son has not gone West as Knocky-luft's son had; he has taken the other popular escape route – to the city – to seek his fortune and to escape the shame of lowly birth as her bastard son. Phoebe's love is intensified with guilt over her inability to protect her son from her own powerless position and over her own selfish joy at having a baby, even if he is illegitimate. Her guilt knows no shame, however. Her explanation offers no apology: "I was jess a clam-fisher, an' knowed nothin' but my baby. His father was a gentleman: come in spring, an' gone in th' fall, an' that was the last of him. That hurt a bit, but I had Derrick" (537).

Davis's development of this character and the motif of suffering patience in this story demonstrates passive female strength. Though an old woman, Phoebe has both physical and spiritual strength. On her first appearance in the story, she announces, "pulling up her sleeve, and showing the knotted tendons and thick muscles of her arm, 'I'm pretty tough, thee sees' " (537). But her greatest strength is her maternal love. She lives the Christian principle of abnegation to the point of literal self-sacrifice.

Phoebe is shown as a woman who has essentially defined her motherhood by being a giver of strength. Talking about her son's birth, she revels in her sacrifice: "I lost much of my strength when he was born; . . . I give it to him. I'm glad of that!" (537). At the story's crisis, when a ship bringing her son home is foundering in a storm, Phoebe again demonstrates the maternal power of self-sacrifice. As other people stand on the beach, helpless to combat the raging surf, she plunges into the breakers: "Old Phoebe Trull had stripped to her red woollen chemise and flannel petticoat, her yellow, muscular arms and chest bare. Her peaked old face was set and her faded blue eye aflame. She did not hear the cry of horror from the wreckers" (541). Phoebe dies, but not without having taught her son and future daughter-in-law the truth of self-sacrificing love: "The true love at home be worth it all. I knowed that always, I kep' it for my boy. He went from it, but it brought him back" (549).

Tensions Resolved

When the little Davis family returned from their restful vacation at the Jersey shore in September, it was to a house of their own on North Twelfth Street. There Clarke and Rebecca began calling their little row house "the Centre of the Universe," as all members of the Davis family would always refer to each of their subsequent homes. It mattered little that there was "no glimpse of green near it" or that it was "flanked by one or two hundred twin brothers" (UVA, 23 September [1864]). The year of crisis in the life of Rebecca Harding Davis was over. With her own home and her own baby, life with her husband reached a calm stability.

During this time Clarke's abolitionist political affiliation and his editorship of the *Legal Intelligencer*, a professional journal, brought them to a number of public lectures. And Rebecca's reputation led them to personal acquaintance with many of the speakers. Davis records brief association with Wendell Phillips, Charles Sumner, James Russell Lowell, and John Greenleaf Whittier. She also became reacquainted with Henry Ward Beecher. She had been impressed by him a few years before during her visit with family friends Captain John C. Frémont and his wife, Jessie, in New York. On that occasion, after hearing Rebecca mention several old favorite hymns from her childhood, he had invited her to Plymouth Church the next Sunday. There she was surprised to discover that he had selected as the hymns to be sung in the service all those she had mentioned. Her lasting impression of this charismatic figure was, however, one of repulsion: "back of the heavy jaws and thick lips and searching eyes swathed in drooping lids, back of the powerful intellect and tender sympathy, there was a nameless something in Mr. Beecher which repelled most women. You resolved obstinately not to agree with his argument, not to laugh or cry with him, not to see him again" (*Bits,* 190).

During these first years of her marriage, Davis continued to produce fiction written by both her personae with regularity. Each year she contributed two or three pieces to the *Atlantic* and a serialized novel plus four or five short pieces to *Peterson's*. The late fall of 1864 also marked the beginning of her career as an essayist. While she was visiting her mother, Clarke, who was overextended in his roles as lawyer, editor, and part-time postal clerk, solicited her assistance with an article for the *Legal Intelligencer*, writing, "Dearest Pet, Will you help your old Boy a little?" (Shaeffer, 205). Helping her husband, she discovered a new, powerful voice within herself, that of a journalist.

This was a happy time, filled with domestic contentment. The only note of sadness occurred at the assassination of President Lincoln. Davis's firm belief in God's active presence caused her to ponder the meaning of such a horrific loss, coming, as it did, a mere week after Lee's surrender had ended the war. She shared her distress with Annie Fields: "I have thought God was dealing with us as with His chosen people of old – by such great visible judgments that we almost heard His voice and saw His arm" (UVA, 20 April [1865]).

Soon after the assassination Rebecca learned she was pregnant again. Charles Belmont Davis, named for a brother of Clarke's who had been killed in battle in Belmont, Missouri, was born 24 January 1866. After this birth, there was illness in the family again. Rebecca spent the winter months nursing baby Charley, who was sick for his first two months, and Clarke, who had pneumonia, along with caring for Hardy, now a toddling "young ruffian" (Langford, 47). She wrote to Annie of her longing to escape from "dull brick houses" to "sweeps of yellow corn" and "lines of purple hills." She was "homesick for the country" even now that she had a "dear little home warm with love and beautiful in its way" (UVA, 30 March [1866]). Though she became resigned to city life, her desire for a rural home, evident throughout her fiction, would remain an unfulfilled longing, assuaged temporarily by summer holidays.

Davis broadened her literary horizon again in late 1866 when she began publishing fiction for a third journal, the new *Galaxy*, under her own name, Mrs. R. H. Davis. The next year she signed her name for the first time to an *Atlantic* piece, but she signed it differently: Mrs. R. B. (Blaine) Davis. Although by the serialization of *Dallas Galbraith* in *Lippincott's* the following year she had reconciled her several identities as Rebecca Harding Davis, she continued for years to maintain simultaneous anonymous identities in *Peterson's*.

Chapter Four

Domestic Bliss (1868-1874)

The Centre of the Universe

By 1869 the life of Rebecca Harding Davis and her family had truly stabilized. Clarke became the managing editor of the *Philadelphia Inquirer*, a position he would hold for the next 20 years, leaving only to become editor of the *Public Ledger*. The same year Rebecca, who had previously dabbled in journalism, officially entered the profession as a contributing editor for the *New York Daily Tribune*; this association lasted 20 years, after which she became similarly involved with the *New York Independent* and the *Saturday Evening Post*.

In 1870 the Davises purchased a home on South Twenty-first Street, another row house, but larger than those they had rented and with a yard. This house, which Charles Belmont Davis remembers as "a home in all that word implies," was their "Centre of the Universe" for over 40 years. There Clarke and Rebecca worked to "create an atmosphere which would prove a constant help to those who lived under its roof" (*Letters*, 1). The only major change in the Davises' lives during these years was the birth of a third child, a daughter named Nora, called Nolly, in 1872.

Davis took great care to make her home inviting to friends as well as family, entertaining frequently. It was always open to friends visiting Philadelphia, such as Ralph Waldo Emerson, who was their guest on several occasions (Harris, 153). In a letter to Emerson, in which Davis extended her first invitation, her developed self-confidence is clear as she recalls their first meeting:

> It was such a relief to see you eat and drink! My oracle's voice came so much closer home to me when I saw he was human as we others. For, as you doubtless have noticed, to us downright commonsensible Western people the gods are intelligible just in proportion as their bones ache or their clothes are cut like our own. Sincerely, I shall not soon forget how kind and gracious you

> were to me, a raw Western girl then and I hope you will be as unselfishly kind now and give us this great pleasure. (Harris, 154 [13 January 1870])

As important as her domestic life was to her, Davis still wanted a professional life as well. She could not stop writing. Once, in later years, in a letter to Richard Harding Davis at the start of his career, she made clear what writing meant to her: "[S]top writing. God forbid. I would almost as soon say stop breathing, for it is pretty much the same thing" (*Letters*, 35). But, as a woman, she firmly believed that her primary identity was as a mother and wife. Although she saw no inherent conflict with women's involvement in professions, she believed that, if possible, a woman should arrange her professional life so that it did not deny husband and children of her necessary, influential presence. This is not to say that Davis, always attentive to social reality, was unaware that most working women were involved in menial labor that they could not arrange to suit themselves. Her editorial career is marked by a campaign to provide vocational education for women to allow them the increased freedom concomitant with skilled employment. But she also recognized that severe financial necessity was not her personal plight.

As far as Davis was concerned, if one pursuit was to be compromised, it had to be her writing; sadly, most readers agree that it sometimes was. Nevertheless, all accounts of the Davis household show Rebecca always at "the Centre of the Universe," while always writing also. Charles Davis's memoir of his brother, Richard, fondly describes the family's happy Point Pleasant summers, in which the boys spent their days roaming freely and Clarke went on "his all-day fishing excursions, while my mother sat on the sunlit porch and wrote novels and mended" (*Letters*, 6).

The writing that most reflects Davis's interests during the late 1860s and early 1870s was never published. It is the journal that she had begun keeping in 1865 as a book-of-days for her children. With little mention of her writing or current events, it records what mattered most to her: nap times and skinned knees and new sailor suits, "Harding's bright face or funny antics" and "Charley's earnest blue eyes." Celebrating "the happy sense of home and love that is under and over all," this journal illuminates a subtle tonal shift in Davis's writing as she settled into domestic life.[1]

Social Protest Novels

Letters to Annie Fields during this period resonate with Davis's successful mediation of motherhood and authorship. Contentment in her own life, however, did not lessen awareness of others less fortunate. One letter, which concludes, "Indoors here, my hands go from pen to babies – very regularly," begins with Davis's continued awareness of inequity in America's cities. Reporting that their Philadelphian "friends are beginning to ship out one after another" for Europe and elsewhere, she mentions also that "the world of the poor is looking at the new monstrosities of fashion," and "the world under that [is] again open mouthed over the last murder" (UVA, 21 April [1866]). Although her topical allusions remain vague, her perception of class disparity is clear.

While the majority of Davis's stories from this period are not focused exposés of specific injustices, those she did write are among her most powerful. The first literary fruit of this comfortable, secure stage in Davis's life is a novel of urgent social concern. Insightful and prophetic, *Waiting for the Verdict* (1867) remains her most ambitious novel.

Waiting for the Verdict

Published first as a serial for *Galaxy*, this multiplot saga of the Civil War explores the possibility of reconciliation between whites and blacks, Northerners and Southerners.[2] In this novel, which confronts the dubious possibility of America's ever being able to compensate for slavery or its ever accepting the total racial integration implicit in true Negro equality, Davis's impulse toward realism creates an interesting tension with her desire to mediate. The possibility of uniting a shattered nation is played out primarily in two relationships: one between Northerner Rosslyn Burley and Southerner Garrick Randolph, the other between black Dr. John Broderip and white Margaret Conrad.

The story begins by introducing both the novel's central characters, Rosslyn Burley and John Broderip, as children. Rosslyn, a bastard and an orphan, is raised by her grandfather, Joe Burley, a New Jersey truck farmer. While Joe peddles his produce in the outlying countryside, she works as a market huckster on the streets of Philadelphia. On the ferry from Philadelphia to New Jersey one evening, they meet Ross's biological father, James Strebling, an Alabama planter who had seduced and abandoned Ross's mother. With him is a precocious young mulatto slave boy named Sap.

Ross next appears, a polished and beautiful young woman, having been befriended and educated by a wealthy Quaker, Abigail Blanchard. While visiting Joe – who, though in his 60s, has enlisted in the Union army – in Kentucky, Ross meets Garrick Randolph, a southern aristocrat who is cousin to James Strebling. Garrick is a complicated character. Although he works for the federal government, he makes no effort to end his own family's ownership of slaves. As a matter of fact, dynastic pride proves to be his fatal flaw, causing him to sell Hugh, an old slave whom his father had promised freedom. Despite their differences, Rosslyn's love for Garrick is steadfast as she allows him time to discover his errors and correct them.

The talk of Philadelphia is an amazing young physician named John Broderip. Though he passes as white, Broderip was the boy Sap, who was bought, then freed and educated in France by another elderly Quaker woman. Broderip enjoys the power and comfort of success. By surrounding himself with luxury and gouging wealthy clients to support his charity cases, he strives to make up for years of abuse and want. No one but the reader knows of his intolerable loneliness, cut off from family and past, living a lie as a white man. When he falls in love with Margaret Conrad, the daughter of a patient, he is forced to tell her the truth about himself.

Though Margaret loves him, she cannot accept his Negroid blood. With his secret out, he is also ruined professionally in Philadelphia. But with his fall comes his moral rise, as he decides to use his charismatic power for the good of his own people by leading a regiment of black soldiers. Broderip's half-brother, Nathan, an uneducated slave, compares him with Moses – "a chile ob de slave woman," who "stole all de learnin' ob his masters, an' den come back an' took his people cross de riber inter freedom" (314). At his death in the Battle of Richmond, Broderip compares himself with Jesus: "it was given to me to die for my people – to me!" (358).

Besides James Strebling, several other lives intersect the fates of the four main characters. Lt. George Markle, of Joe Burley's army troop, is a genuinely good man who also loves Margaret Conrad. Nathan is a slave on the Strebling plantation. While hiding as a runaway, Nathan saves Markle's life. In the course of the novel the reader discovers that Nathan is Broderip's brother and that they both are the sons of Hugh, an old slave belonging to Garrick Randolph's family. Nathan has run away to join his common-law wife, Anny, from another plantation, and their son, Tom.

Although most of the novel's action takes place during the war, its concerns are focused on the aftermath. The title is explained clearly by Nat, the runaway slave, when Markle assures him of Union victory and the sure end of slavery: "But dat's on'y de beginnin'. Dat was a great wrong de white folks did to us. How's dey goin' to make it up to us?" (168). All the novel's themes cluster around this central question.

Davis asks whether America, finally freed from its shackle of slavery, will be able to realize the ideals on which it was founded. She does not hold out much hope for legislated immediate results. As Rosslyn argues, it "is a fable that all men are born free and equal in this country" anyway (229). She maintains that few Americans, even among abolitionists, really believe in racial equality as a fact and that national acceptance of interracial procreation will be the only final proof of truly realized equality. As Joe explains, however, when slavery is not present to clarify the hierarchy as in the South, "there's no danger of amalgamation with us. The antipathy's too strong between colors" (346).

The verdict will further declare whether Americans are committed enough to their ideals to support the necessary generations of affirmative action to restore to health and wholeness "men and women whose brains and bodies were diseased and incomplete from generations of barbarism and slavery" (331). Davis suggests that Americans must responsibly confront the fact that the races are indeed not equal because generations of slavery have done great damage – in her view, both genetic and cultural. She asserts that blacks have been handicapped by being denied any productive cultural context: "They have neither philosophy, nor records of a great past, nor coherence to work for a place among nations" (313).

Davis implies that the only way Americans will come to accept their nation's founding ideals will be through personal interracial relationships. Although the possibility of interracial marriage fails in Margaret Conrad's rejection of Broderip, the possibility of interracial friendships is affirmed in several cases: Nathan and Markle, Broderip and Margaret's father, Rosslyn and Anny. The two women most successfully transcend the boundaries of a classist, racist society. Explaining to Anny, "There can be no alms-giving from me to you. . . . We all owe to each other a debt, and I but try to pay it," Ross voices Davis's vision of national healing (353). She also anticipates the metaphor of a promissory obligation that Martin Luther King, Jr., would use a century later.

Rosslyn demonstrates Davis's solution of personal assistance and her faith in familial affection when, at the close of the Civil War and the close of the novel, she reunites Nathan, Anny, Tom, and old Hugh. She also provides them with a home and a livelihood. Speaking for the consensus, her father questions the feasibility of her plan to effect any real change: "But there are four millions of people impatient to be helped up – and up. What signifies four?" To this, she responds with the voice of the author, saying, "If we all lift a few – " (349).

The essential ingredient for redressing the wrong of slavery is education. Repeatedly in this novel education provides the key to self-salvation. It allows Ross to leave the market stalls and become a commercial artist; it allows Broderip to leave his master's horse stalls and become a surgeon. Nathan is keenly aware that, just as ignorance has been the primary tool of black oppression, learning will ensure true freedom. He eloquently explains the value of language to Markle: "Suh, we've bin kept ign'rant so dat we might be dumb. We can't speak words dat de white folks 'ud listen to. We can't write 'em" (163). But perhaps even more powerful is his response to Broderip's doubts that blacks will be able to overcome their slave mentality: "Dey neber know'd dey was so great a people, de slave in M's Jeems' plantation neber had no way ob touchin' de slave in Georgy. 'Pears to me when dy kin speak to each oder by newspaper an' books, like de white men, dey'll feel dere strength, an' use it" (314).

Waiting for the Verdict concludes its indictment of slavery in the South and racism in the North with the formation of a composite family, brought together by Rosslyn for the mutual welfare and dignity of all. The northern-raised daughter of a Southerner, Ross creates a home that will be a comfort to all. Her home is composed of her husband, an aristocratic Southerner and Unionist; her grandfather, a truck-peddler and Union soldier; her husband's aunt, a southern belle; her infant son; and the orphaned daughter of a murdered teacher of freed slaves. She augments her own multigenerational, multicultural family with another, the estranged family of freed slaves who are related to her half brother, the son of Rosslyn's father and a black woman who was a slave. The two families form a new community that integrates America's disparate parts. In its resolution, *Waiting for the Verdict*, like *John Andross*, Davis's other great protest novel of this period, reflects her increasing faith in the power of familial love.

In Rosslyn's social model Davis demonstrates a way to reform society according to Christian ideals. Furthermore, in the novel's happy ending she promotes spiritual, not material, rewards. Garrick Randolph, Ross's husband, lightly complains about the fate that has reduced their fortunes, saying, "It is hardly fair. All dramas, from the old fairy stories to the last novel, end in a glitter of gold." To this Ross responds with Davis's sentiments that in "the real ones which God orders," the dramas "oftenest end in love, plenty of hard work, and the poor at your gate" (351).

Although the novel does not end well for everyone, those who have not found happiness have gained wisdom. Perhaps to atone for her rejection of Broderip, Margaret is teaching freed blacks in the ghettos of Philadelphia. On his way home, Markle brings her word of Broderip's heroic death and reaffirms his own love for her. They part friends as he continues on home with his own plans to "find Christ's work to do." (361).

The novel concludes with a sentimental, domestic vision: "The windows of the little tenant house were open, and within he saw Nathan's smiling face with his wife's close beside it, both listening to some talk of Tom's, while the gray-headed old man nodded solemnly in the corner. A little farther on, the red light streamed from Ross' happy home" (360). These two families – mixing generations, cultures, and races – will live together happily. They have formed the beginning of a community, based on mutual interdependence.

Although Davis offers some remedies to the problems exposed by her novel, she does not pretend to have all the answers. Much of this book's power lies in its open ending with many unsolved issues. Anny's maternal anxiety about her son, for instance, leads her to doubt the success of Ross's approach to the problems of racism. At the close of the novel, Anny voices the author's concern about the stability of an America that continues segregated and unequal:

> Freedom and clo's, and a home of our own, is much. But it's not all. Forgive me. A mudder kerries her chile's life on her heart when he's a man, jes as before he was born; you know dat. I wondered what was my boy's birthright in dis country. . . . Dar's power in Tom's head, Missus, and dar's bad passions in his blood, and ef dar's no work given to de one, de oder has its work ready. He must be a man or a beast, an' dat soon. I tink of it night an' day. I'm his mudder. Dar's four millions of his people like him; waitin' for de whites to say which dey shall be – men or beasts. Waitin' for the verdict. (354)

Davis hoped this novel would speak to postwar America as Harriet Beecher Stowe's *Uncle Tom's Cabin* had to the prewar nation. Her correspondence on *Waiting for the Verdict,* however, deals largely with the personal horrors of serial publication. The editors, who had solicited her for their new magazine, began to renege on their promises that she "was not to be limited as to length" when they decided in the middle of her run to change the magazine format. Her expanding work became inconvenient for their shrinking size. Despite angry letters, she eventually followed their demands, realizing that "whether it mutilates the story or not," was "a secondary consideration" to her publishers (Shaeffer, 144). After this experience, Davis swore never to write for *Galaxy* again, and she renewed her vow never to serialize large works in the future. But her serial for *Galaxy*, which earned $3600 before book publication, was undeniably lucrative (Langford, 49). She did write for *Galaxy* again, though nothing lengthy, and she continued to serialize every novel she wrote.

"In the Market"

Many of Davis's female protagonists agonize over the uselessness that middle-class propriety forces upon them as they are expected to await passively their only acceptable destiny – marriage. "In the Market," a story published in *Peterson's* in 1868, "by the author of 'Margret Howth,' " specifically attacks marriage mores as immoral and unjust.[3] Davis's choice of journal in this situation seems more political than aesthetic. Her target audience was the typical reader of *Peterson's*, with its conglomeration of dress patterns, recipes, and fiction: "girls, especially, who belong to that miserable border-land between wealth and poverty, whose citizens struggle to meet the demands of the one state out of the necessities of the other" (49).

The story concentrates on two sisters in a large working-class family, whose time has come to be brokered on the marriage market. Clara dutifully marries a man she does not love rather than remain a drain on her family's resources. Margaret, however, refuses to be part of what she sees as "legal prostitution," declaring that God "never meant that marriage should be the only means by which a woman should gain her food and clothes, and provide for her old age" (54). Alienating family, community, and lover, she "unsexes herself," to achieve economic independence. Refusing even to pursue teaching or sewing because, as female employments, they are "consequently poorly paid," she goes into business for herself as a farmer and distributor of medicinal herbs. When, after several difficult years, her enterprise begins to profit, she is even able to expand and to hire more "help (women's help)" (55).

By the end Margaret has regained acceptance, and she has also married, but for love to an equal partner, who respects her work. The narrator reports that "Margaret never gave up her business," and that "her daughters have each been given a trade or profession" (57). Davis's political intent is again clear in the conclusion as Margaret reminds her community and the reader that every young woman could also do what she has done: "I have only the ordinary faculties of common sense and perseverance. Any woman has enough power given her to stand alone, if need be" (57).

"Put Out of the Way"

Two years after "In the Market" *Peterson's* published "Put Out of the Way," a serial "by the author of 'The Second Life.' "[4] Though written as a sensational thriller, this novella was also a well-researched exposé of legal and medical abuses in the treatment of the mentally ill. It is thematically linked with Davis's more realistic protest fiction of the period. In this story, Davis urges reform as she exposes inheritance laws and insanity laws built on reason, not affection, and perpetuated by efficacy, not morality.

The specific problem on which the plot turns is graft among physicians who can legally institutionalize people without due process. The issue is explained by the villain Col. Leeds, a gentleman of social, economic, military, and political position who understands how to use his power: "There are Bastiles in the United States, by the aid of which any inconvenient person can be put out of the way for life. It is a quiet, safe means, which a gentleman can use with no fear of punishment. . . . Only pay enough, and get up your case right, as the lawyers say, [and] you have science and philanthropy both to assist you" (435).

Davis's writing of "Put Out of the Way" was inspired by Clarke Davis's editorial exposés on the subject. In 1868 he had published "A Modern Lettre de Cachet" in the *Atlantic*, which documented abuses in the Pennsylvania laws.[5] Together, their different treatments of this matter were instrumental in the eventual revision of the Pennsylvania laws; these reforms were used as models by many other states.

John Andross

In 1873 Davis again wrote a novel of social protest. *John Andross* demonstrates Davis's continued concern about the effects of industrialism and capitalism in America.[6] This time her focus was on the graft and corruption in what would become known as the Gilded Age, particularly the whiskey-ring scandal of President Grant's administration (1869-77). Set in Lock Haven, Philadelphia, and Harrisburg, the novel focuses on the Pennsylvania ring and its crimes, about which Davis was well informed.

In 1869 the *Philadelphia Public Ledger* ran an editorial on the recently attempted assassination of James J. Brooks, a law officer who apparently could not be bribed. The editorial calls attention to the criminal action of "the combination styled the 'whiskey ring,'" which has proven "as potent in procuring immunity for those who commit crimes in its service, as it is pervading in having its emissaries, tools and agents everywhere, from the floors of Congress to the courts of justice." Detective Brooks survived and in 1873 published in Philadelphia his own account of the ring's illegal activities entitled *Whiskey Drops*. Davis's novel, which began running as a serial in *Hearth and Home*, a periodical edited by Harriet Beecher Stowe, in December of that year, draws many of its facts from Brooks's exposé.[7] In fact, she has one of the novel's characters allude directly to the event. He describes a man who was "shot by the order of the Whiskey Ring, and when the actual murderers threatened to betray their employers, the poor wretches had been killed"

(298). In the novel, this story is told to convince another character that, though these are neither the "dark ages" nor the "days of assassins," greed can and does motivate murder among ostensibly respectable citizens.

In *John Andross*, which can arguably be claimed as Davis's best novel, we see her growing facility with dramatic narration and her movement away from the didactic moralizing that undermines *Margret Howth* and *Waiting for the Verdict*. In *John Andross* Davis returns to a single plot, involving a relatively small cast of characters. This is not a simple novel, however. The suspenseful story is filled with complications, and the characters are remarkably complex. Reviews, such as one appearing in the *Atlantic* in 1874, during William Dean Howells's editorship, show that readers saw in this novel the power of both the specific and the universal. The reviewer praises *John Andross* for being "an American novel in which the American part does not outweigh everything else; it has those qualities more important than geographic accuracy" (115).

The most outstanding quality of this novel is its complex, paradoxical characters. The good are clearly flawed and the bad all reveal some redeeming quality. The two protagonists of the novel are John Andross, known to his friends as Jack, and Dr. Clay Braddock. The charismatic Andross is admirable, but not heroic: he steals to protect his family honor, and he rationalizes his crimes, at least temporarily. Braddock, who seems to be an unordained doctor of divinity, is truly honorable, but vain and a bit of a prig. The plot details certain temptations that these men face and the way they respond, as well as difficulties that arise from their own errors in judgment. Their most glaring misperceptions concern women. While interesting, the primary female characters are less complicated. Isabel Latimer, Andross's friend and Braddock's fiancé, embodies those values that are true and lasting; the egoistic and materialistic Anna Maddox, Andross's love interest, personifies the shallow false values of the age.

The story begins as Dr. Clay Braddock, a young officer at the Gray Eagle Iron Works, returns to Lock Haven to discover that his friend John Andross has disappeared. Andross, a talented and likable young man, has a mysterious past. Braddock had discovered him some years before, penniless, surviving as a coal burner. Sensing Andross's potential, Braddock secured him a position as a clerk at the Gray Eagle Furnace. Now, discovering that $6000 is also missing,

Braddock suspects Andross of theft, but loyally replaces the money with his own life savings. Until the end of the story Andross, who has taken the funds, remains unaware of the debt he owes Braddock and fears being found out before he can replace the money. Braddock searches for Andross and eventually finds him safe at the mountain home of his fiancé, Isabel Latimer, who discovered him unexpectedly wandering in the wilderness.

Eventually, dramatic irony is established as the reader learns Andross's history while the other characters remain ignorant of it. Though of a good Philadelphia family, his father died in debt from bad investments while Jack, as he is known, was in college. Houston Laird, a friend of his father, continued to finance his education and then set him up in business. Laird, a "railroad king," is president of the National Transit Association, but his interests and influence range wide into what sounds like a mob syndicate. He made Jack first a plant manager whose real job was to ensure workers' votes for the right candidates, then a lobbyist at Harrisburg to secure Laird's interests, and finally a financial officer overseeing payoffs. When Andross tried to leave the corporation, Laird blackmailed him, threatening to reveal a forgery that his father had committed while in debt to Laird and thus to destroy his father's name. Realizing that Laird, never a friend, had managed to control his father as he now controlled him, Andross escaped by giving up everything. After Braddock offered him a decent job in the remote Nittany Mountains, he happily began to build a new life. He now even has a budding romance with the belle of the region, Anna, daughter of Judge Maddox, the owner of the Gray Eagle Furnace. Unfortunately, his identity is accidentally discovered one day by a Philadelphia reporter named Kenny. In desperation, Andross steals the payroll money from Maddox to buy Kenny's silence and then flees to the mountains.

Andross's attempt to buy anonymity fails. Accompanying Braddock is Julius Ware, a disreputable journalist who hopes to blackmail Andross as Kenny has. Soon Laird himself comes in search of Andross, offering him a seat in the state senate. Andross is pressured from all sides to return to Laird. Isabel's father, the honorable but naive Col. Thomas Latimer, and the not-so-honorable and naive Judge Mattox are taken in by Laird's savvy charm. The self-centered, shallow, but adorable Anna Mattox threatens to reject Jack if he refuses Laird's offer of money and power. Finally Jack accepts.

By December, six months later, the scene of action has shifted to Philadelphia. Andross has become a popular and respected state senator. Finding himself surprisingly unhampered by Laird, he deludes himself into thinking he is his own man. Judge Mattox, after closing the furnace company and investing his money with Laird, has moved with Anna to the city, where she is courted by anyone with money. Braddock, now out of work and money, has come to the city also. Having spent his savings to protect Andross, he has mysteriously canceled his and Isabel's wedding plans. Julius Ware is back in the city, too, but not as a reporter; he has become a preacher, living a life of faith, supported by donations. When Laird, in an effort to appear in compliance with the law, convinces honest Col. Latimer to take the position of collector of liquor taxes, Isabel and her father also come to the city.

In the course of the season, Laird encounters two crises. First, Col. Latimer, assisted by the streetwise detective Nick Bowyer (modeled on Brooks), proves to be more effective than Laird planned. Instead of taking bribes, he and Bowyer arrest those who attempt bribery and close down distilleries that do not pay the tax. In response, Laird endorses the hiring of a thug to teach Bowyer a lesson. Other less savory members of the ring decide that assassination of both Bowyer and Latimer is the only sure answer. Next, Andross, disregarding Laird and his party, plans to vote against a bill necessary to the ring's survival. Much of the plot turns on the machinations of Laird, Judge Maddox, and Anna to bring Jack in line, Anna's manipulation of Braddock to assist in those efforts, and Isabel's struggle to save her father. By the end it looks like Jack has been successfully coerced into voting for the ring. But when, at the eleventh hour as the vote is being taken on the floor of the senate, Andross discovers through Isabel that he has also unwittingly assisted in the plot to assassinate Col. Latimer, he recants. Voting no, he resigns from the senate, confesses his theft to Mattox, and begs Anna to accept him as a man without power and wealth, only honor. At this point she announces to Andross, the onlooking Braddock, and her father that their engagement, only a ruse to secure his vote, was never real because she has been secretly married to Julius Ware. Shocked now at nothing, Andross leaves with Isabel to save her father; they are followed by a humbled Braddock.

While the novel takes a few more twists and turns, this is essentially the story's climax. They save Latimer, and Isabel accepts Braddock back. Andross, finally discovering his debt to Braddock, repays him; and Latimer, Braddock, and Andross buy the Gray Eagle Furnace. When we see them again after five years, it seems that everyone is living happily ever after: Clay and Isabel are married and have a son; the furnace is thriving. Only Jack, unable to get over the loss of Anna, seems discontent.

Davis concludes her novel of protest against greed and decadence in post-Civil War America with a sardonic tone and a naturalistic vision. The Braddocks, the Wares, and Andross are all vacationing at the shore. Anna, who had used her sweet frail dependency to secure a life of pampered security in which love played no part, has become an obese shrew who must work to support the husband she adores. The only constant is that she remains as shallow and inane as ever. As Jack and Isabel stand on the beach watching Anna and Julius Ware floundering in a little boat hardly out of the surf, they are more amused than concerned. But when the boat capsizes and Ware, thinking only of himself, swims ashore, Andross dives into the surf to rescue Anna, who has panicked. Depicted with bitter irony, this ludicrous mishap swiftly turns into disaster. Although he can almost touch bottom, Jack is exhausted by the waves and by Anna's uncooperative 200-pound bulk. When he finally brings her ashore, Anna goes immediately to Ware, without a backward glance at Jack, who is left on the beach close to death. Prostrate on the sand, he finally sees his false ideal as she is "in soul as well as body, and in that moment her hold on him [is] gone forever" (324). Though Isabel has gone for help, Davis leaves the reader unsure of her hero's survival. Instead she asks, "Could he bear it?" until help arrived, and then concludes enigmatically: "meanwhile the tide flowed steadily inward, but gave no answer" (324).

Davis's criticism is aimed at several targets that were dominant features of nineteenth-century America. In her exploration of the shallow materialism of a society valuing wealth over honor, she focuses on corruption in politics, journalism, and religion as well as in business. In a world where money is power, it is "a struggle with all of them for emeralds, or houses, or stock" (283). Until the very end, Isabel is a voice crying in the wilderness, defining success morally, instead of materially. She defines the "successful man" as any man who "fights against his besetting folly or his weakness, and conquers it" (321).

As always, Davis's largest target is hypocrisy, in this case most clearly epitomized by Houston Laird, whose duplicity also makes him a fascinatingly complicated character. The head of "one of the most powerful [rings] in Philadelphia and New York," Laird, a "tender husband and father," who is also "head of Christian associations, aged workmen's homes, hospitals" (79), does not scruple against bribery, graft, or even murder. Davis also exposes as fallacies certain popular beliefs fostering hypocrisy, such as the myth of a self-made destiny or the myths of the ideal woman and ideal marriage. Finally, she questions the ability of a sensation-hungry democracy to correct these social ills.

While Davis's indignation at abused power and her anxiety over what she describes elsewhere as "the disease of money-getting" infuses this novel, its tone is markedly different from the urgent passion of her earlier protest pieces, such as "Iron-Mills," *Waiting for the Verdict*, or even "Put Out of the Way." In *John Andross* we see Davis's movement toward satire as she exposes the flaws of her main characters: Andross's ability to rationalize his moral compromises, Braddock's priggishness. Probably nowhere, however, is her satiric eye more unblinking than in her depiction of both men's infatuation with Anna Maddox, "that ideal of all men, a yielding woman" (104). Her target is not so much a vapid Anna as it is the shallow vanity of men: "The truth was, the charm in Anna was in this matter of protection. Isabel was so healthily tough and sensible" (218).

Davis's increased emphasis on the realistic techniques of dramatic plots, complex characters, and satiric tone did not diminish her fascination with philosophical themes. The central concerns of this novel are the limits on free will and the nature of fate. Ruling out a Calvinistic vision of fate, Davis recognizes the power of environmental and economic determinism as Andross reveals the moral challenge of the future: "You might fight against a man. But a powerful corporation meets you with the brain power of a multitude of men, but with no conscience, nothing to which you can appeal. It buys the law. It buys public opinion" (53).

Her protagonists struggle with varying degrees of success to live honorably in a society bent on corrupting them for its own survival.

Domestic Reform

Clearly, Davis maintained her critical scrutiny of American life while at home tending children. Domestic contentment, however, increasingly marks her fiction in the 1870s. Since Fields's first request for her to alleviate some of the gloom in her fiction, her writing had gradually increased in sentimental optimism. Also, since Clarke's initial influence, much of her work tended toward moralistic didacticism. With motherhood, the degree to which both these qualities affected her writing increased.

Domestic affirmation and social protest continued to coexist as themes in Davis's fiction; after the birth of her two sons, however, her focus seemed to shift away from the symptoms of evil in social injustice and more toward its primary cause, egoism. Although Davis would occasionally make a specific problem the thematic center of her fiction, as she did in *John Andross* and "Put Out of the Way," *Dallas Galbraith*, written in 1868, a year after *Verdict* appeared, marks a change in emphasis from exposing social ills to concentrating on individual sentimental transformations. Her stories continue to emphasize the recantation of a self-reliant protagonist for the joy of home and family, first developed in *Margret Howth*, but the characters' transformations less frequently involve larger social problems. Like Dallas Galbraith, many of Davis's protagonists seem to reflect the author's state of mind at this time, in which spouse and child are "only another name for God's tenderness."[8]

Dallas Galbraith

As with the request by *Galaxy* for *Waiting for the Verdict*, the editors of *Lippincott's Magazine* solicited Davis to inaugurate their new journal, which began in 1868. *Dallas Galbraith* was serialized as the lead story in the first 10 numbers of that magazine and then published as a single volume.

This novel, Davis's third, received less favorable reviews than her previous books; the perceived fault seems to have been her increased sentimentalism and didacticism. Henry James, writing for *Nation*, criticized *Dallas Galbraith* for appealing "to the conscience" instead of "to the reader's sense of beauty," as an "objective" novel does. He faults Davis for "instructing us, purifying us, stirring up our pity."[9]

Regardless of sentimental or realistic biases, though, *Dallas Galbraith* is a less compelling novel than her others. The long multiplot narrative contains unnecessary complexities and often lacks plausibility. Regrettably, Davis employs a melodramatic stock villain, George Laddoun. And her hero, Dallas Galbraith, though interesting in many aspects, lacks the mixed, flawed nature of Davis's other protagonists. The strength of the novel lies in the psychologically subtle yet complex development of several other characters, particularly the females. Honora Dundas, the young woman whom Dallas loves, and Dallas's grandmother, the matriarch Hannah Dour Dundas, are among her best.

In this novel Davis gives full reign to philosophical questions treated less directly in her previous writing: free will and fate, the possibility of self-creation, the reality of environmental determinism, and faith in divine plenitude. It also affirms the sanctity of the domestic sphere for men as well as women. Still, while often thoughtful and provocative, the novel frequently slips into abstraction since it is not grounded in attention to a particular social harm.

Dallas, an abandoned child and a victimized adult, is a talented and honorable man who, like Job, seems tormented by adverse fate. Though sometimes bemoaning his cursed destiny, he steadfastly upholds his own code of morality despite horrendous costs. He values nothing so much as home, family, and community – all of which are denied him until the novel's end, when his faith and goodness finally bring him domestic fulfillment.

The story begins in the remote seaside village of Manasquan, New Jersey, an area Davis knew well from her Point Pleasant summers. Dallas Galbraith, a homeless youth of 16, assists Dr. George Laddoun, who as a young medical student had rescued Dallas from the Scranton coal pits. Well liked by everyone, Dallas is particularly close to Lizzie Byrne, Laddoun's fiancé. Later we discover the Dallas had run away from an abusive step-father when his mother, who was also being abused, could no longer protect him. Dallas's peaceful life is disrupted when it is discovered that years before he had unknowingly helped Laddoun steal by forging a bank note. Rather than implicate his benefactor, Dallas takes the blame and serves a five-year prison sentence. Laddoun keeps quiet and goes free.

The scene then shifts to the Stone-post Farm, home of Dallas's paternal grandparents, Hannah and James Galbraith. It is Thanksgiving Day, five years later. Dallas's mother, who was widowed as a young mother when the wastrel Tom Galbraith died, has been widowed for a second time. Believing her son long dead, she has accepted the Galbraith's invitation to live with them. Coincidentally, Lizzie Byrne, who broke off her engagement with Laddoun in disgust after the trial, has become employed as a maid at the Stone-post Farm. She has remained in contact with Dallas, and hopes to arrange a reunion between Dallas and his family. Also residing at the Stone-post Farm is the Galbraith's adopted daughter and heir, Honora Dundas, an intelligent, independent young woman.

Reunion is difficult, however, when Dallas discovers how thoroughly prejudiced his grandmother and Honora are against anyone who has been a convict. Through the story's many twists and turns, Dallas strives to live honorably as he also seeks love and acceptance from his family and Honora; they eventually learn to see past the superficial facts of a person's life to truer qualities. The individual pride and prejudice of these characters aside, the reunion of the Galbraiths is complicated by the ongoing malevolence of George Laddoun, who is bent on destroying Dallas's happiness. Laddoun's inexplicable motivation is the real weakness of the plot. Perhaps Davis hoped to reveal through him a perceptive observation of human psychology, having to do with guilt that drives someone to compound a crime, attempting to validate it, but she does not succeed. Rather, Laddoun seems a melodramatic villain whose only purpose is to persecute the hero.

While this novel does uphold sentimental tenets, it does not celebrate conventional male and female roles. Both males and females in this novel defy gender codification, as Davis's sympathetic characters always do. Dallas Galbraith is the ideal feminized hero. A young man who "with all his stout muscle and hot blood, [is] as easily abashed as a girl," he has a "girlish face" (11, 14). His behavior is such that women forget he is not a woman (23).

Honora Dundas, the young woman who becomes the love interest in *Dallas Galbraith*, is like many of Davis's other pivotal female characters in that she feels stifled by her female sphere. She is "not one of the world's bits of useless porcelain which it delights to set aside and guard" (17). But she is trapped in the protective custody of her loving family. She is perhaps more fortunate than most in that she has a loved one who recognizes her situation: "Her uncle silently noted it all, and felt a deep, tender pity for her. There was no career open for women but that of wife and mother; and until that came to them, he thought that even the least morbid among them suffered from unused power and mental hunger" (10). Yet his sympathy is not enough to counteract received values: "He would have been ready to strike any one who would propose that Honora should find work and happiness outside of this tardy husband. He had a most delicate appreciation of woman's sphere, and drew the limits narrowly" (10).

Female rebellion against restrictive mores, a recurring theme in Davis's fiction, is emphasized in this novel. In the second installment of *Dallas Galbraith*, Honora is introduced in terms of this theme: "If she had been a man, she would have had politics or a trade or profession – some interest below and broader than her own petty cares – to sink them in. As it was, she sewed. She did not find in the needle that infallible medicine for a woman's mind diseased which men consider it" (9).

Discontent with the restrictions of the female sphere is expressed in every installment and voiced by many other characters. In the February number, Lizzie Byrne, the long-suffering fiancé of George Laddoun, says, "If I were a man, I'd force justice from the law, I'd never whimper" (133). In March, the narrator introduces Madam Galbraith: "If she had been a man, she would have worked off the rank, nervous vitality of her brawny body and brain in some struggle for freedom – Cretan or Fenian" (233). In April, a frustrated Honora says, "If I were not a woman, I would know first what the world is which we live in" (365). In June, a male character congratulates himself, "I'm not a woman, thank God!" (579). In July, Madam Galbraith again voices the discontent shared by Honora, Lizzie, and so many of Davis's women: "If I had been a man, I would have made my mark upon the world. But when I am gone, there will not be a sign on the earth that I have lived" (18). The discontent of these characters, as for most of Davis's females, results from their being capable, intelligent, energetic women who are frustrated by their limitations, humiliated by their dependency, and angry at their decorative uselessness.

In contrast with the admirable females is Dallas Galbraith's mother, Mary Duffield, a thoroughly unsympathetic character. Compared with the patient Lizzie and the passionate Honora, Mary

Duffield is weak and unattractive. But, like Anna Maddox in *John Andross*, she is depicted as the epitome of conventional female perfection. She is a hollow woman, surviving only for her creature comforts. Content to be waited on by the Galbraiths, she is impervious to the misfortune of others: "Whatever storm of joy or sorrow might rage about her, Mrs. Duffield remained like Gideon's fleece, miraculously dry, white and cool" (27).

While much of *Dallas Galbraith* is structured on the protagonist's troubled courtship of Honora Dundas, Dallas's primary quest is not simply for a wife. It is for all that she makes possible: home and family. He is an individual seeking a milieu in which he can honorably define himself. Although his quest is perhaps more noble than that of Stephen Holmes in *Margret Howth*, it is equally misguided. He errs at first in defining himself singly, heroically. As Honora and others learn to accept Dallas's internal value instead of being misled by reputation, Dallas learns that he is best defined through family. By the novel's end, he has clearly learned this lesson: "As he goes to his home in the quiet evening, his own life becomes present to Dallas Galbraith as never before in all its full and completed meaning; and seeing in that home, in his wife, and child . . . he knows the share his life has borne in the great scheme of order" (373). Dallas, finally a family man, affirms "the Eternal Order" of "inevitable Good at last" (372).

"A Pearl of Great Price"

"A Pearl of Great Price" (1868) offers a darker vision of these truths denied.[10] The virtuous female protagonist in this story fails to realize that marriage and family are the noblest life choices. Like Dallas Galbraith, Bertha Müller, is both morally superior to the rest of her society and an outcast: "a homely, irreligious girl, held as of a lower caste by all the belles of the village: a trifle coarse, perhaps" (608). Like many of Davis's heroines, she is not a beauty. Having learned "to dress without looking in the glass, morbidly trying to forget her homely face," Bart, as she is simply called, suffers from feelings of inadequacy, according to conventional standards of ideal womanhood (611).

Bart is not unloved, though; she has a fiancé – Sidney Kirke. Faced with what she sees as a choice between love and honor, Bart chooses honor, rejecting love and marriage to a man who truly loves her. She is committed to operating the family mill to fulfill a debt incurred by her dead father. But the fault is not entirely hers; it rests also on her fiancé and his rigidly conventional perception of marriage. Marriage would necessitate her leaving the mill since Sidney resides in another town. When she is not moved by his logic – "*I* cannot remain. You belong to me" (613) – he leaves her. In time, Bart accepts that she is "a single woman now for the rest of her life" (617).

Denied fulfillment through motherhood and family, Bart accepts a larger, though not as satisfying, role as the primary nurturer of her entire community, for which she becomes "the heart and mainspring" (79). Sidney marries another; years go by; and Bart and Sidney are both old people – he a widower – when they meet again. Seeing Bart's home, to which a man could come "for rest of strength, and it would never fail him," and realizing that Bart "belonged to it as the heart to the body" (85), the world-weary Sidney is now glad to live with her after they marry. They are finally together, but they are old. The fruitful years they might have had have been wasted.

Branching Out

New Genres, New Periodicals

As Davis's personal world narrowed to encompass little more than home and family, her literary world broadened. In 1869 she began her career as an periodical essayist. During this period when she was less able to concentrate on serious fiction because of attending to home and family, journalism offered her a way to continue writing and enjoying an income. She became a contributing editor to Horace Greeley's *New York Daily Tribune*, for which she would write regular features, unsigned, for the next 20 years. She also began publishing essays as well as fiction in *Putnam's Magazine*.

"Men's Rights," one of these early *Putnam's* essays, treats the "woman question," which so consumed nineteenth-century thought. Though somewhat facetious, the title also indicates Davis's rhetorical strategy of resolving polarity through synthesis. Negotiating between opposing positions, she argues against a "new path needed for women" other than that of home and family but for "a widening of the old one," to include trained work for wages (219). Ironically maintaining her "perverse inclination to the other side of the question" (212), she argues that the binding proscriptions by which the domestic sphere restricts a woman's natural growth perverted her generation of women. Tongue in cheek, she defends the right of men to have female partners who are healthy, whole human beings. To this end she encourages women to rebel against those aspects of popular domesticity that contribute to their moral, intellectual, and spiritual decay and men to support their rebellion. At the same time, she asserts in an equally left-handed fashion that, rather than dwelling on "the guilt of man," the solution lies in clarifying "the responsibility of women" to work for change (216).

This provocative essay also asserts several recurring themes from her fiction. Citing Shakespeare's Miranda and Juliet, Thackeray's Amelia, and "all of Dickens's heroines," she exposes the false ideal of womanhood as embodied in fiction by male authors: "the whole mob of perfect and silly Madonnas, are but so many exponents of the man's ideal woman, – the woman who, with accidentally more or less brain (it matters little whether less or more), lives solely in and for man" (218). She also exposes the anguish of women who lead unfulfilled lives, explaining that "suffrage, or work, any of the popular cries among us, are but so many expressions of the same mental hunger or unused power. Unused, and therefore unwholesome power" (214).

Ironically, just a year after the appearance of "Men's Rights," a subtle yet uncompromising feminist argument, and two years after the publication of her story "In the Market," Davis was mistakenly advertised as the author of an antifeminist tract entitled *Pro Aris et Focis* (*A Plea for Our Alters and Hearths*). The *New York Daily Tribune* immediately published the following disclaimer, couching in sarcasm the outrage felt by the paper and its new contributing editor: "A recent work entitled "*Pro Aris et Focis*, by the author of *Waiting for the Verdict*," has been absurdly attributed to Mrs. Rebecca Harding Davis. That admirable novelist and magazine writer had no more to do with it then she had with the Hindoo Vedas or the books of Confusius; and not wishing to wear unearned honors she desires to have the fact known."[11] Regrettably, many modern scholars have perpetuated this misattribution, causing Davis to be seen erroneously as a vocal antagonist to suffrage and economic independence for women.

Like later realists Stephen Crane and Theodore Dreiser, who moved easily from journalism to fiction, Davis, with her desire to write only of real life, moved easily from fiction into journalism. Her desire to dramatize the profound significance of mundane experiences in essays as well as fiction led her to mine factual records – historical documents and current newspapers. While stories like "Ellen" and "Blind Tom" demonstrate this facet of her writing early in her career, it was a mode that blossomed when she began writing essays. She was particularly fond of searching old manuscripts in the archives of the Philadelphia Public Library. In "A Faded Leaf of History," which Davis wrote for the *Atlantic* in 1873, she recounts a story recorded in a 200-year-old pamphlet, "printed by Rainier Janssen, 1698."[12] This particular history also reflects Davis's focus on the sanctity of motherhood at this time in her life.

Although she assures her readers, "I have left the facts of the history unaltered, even in the names" (45), Davis's selection and emphasis shape the facts to serve her thesis. As she later confesses, "if I were to try to reproduce the history of the famished men and women of the crew during the months that followed, I should but convey to you a dull and dreary horror." (49) Her account demonstrates the presence of a sentimental, maternal God of love.

The manuscript, however, does not discuss theology. Written by a recently arrived Quaker by the name of Jonathan Dickenson, it tells the record of a small party, primarily his household, on its way to Penn's colony, who are shipwrecked off the coast of Florida. The survivors spend a harrowing winter of deprivation and fear at the mercy of both nature and savages. After three months of wandering in the wilderness, they are rescued by the governor of Catholic, Spanish St. Augustine, and eventually they arrive in Philadelphia.

Mary Dickenson, a young wife and mother, is the most real character in this history for Davis, and her plight is the most poignant. Unlike the sailors, who have chosen this life, or her husband, who has chosen to build his fortune in the New World, Mary is just a woman "whose highest ambition [is] to take care of her snug little house" but whose fate has determined that it must be in a new land (48). Her situation, though one of extremity, is not really different from her normal life. She is at the mercy of savages for her survival and the welfare of her baby just as she has been at the mercy of her husband's decisions. She and her baby must trust. Just as Friend Dickenson, who assumes evil from the savages and so deals with them dishonestly, usually has his expectations fulfilled, the mother and baby, in their need, elicit care and nurturing from everyone.

Davis's narrative relates a sequence of episodes in which deprivation and brutality are exacerbated by alienating male behavior and are assuaged by befriending female behavior. In a typical instance the men, failing in their pretense of being Spaniards instead of Englishmen, have enraged a party of warriors. After the savages strip them of all clothing and ransack their trunks, the chief, or "Cassekey," notices the starving baby and his exhausted mother. Shortly, the captives begin a forced march to the Indian camp, assuming they are on their way to be eaten by cannibals. Davis quotes the original passage (replete with double consonants in use in the seventeenth century) describing their reception at the camp:

> Herein was the Wife of the Canibal, and some old Women sitting in a Cabbin made of Sticks about a Foot high, and covered with a Matt. He made sign for us to sitt down on the Ground, which we did. The Cassekey's Wife looking at my Child and having her own Child in her lapp, putt it away to another Woman, and rose upp and would not bee denied, but would have my child. She took it and suckled it at her Breast, feeling it from Top to Toe, and viewing it with a sad Countenance. (48)

The themes of this first episode are repeated. In each instance female nurturing and trust redeems male distrust and destructiveness.

Davis is struck by Dickenson's blindness to the evidence of truth in the experience he records. Describing loving providence as "Mother Nature," whose care is replicated in human care, she maintains that "it was the child and its mother who had been a protection and shield to the whole crew." Dickenson, however, has seen "only another inexplicable miracle of God" (49). Though the celebration of motherhood implicit in his history seems to have eluded its first historian, it does not elude Davis. The "mystery of that Divine Childhood that was once in the world" is revealed by the facts of this old record: "how in tribes through which no white man had ever travelled alive, [a baby] was passed from one savage mother to the other, tenderly handled, nursed at their breasts; how a gentler, kindlier spirit seemed to come from the presence of the baby and its mother to the crew" (50).

Focused, as she was at this time, on her children, Davis also began writing juvenile fiction in 1870. For subjects she often drew from history, as in "A Hundred Years Ago"; from legends, as in "Naylor o' the Bowl"; from tall tales, as in "Hard Tack"; and from her own youth, as in "The Paw Paw Hunt." Publishing regularly in well-respected young people's journals like *St. Nicholas* and *Youth's Companion*, she would continue writing children's fiction throughout her career – "Two Brave Boys," her last published piece, appeared in *St. Nicholas* two months before her death.[13]

Character Sketches

During 1873 and 1874 *Scribner's Monthly*, which promoted regional realism, featured a series of eight local character sketches by Davis. Interestingly, Davis again attempted a fictional persona with these sketches. Although she had already published two serials – *Natasqua* and "Earthen Pitchers" – in *Scribner's* under her own name, all these character sketches, which are told by the same fictional narrator, are signed "by R. H. D.," an identity she had never used before. It appears she hoped that by melding author and narrator her sketches would gain verisimilitude. These stories, with their emphasis on clear delineation of characters who have been shaped by a particular milieu, demonstrate Davis's continual striving toward realism. In these seemingly trivial lives the narrator discovers pathos and drama. She also discovers in the lives of her subjects the fallacy of preconceived stereotypes.

One of the first of these sketches is the "Pepper-Pot Woman," set in urban Philadelphia.[14] As she walks her beat, yelling "Pep-per-y-Pot!" Aunt Sarah is one of the "numberless middle-aged women, in ragged calico gowns, and with greasy tray-pads on their heads, who fill the market wharves at early dawn like a flock of gray, ill-smelling birds" (541). What most fascinates the narrator about Sarah is not her hard life but her total acceptance of whatever is natural – whether in people or in fate. As a result she seems to exist outside of civil law. She has had "one or two husbands in her day, and been married to neither of them" because living with them seemed "natural" (541). She has raised five children to adulthood, none of whom are related to her or to each other, because, as she says, "The children were left, and somebody had to take 'em; it was more natural for me than women with their hands full" (542). When Nan, one of her daughters, starts "turnin' to the bad," Sarah seems saddened, "but she makes no effort to interfere" (543).

The story's narrator and her husband, solid members of the mainstream, are affected by their knowledge of Sarah. She has altered their perceptions. At one point the narrator's husband attempts to explain her influence to their minister: "There is a certain old huckster-woman who has done more to shake my faith in the established heaven and hell than any skeptical arguments. I cannot find room for her in either; I cannot accommodate her to any other place than the back streets of Philadelphia" (342).

Like Sarah, the pepper-pot woman, Dolly, the subject of a sketch which appeared several months later, depicts another character who innocently and unknowingly disturbs someone else by defying preconceived notions of propriety.[15] In "Dolly" the narrator tells the tale of Dolly and the narrator's friend George Fanning, her befuddled suitor. The narrator does not miss the irony of poor George's bewilderment at the refusal of his heart's desire, Dolly, to live according to the romantic image he has of her.

The story begins with George's falling in love with the idea of innocence as it is embodied in a young Moravian convent girl. "Did you ever see innocence or unselfishness shine so transparent in any face?" George asks, comparing his "Dorothea" to "one of Corregia's Madonnas." To which the cynical narrator comments aside, "I thought Dolly much less insipid than any of those virgins, who surely were only immaculate from sheer lack of ideas" (90). George goes away to pursue his life, carrying her picture with him, planning to return in several years and find Dolly exactly as he had left her. George's first bewilderment is to discover on his return that Dolly has left the convent. He is sad, but he has his fantasy; and that, the narrator assures his reader, is what he likes best anyway.

The obstacle to George's fantasy is that Dolly, the reality, never conveniently disappears. And worse, she never seems to suffer for not staying locked in the protective casing of the convent, or the picture frame, or George's imagination. When they happen to meet again years later, she is radiant as one of the performers in P. T. Barnum's hippodrome. George hurries backstage with some confused thoughts on "the best way to appeal to unrepentant Magdalenes" (91), but he is caught up short when she greets him heartily, talking of her husband, who is homesteading out in Nebraska, and introducing him to her son and baby daughter. As she happily explains that her performance pay is going to purchase the Nebraska farm property, she is innocent of the way her refusal to fit neatly into preconceived notions of morality wreaks havoc on George's psyche: "The appeal to poor lost creatures or unrepentant Magdalenes seemed strangely inappropriate just then" (92).

"The Poetess of Clap City," another of these sketches, depicts a would-be poet who has forsaken her art to be a wife and mother. The story of Maria Heald, the poet in whom everyone saw "the earmark of genius," confounds the reader's expectations for a happy ending.[16] In this sketch, as in all the others, irony lies in the discrepancy between sentimental assumptions and reality.

The narrator begins this tale by explaining that "an accident happened to Maria which will occur to women with vocations – she married" (613). Her husband, "a silly, affectionate fellow" (613), turns out to be a drunk as well. Maria's life is hard, but she accepts her fate without surrendering to it. Postponing fulfillment of her artistic desire, she manages to support her family as a truck farmer, to provide a nurturing home for her children, and to finance her husband's periodic treatments for alcoholism. The one thing she will not do, however, is write for a living; as she explains, "I could not bring myself to sell my birthright for a mess of pottage" (614). As the years go on, she is sustained by her dream of the great poem that is within her. When after long years her husband dies, she proves to be a shrewd investor as well as an able provider and achieves a position of comfort for herself and her grown children. Finally, in possession of time and energy for herself, she writes her poem, "her life work, the expression of herself" (615). The story concludes with the narrator's report that it has made the rounds to several publishers who had earlier urged her to write. All now agree that "it is trash" (615). Ironically, Maria's refusal to compromise her talent has allowed it to atrophy.

In a sketch called "The Middle-Aged Woman" Davis explains why her focus in nearly all of these vignettes is on women:

> Choose any artist that you know – the one with the kindliest nature and the finest perceptions – and ask him to give you his idea of the genius of the commonplace, and my word for it, he paints you a middle-aged woman. . . . In middle-age she is the unromantic center of an unromantic world of daily dinners, anxieties about children, and worries about cooks and chambermaid. . . .

> This woman, just at the age when the poet and novelist will have none of her, is the fittest subject for the student of human nature. . . . whoever would gain a clear idea of the condition of American society, too, must take the middle-aged woman as the index.[17]

Davis proceeds to portray two very different women, claiming, "take a woman of forty anywhere in the States, and you have an embodied history and prophecy of the social condition of the country, practical and minute as you can find no where else except in a daily newspaper" (346).

Some women's lives in America, she points out, are still primitive, like that of Mistress Pitloe, who lives deep within the Nantahala range of North Carolina. As she travels out of the mountains, Davis points out that she also travels through time. Mistress Pitloe lives a more seventeenth-century life in her "house made of a dozen log huts squatted together with open passage-ways between." A "tall, raw-boned woman of fifty," she is the wife of Squire Pitloe, a colonel in the war, wealthiest farmer in the county, and a knowing politician. But she "has not left the farm for five years; her chances for reading consist of the Bible and a yellow pile of Baptist tracts" (346). Both in the field and in the house she serves her husband: "she eats with the servants, and is held in effect their social companion and equal." In Mistress Pitloe, Davis offers her nineteenth-century readers insight into another American woman whose life is most likely different from theirs: "It has not yet occurred to her that emancipation waits for her. She is no more inclined to question the limitations which make a beast of burden of her, than she is to quarrel with the monotonous hill-ranges, clad in the funereal black of the balsam, that have shut her in since her birth" (346).

Although also a middle-aged wife and mother, Mrs. Pettit, a writer who has just been made an editor in New York, would seem a different species from Mistress Pitloe. This sketch depicts a nineteenth-century version of the superwoman myth. A professional success, as well as a domestic one, Mrs. Pettit's life is also very different from that of Davis's average reader: "There is probably no subject or fact known to modern thought with which she is not thus brought in contact in the course of the year. At 4 P.M. she locks her office door, and goes home, and there is not a more picturesque, or better-dressed woman, or daintier dinner in New York, than those which welcome her husband, and her boys an hour later" (347).

This piece is typical of Davis's commitment to mediating difference – the nation's need of it and literature's power to achieve it:

> After all, Mrs. Pettit, pen in hand in her office, and Mistress Pitloe holding the plow, have only taken different handles of the same electric battery. As far as each is able, she is making life healthfuller and cheerfuller [*sic*], and nearer to God for her husband and children and neighbors, whether these last mean a few half-breed Indians or the hundred thousand readers of a magazine. It is precisely the same work as that of countless other unpicturesque, middle-aged women, from Maine woods to Pennsylvania villages, or California ranches. (347)

Satire

Davis's fiction of the early 1870s shows her exploration in another direction as well. Irony, which had always been detectable here and there in her writing, governs the tone of several stories of this period. In them Davis developed the satiric voice that would shape her late fiction. These early satiric pieces are interesting as further instances of Davis's mediation of opposing impulses. Davis was a Christian woman with optimistic faith in God's benevolence, yet she also had a fairly splenetic vision of society and a satirist's disgust with hypocrisy. Although she maintained the critical stance that humans are all of a mixed nature, she dwelt more on the unattractive in her protagonists than the attractive in her antagonists. The tension between optimism and pessimism, irony and urgency sometimes appears to compromise the integrity of her fiction.

Natasqua

In 1870 Davis again helped inaugurate a new periodical, publishing *Natasqua* in the first three numbers of *Scribner's Monthly*. This serial, which was later published as a paperback novelette, is not among Davis's best.[18] It is essentially a love story with melodramatic elements, such as secret pasts and abductions. The story is set in a sea-side village on the Natasqua River, modeled again on Manasquan, New Jersey. The romance between Richard Dort, a young crab fisherman, and Romy Vaux, the daughter of a shady New York journalist, is frustrated by the ambitions of Romy's status-hungry father. The lovers' struggle reveals a larger conflict between the honest, hard-working villagers and the false, parasitic New Yorkers.

The strongest element in this little novel is its satiric depiction of Romy's father, Major Vaux, who has changed his name from Joseph Fox to be "genteeler" (289), and her stepmother, Fanny Vaux, who happens to be Richard's real mother. Major Vaux is Davis's first characterization of the ignoble American type she felt most embodied the decadence of the late nineteenth century. She would further develop this type in Houston Laird and Julius Ware for *John Andross*, as well as many others. In Vaux, as in Ware, she places the huckster in the arena she knew best, journalism.

Major Vaux, a newspaper adman who wields power through "puffs," is motivated by no values other than greed and expedience. While he is the villain of the story as the chief agent against the lovers, we are invited to laugh at him more than to fear him. As the advertising agent for over 100 daily journals, who proudly brags, "We hold the public by the ear, as it were, like an overgrown donkey, and lead it where we will," his power is daunting (62). But his lack of awareness is humorous. Encamped at the shore with his family and servants, he prides himself on his kinship with the primitive. When "whisked into the tent and before a *beaufet* [*sic*] covered with liquors," however, both Richard Dort and the reader alike are "bewildered" by his very unnatural opulence. Amid "a glitter of silver presentation-cups" and "exquisitely shaped glass," Vaux holds forth: "You see us in the rough, sir, in the rough! We find it good once in the year to lose ourselves from the trammels of state and fashion and throw ourselves upon the bosom of Mother Nature. Hence, our tent, our couch of skins, our barbaric cookery"(63). His tastelessness knows no bounds as he dresses his wife to impress the world in "clothing of scarlet and green flying fringes, tassels, an Arab mantle, [and] wisps of false hair hanging dishevelled, according to the highest art of coiffeur" (61).

While Davis treats Major Vaux with a light Horatian touch, she portrays Fanny Vaux in a much darker juvenalian way. Like Dallas Galbraith's mother, Mrs. Vaux is a weak woman. Totally intimidated by her boor of a husband, she speaks to him "in a shrill frightened falsetto" (62). But she is also kept high on a pedestal by him. For Davis, the pampered, fragile woman who was an irresponsible mother was another symbol of decadence in post-Civil War America; and she was no laughing matter. Nonetheless, Davis reserves some sympathy for this "meek scared little woman," whose sole function seems to be "the cap and crown of [her husband's] social success" (65). The ultimate blame falls on society, which has not left a woman like Fanny Vaux many options. As Henrik Ibsen would show several decades later in *A Doll's House*, Davis demonstrates in this story that marriage mores in the nineteenth century could turn a woman into "a doll, a milliner's block" (161).

"Balacchi Brothers"

"Balacchi Brothers" (1872), which was reprinted several times in Davis's lifetime as an example of the new realism, contains numerous satiric elements.[19] Davis's primary target here is the narrow bigotry upheld by conventional mores, particularly as they denigrate performers. This theme recurs in several stories. Davis was highly sensitive to this form of hypocritical intolerance. Married to an aficionado of the theater, she enjoyed close friendships among Philadelphia's theatrical set, including such notable families as the Drews and the Barrymores. Great acrobats and also decent men, the Balacchi brothers are treated like pariahs. In the rural villages "good" Methodists and Presbyterians "looked on the theatre as the gate of hell," with the Balacchis "swinging over it." Regardless of the men's rectitude, natives assume they are "half-naked, drunken play-actors" (69). As George Balacchi's estranged sister proves, sophisticated city folk are no less bigoted. There, codes of propriety exclude performers, "dissolute and degraded, the very offal of humanity," from polite society (71). The playbill announcing the Balacchi brothers' acrobatic performance satirizes the hypocrisy of society's superficial gentility. In addition to several "posture girls" to hold ropes and trapezes, their company includes a pianist so that, as the manager explains, he can "cover you fellows over with respectability": " 'Concert' was the heading in large caps on the bills, 'Balacchi Brothers will give their aesthetic *tableaux vivants* in the interludes' " (68). Pious and proper citizens could attend a concert in good conscience; it did not matter that the "interludes" were most of the show.

Kitty's Choice, or Berrytown

The year 1873 saw the publication of two novel-length serials, "Berrytown" (later published as *Kitty's Choice, or Berrytown*) and "Earthen Pitchers." Though very different in plot, these stories are thematically similar. Upholding a commonsense philosophy, they argue against idealism and Puritanism. Instead, they assert that corporeal existence, being part of God's plan, should be valued, that loving, providing physical comfort, and finding contentment on earth are ways of righteous living. They both also satirize philosophies and behaviors that deny this truth.

The most satiric story of this period, *Kitty's Choice, or Berrytown* also shows the tension in Davis's writing at this time between the sympathetic critical realist she had always been and the more detached satirist she was becoming.[20] Primary among the many targets of her derision in this novel are self-righteous reformers and malcontent feminists. But efforts to create realistically complicated characters and situations, containing both good and bad elements seem to blur the focus of her satire.

The most uncompromising satire is aimed at the misguided notions impelling the nineteenth-century communitarian movement.[21] The story is set in the fictional Berrytown, a utopian community reminiscent in name and description of Bronson Alcott's Fruitlands, where the "the intolerance of these apostles of toleration is unaccountable" (410): "It was the capital of Progress. . . . Thither hied every man who had any indictment against the age, or who had invented an inch-rule of a theory which was to bring the staggering old world into shape. Woman-Suffrage, Free-Love, Spiritualism, offshoots from Orthodoxy in every sect, had there food and shelter" (401).

More complicated is Davis's ridicule of "the new woman," Maria Muller. A Margaret Fuller type, Maria is a surgeon, a suffragist, and a member of the Inner Light Club for Advanced Women. Although her egoism makes her an apt satirical target, Maria is presented sympathetically in her refusal "to be the fool or slave of a lover or a husband or son" (407). Yet when she sincerely falls in love, her previous feminist stance is derided as she dons "flounced white muslin and rose-colored ribbons" (697).

The Inner Light Club, a gathering of transcendental feminist reformers under the guidance of a Herr Bluhm, combines both the satiric targets of the novel. With "faith in the superior integrity and purity of woman's mind," the group debates such controversial questions as "Shall marriage in the Advanced Consolidated Republic be for life or for a term of years?" But their open-mindedness is suspect: "The profoundest thinkers in the society would bring to this vital question all their strength and knowledge, and, as they had all made up their minds beforehand against bondage and babies, the verdict was likely to be unanimous" (38). Even this group, however, is described somewhat sympathetically as being composed not of the popular caricature of women with "hair cut short, sharp nose and sharper voice," but rather women with "calm, benign faces" who, "having fought successfully against slavery, when that victory was won had taken up arms against the oppressors of women with devout and faithful purpose" (39). This passage seems to reveal the problem with Davis's satire at this time; satire requires caricature and Davis still strove for photorealism. Furthermore, her efforts to show realistic complexity in her characters sometimes led to unsatisfactory delineation.

Hugh Guinness, the man who ends up being Kitty's choice, is also blurred as a character. Certainly, his role in the plot requires that he be admirable. Yet at significant moments, he demonstrates a repelling lack of sensitivity. His response to the advanced ideas on womanhood propounded by "followers of the Inner Light," for instance, seems inconsistent. To the unsavory sophistication of their social concerns, the love story's hero asks, "If women are not pure and spotless, what have we to look up to?" (40).

The satiric norm for this novel is the protagonist, young Kitty Vogdes of Berrytown. Like all of Davis's admirable women, she "has a good deal of common sense" (47). Unlike others in her effete community, Kitty is "a hearty eater," with "nerves laid quite out of reach under the thick healthy flesh"; she knows "nothing of the hysterical clairvoyant moods and trances familiar to so many lean, bilious American women" (586). Even Kitty's character is confused and muddied at the end, though, as she too becomes the butt of satire. The plot has traced Kitty's development from a sheltered young girl into an assertive woman. While she is admirable through most of the story, in the last few paragraphs even she is compromised. Hugh and Kitty, now with children, along with the grandfather, old Mr. Guinness, are living what appears to be happily ever after on a farm away from Berrytown. Maria Muller, who travels much, often stays with them also. Kitty seems to be the perfect wife and mother, yet when she complains that the childless Maria "nurses that [pet] dog as if it were a baby. It's silly! It's disgusting!" she seems disconcertingly shrewish and unsympathetic (48).

Like Mark Twain, her contemporary, Davis seems bent, ultimately, on satirizing the romantic assumptions of her own plot. In the story's climactic homecoming, Kitty happily leads her husband to what the reader knows is her own private sanctum, "a little recess or cave, and a gray old bench on which was just room for two." At this moment Hugh's desirability, Kitty's wisdom, and the story's happy ending are all called into question: "It was nothing to him but a deserted spring-house. It was the one enchanted spot of Kitty's life" (47).

Sometimes, particularly in those stories where she was developing her satiric voice, Davis's mediation between sympathy and derision is not entirely successful. This is the case in *Kitty's Choice*, where the reader is forced at the end to look with satiric distance at a character who has been presented as a sympathetic ideal.

"Earthen Pitchers"

The satire of "Earthen Pitchers" leads one to suspect that problems with the clarity of her vision were not accidental but rather the unavoidable result of her ambitious attempt to satirize herself. This serial, which regrettably was never published as a novel, is fascinating and thoughtful, but its tone is even more unsettling than that of *Kitty's Choice*.[22] In this story of interlocking love triangles, Davis attempts to undercut the apparent moral of her novel that if you "are a woman," you "cannot shirk your real work [domesticity] for any whim [art]" (717). The real satiric target of this love story is love, or rather our erroneous expectation of love – the foolish life-shaping choices it causes us to make, its inability to provide the total happiness we want from it. Most troubling, though, is the issue of compromise. The two young women in this story willingly compromise their talent and ambition to accept their feminine role as vessels (pitchers) of mundane material (earthen) comfort. While this choice is one Davis usually celebrated, here, at a time when she was living out this exact compromise, she calls it into question.

The story traces the frustrated courtship of four characters. Jane Derby is a "sharp woman pushing into a man's place [journalism]" (77), who is "built for use and not for show" (80). She desires Niel Goddard, an artist of little rectitude, because he is the only man who has ever seen past her homely mannishness to appreciate her as a "womanly woman" (80). Niel, not very steadfast in any desire, is infatuated with the remote singer Audry Swenson. Niel is actually more in love with his own image of Audry than with the real woman. "Nature," he says, "could have created no more perfect type of the vestal virgin to dedicate to Art" (600). For Niel, Audry's attraction is that of a muse; he recognizes her "fund of original power" and plans to use her as "a fountain of life ready to my hand" (598). Audry is deaf to his proposal that she be an inspiration and a helpmate, explaining, "I can never marry," because "my art is all there is of me" (599). Also pursuing Audry is Jane's country cousin, Kit Graff, a patient, unassuming farmer.

A train wreck, Davis's favorite crisis device, causes both Audry and Niel to reevaluate their choices. Niel, realizing that Jane is the only woman who has ever loved him enough to sacrifice all for him, proposes; Jane, pausing only a moment to consider "all the Audrys past, and all the Audrys to come," accepts (716). Though Audry at first responds with "the look of a caged animal" to the idea of marriage to the wounded Kit Graff, her noble but simple childhood love, she agrees to marry him to give him reason to live. She accepts his proposal, but, more significantly, she accepts the traditional vocation of her womanhood over her desire to be a singer.

When all is said and done, the reader is assured that each woman has the man she wants and the life she wants; but the reader is hard-pressed to find joy in the darkened comedic resolution or sincerity in the narrator's stance. For both Jane Derby – the worldly, pragmatic journalist – and Audry Swenson – the innocent, idealistic musician – marriage and motherhood directly undermine creativity and autonomy. Jane leaves the city and the newspapers to run a farm and raise children, while Niel goes to the city and even to Europe with whoever is his "intimate friend of the moment." She ignores "the young women who run after her brilliant husband . . . knowing they cannot touch her hold on him" (718).

Jane's sacrifice for a man who does not consider her needs is sad; but Audry's sacrifice for a man who, though he adores her, is incapable of understanding her – a man "who cares little for music" (721) – is somehow even sadder. Tainting the happy-ever-after ending is the knowledge that her desire to sing, though repressed, is still painfully present. Now she uses her talent only to sing her daughter lullabies and to help support the family with music lessons. The story concludes as Audry, who has always had an affinity with nature, particularly the sea, experiences a rare moment of the old transcendent intimacy:

> For a brief moment the tossing waves, the sand dunes, the marshes put on their dear old familiar faces. Old meanings, old voices came close to her as ghosts in the sunlight. . . . She buried her hands in the warm white sand. She held the long salt grass to her cheeks. She seemed to have come home to them again. . . . She began to sing, she knew not what. But the tones were discordant, the voice was cracked. Then she knew that whatever power she might have had was quite wasted and gone. She would never hear again the voice that once had called to her. (721)

Like Maria in "The Poetess of Clap-City," the two women in "Earthen Pitchers" are forced to confront the fact that undeveloped power atrophies, and wasted talent is irrevocably lost. As in *Kitty's Choice*, the ambiguous resolution of this story calls into question its own suppositions. In this love story satirizing the efficacy of love, the protagonists' choices regarding marriage and family are never regretted, but they are recognized by both the narrator and the characters as unfulfilling.

"Earthen Pitchers" highlights the fact that these early satires were written at a time when Davis was enjoying a fulfilled life as a happily married mother of three children. But it also suggests that Davis, though always writing, like her characters often compromised her talent, producing less and less of the intense, demanding fiction of which she was capable. Instead of submitting to the respected journals that continued to solicit her work, she was more likely to send potboilers to popular children's and women's fashion magazines. These are what she had time and energy for. Still, the continued, though less frequent, appearance of strong work by Davis in better journals demonstrates that she still knew and valued quality in her writing.

Chapter Five

Homebound (1875-1889)

Material from Home

Throughout the 1880s Rebecca Harding Davis continued to pursue less ambitious projects that would not compromise her role as wife and mother. Except for one novel, *A Law unto Herself,* in 1878, she did not publish a new book until 1892. She continued writing essays regularly for the *New York Tribune,* however, and occasionally for other presses, particularly the *Independent,* another liberal New York weekly. She also wrote a tremendous number of children's stories, publishing from 5 to 15 juvenile pieces each year. While clearly having put her family ahead of her work, she never stopped writing, even temporarily. Instead, she gleaned much of her material from experiences on family trips and events that were part of her daily life.

The pattern of Rebecca and Clarke's family life appears to have continued its uneventful course, with the couple offering each other mutual support in their literary endeavors. While Rebecca was gaining a national reputation as an essayist, Clarke enjoyed moderate success as a fiction writer. His novel *A Stranded Ship,* first published in 1869, was reprinted with additional stories in 1880.[1] Both encouraged their children as well as each other. When their eldest son, Richard Harding Davis, revealed his literary aspirations while still in school, Rebecca had his first volume, *The Adventures of My Freshman,* privately printed; the doting parents bought all the copies.[2]

With her attention on home and family, Rebecca Harding Davis's life at this time seems to have become once removed from the outer world of affairs. Correspondence with her publishers indicates that, when she occasionally had business in New York that had to be handled personally, Clarke usually went as her agent. Except for family vacations, she seldom ventured from home. While there are numerous references in the journal and in correspondence to Clarke's attending the theater, there is no mention of Rebecca's accompanying him. A frequent and gracious hostess, she does not seem to have been antisocial, just preoccupied by the demands of home and children. Happily assuming her role as the center of the Davis family's "centre of the universe," she nonetheless continued to send forth her writing into the world.

The Centennial Exposition

Philadelphia was the site of the 1876 Centennial Exposition. Davis reported to Annie Fields in Boston that Clarke was one of its "most active managers." Rebecca was also supposed to have been involved, yet she apparently hardly attended. As she wrote Annie, "I know less about it than even you. . . . I was only down there one evening, though I believe my name was on a committee" (UVA, 6 November 1876). Harris points out that Davis, always a critic of industrialism, probably had reservations about the exposition's celebration of technological progress (192-93). Regrettably, she seems to have missed the historic suffrage demonstrations that Susan B. Anthony and Elizabeth Cady Stanton led in protest of the Declaration of Independence, taking over the platform to read their Women's Declaration of Rights; there is no record that she even saw the Women's Pavillion.[3]

Instead, Davis seized on the public's interest in colonial Philadelphia and its role in the founding of America as an opportunity to write, publishing three different researched pieces on historic Philadelphia.[4] Her "Old Philadelphia," appearing in *Harper's,* is a well-documented portrait of the ancestors of various contemporary residents of the city who colonized the wilderness homeland of the Lenni-Lennappé. With stories of these early settlers, Davis emphasized Philadelphia's unique heritage of "brotherly love." The earliest colonials were Swedes, who came with Gustavus Adolphus in 1637 to establish a utopian community, "where every man should have enough to eat, and toleration to worship God as he chose" (705). Then in 1682, William Penn, with his Society of Friends, established an English colony on similar principles. This article demonstrates Davis's ability to show the great as ordinary and the ordinary as great. It also illustrates her sense of the present imbued with the past.

In "Old Landmarks in Philadelphia," a piece run in *Scribner's Monthly,* Davis emphasizes the provincial quality of Philadelphia.

While W. C. Fields and others have since found this same characteristic to be a detraction, for Davis it was one of the city's unique charms: "The city of the Friends, as she opens her gates to entertain the world this summer, finds she has but a sober display of household goods and gods to make. . . . She has accumulated fewer showy churches, theaters, or monuments than her Western sisters. . . . She has naturally neglected to provide a variety of public amusements for a people noted through the States for their domestic and sober habits, and forgotten to build monuments to great dead men in her anxiety to make of herself a comfortable home for obscure living ones" (145).

The *Lippincott's* piece, "A Glimpse of Philadelphia in July, 1776," is different. Like "A Faded Leaf," it is a fictionalized account from an old manuscript. The source for this history is a personal diary kept by a Mr. Henry Keen Waldo, member of the Virginia House of Burgesses from Queen Anne's, who had come to Philadelphia in 1776 for the Continental Congress. Although Waldo was an advocate of Thomas Jefferson and Patrick Henry, the diary reflects his private domestic life rather than his public political one. It is the record of a concerned father who brought his unmarried daughter with him to the city. With only brief references to the historic controversies of the Congress, the piece documents the homes that Waldo and his daughter Betty visit and the people they meet.

Davis develops as her plot the courtship of Betty Waldo; thematically, she highlights the broadening experience of mediating cultural difference. The extravagant and aristocratic Virginian records his discoveries of admirable qualities in the sober Quakers of old Philadelphia; he also sees in the bustling city portents of national change: "[F]rom the Northern Liberties came the music of the city battalions at drill, now passed a dozen painted Indians in hunting-shirts, not lounging lazily under a load of peltry, but erect, keeping step to the tap of the drum; again, a band of fighting Quakers, young fellows, cockaded, in blue and buff; . . . the very gangs of 'prentice-apron lads in their smock shirts and leathern aprons crowded about Dock Creek, and the black slaves at work in the reeking kitchens gabbled together of Washington's hungry soldiers" (30). In the eyes of Davis's fictionalized colonial, old Philadelphia symbolizes the American spirit: pluralistic, proud, and free.

The New Jersey Coast

Davis's desire to research facts and to discover in them illuminating insights seems to have been greatly satisfied by her movement into journalism. During her sojourns on the New Jersey coast Davis found more material than the colorful characters who populate novels like *Dallas Galbraith* and *Natasqua* and children's stories like "How the 'Gull' Went Down" and "The Shipwreck."[5] Fascination with the human drama of shipwrecks and inquiry into the odd little rescue stations on the beaches led in 1876 to two significant expository pieces for *Lippincott's* – "The House on the Beach" and "Life-Saving Station."[6] In both articles the author recounts what she and her little party of summer tourists learn about the history and present conditions of marine safety. Their education begins when they discover a little two-story wooden shed on the beach, which turns out to be one of 108 similar facilities recently established by the government; the upstairs being a weather and signal station, the downstairs a life-saving station. Their guide is a weathered old fisherman named Captain Brown.

The first article to appear was "The House on the Beach," which focuses primarily on the U.S. Signal Service Bureau, a forerunner of the National Weather Service. Pointing to a wreck offshore and to the little shed, Davis asserts a theme recurring in all her writing: "[I]f we choose to look more deeply into things, we may find in the old hulk and commonplace building hints as significant of the Infinite Order and Power" (72). Recounting the history of meteorology as far back as "Aristotle and the Chaldeans," she points out that tales of Greek and Judaic heroes "are no longer myths to us when we remember that they were wet by the rain and anxious about the weather and their crops, just as we are" (73). While human vulnerability to the elements had been a universal experience, Davis explains that in her time, because of the heroism of scientific explorers and the establishment of the Signal Service, sea travel had become safer than ever before.

"Life-Saving Stations," the second installment, explains contemporary advancements in sea rescue operations. Old Captain Brown's tales of past wrecks on the Long Island and New Jersey coasts provide human interest. But the article's impact lies more in its documentation and statistical data. Her research was so impressive that

Encyclopedia Britannica asked her to write a seven-page entry on the U.S. Life-Saving Service for its supplement to the ninth edition.[7]

Theatrical Friends

Both at home in Philadelphia and during the summers at Point Pleasant, the Davises' circle of friends seems to have been composed primarily of theater people. Davis's father had been a amateur scholar of Elizabethan and Restoration drama. Her husband, Clarke, was a respected theater reviewer, whose criticism of Shakespearean productions is included in Horace Howard Furness's *Variorum* edition of the plays. Richard Harding Davis, Rebecca's eldest son, became a popular playwright. Although she never wrote for the theater herself, Davis enjoyed the art and respected the craft. As she showed in "Balacchi Brothers," her indignation at hypocrisy was stirred by polite society's ostracism of performers. She was particularly indignant over the way people questioned the virtue of actresses.

"Across the Gulf" (1881) develops this concern.[8] When the Reverend William Imlay falls in love with Jane Shannon, a young actress, he is forced to negotiate between two worlds: the genteel world of his mother and "the brilliant wicked hell below the decorous world in which [Janey] lived, to which pertained all of Satan's doings, – cards, fashion, dancing, and, above all, theatres" (59). Ultimately, he proved too dependent on social opinion to follow his heart. Davis is less sentimental in her development of Janey than she was with previous characters who were female performers. As with Lizzie Gurney, Dolly, and others, she still provides Janey with a morally redeeming motive: she is supporting her father and brother. Davis emphasizes, however, that Janey simply likes acting and living with an extended family of actors. Though kind and decent, she is also ambitious and thrives on the independence of earning a good salary. When Imlay offers to save her, saying, "I came, to persuade you to leave this mode of life," his words fall on deaf ears. "No," she replies with simple dignity, "it's my trade" (70).

A Law unto Herself

In *A Law unto Herself* (1877), her only novel of this period, Davis asserts the validity of civil or filial disobedience when morality and legality are in conflict.[9] Jane Swendon, the protagonist, is a woman of absolute integrity who feels impelled to defy the law. Before the death of Captain Swendon, Jane, loving her father dearly and wishing to be an obedient daughter, stays by his side during his last days, tortured by his ignorant confidence that he is wise to marry her to a despicable charlatan. The dramatic irony is truly painful as her father gives his righteous assurances: "I will not leave you until I have taken care of you, Jenny" (626). Confronted with her father's repeated pleas, she finally agrees to marry a man she despises. Realizing that she cannot throw her life away for anyone, however, she is forced to deceive her father to be true to herself.

More shocking from a legal standpoint, however, is the heroine's knowing destruction of a legal will to regain a fortune that she believes rightfully belongs to her ill father. The Swendons have lived in poverty since Jane's mother, Virginie Morôt, was disinherited for marrying Jane's father, a sweet, brilliant, but penniless inventor. Instead of willing his money to Virginie, who eventually died unable to afford medicine, old Morôt left it to a dissolute cousin, Will Laidley, who offers no aid to the destitute Swendons. Now on his own deathbed, Laidley is apparently planning to appease his guilt by willing the fortune back to the Swendons when he is convinced by Pliny Van Ness, a fraudulent philanthropist, that his redemption will be more likely if he gives all his money to "God's service." As depicted, this change of heart is ignoble, but entirely legal. Desperate to help her ailing father, Jane sincerely tries to convince her cousin that "it is of the living, not the dead, you ought to think" (181). But when he refuses to see his error, she calmly takes the new will and before his eyes burns it in the fire, declaring, "You shall not wrong him [her father]" (182). When Laidley dies before he can remake the second will, everyone assumes the previous will to be valid, and the Swendons receive the inheritance. Unaware of what has transpired, Jane's father is disturbed by her steadfast enmity and her refusal to seek any last-minute reconciliation with her cousin before his death. She maintains, "I have done nothing to him which I would wish to set right" (182). The reader, aware of the statement's full import, is perhaps more shocked.

As usual, the best aspect of this novel is characterization. Bruce Neckart, Jane's ambitious lover, Captain Swendon, her misguided father, and Pliny Van Ness, her despicable betrothed, are all multidimensional, memorable characters. But Jane is by far the most complicated and thematically significant character in the novel. The story asserts the sanctity of the individual over society, the natural world over the world of commerce and politics, and common sense over intellectualism. The embodiment of all these attributes is Jane Swendon, a totally honest woman who "never comes into town: she is not a woman of society"; she seems "only a part of the shore, as much as sea or sand" (177). The one who learns the truth of her values is Bruce Neckart, a workaholic who is "a controller of a great journal" and a "leading politician" (170).

While embodying natural virtues and individual integrity, Jane is not an idealist. Firmly grounded in this world, she demonstrates one of Davis's most frequently recurring themes: "No matter what our sympathy, our help for each other can seldom come any closer than skin or stomach, after all" (292). This philosophy directed Davis's belief in individual reform, shaped her realistic sensibility in literature, and it determined the choices in her personal life.[10]

In many ways this novel repeats the strengths and weaknesses of "Earthen Pitchers." While creating memorable characters, Davis's dual impulses toward sympathy and satire also lead to a degree of ambiguity. Two interesting characters who demonstrate this tension are women outside the realm of propriety: Charlotte Van Ness, Pliny's first wife, and Cornelia Fleming, a rather bohemian friend of the Swendons, who also loves Bruce. While both women are antagonists of sorts, Davis seems to admire their grit, if not their values.

A con artist and actress for hire, Charlotte Van Ness also appears throughout the course of the novel as Madame Varens, a medium, and as the Russian Princess Trebizoff. Her role in the machinations that beset the protagonists could easily make her villainous, but Davis provides her with maternal impulses that render her sympathetic and with a resilience that is even heroic. For example, her threat, when Jane Swendon debunks her sham séance – "I owe you an ill turn, and I shall pay it" – is softened when she follows that declaration with "I had a way to support myself and my boy for a year, and you have taken it from me" (48).

Cornelia Fleming, an artist and a "New Woman," is a foil for Jane, who in her own quiet way is actually more self-reliant. When she fails to find love and fulfillment through marriage, Cornelia replaces these with art. With "her hair cut short" and her "man's collar," she attempts an alternative lifestyle but fails to do so successfully: "A good fellow, Corny," the other artists say, "but what a pity that she is not a man" (731). While she is drawn to invite ridicule in many ways, Cornelia is also presented sympathetically as "sensitive and delicate in the extreme," even though others might "mistake her for one of the strong-minded Advanced Sisterhood" (724).

Subsequent melodramatic plot developments in this novel do not do justice to the potential of its complex characters. To escape being forced by her father into marriage with Pliny Van Ness, who has fooled everyone, Jane flees, only to be relentlessly pursued by him all over the United States. Meanwhile, Bruce Neckert, who believes he is fated to become insane, like his mother, sails for Europe only to have Cornelia reveal the identity of his real parentage, which removes any impediment to his marrying Jane. With improbable alacrity he crosses the Atlantic, marshals forces to destroy Van Ness, and finds Jane hiding in the Blue Ridge Mountains of North Carolina, just in the nick of time.

Regardless of its melodramatic plot, *A Law unto Herself* is noteworthy for its insight into female psychology. From Margret Howth to Audry Swenson in "Earthen Pitchers," Davis was always fascinated with interiority, trying to depict an inner private personality in her female protagonists that is unknown to others. With Jane Swendon, Davis pursues this idea in depth. The novel's conclusion reveals Jane's interiority as a form of passive rebellion against paternal, conjugal, legal, and ideological control. When in the final scene, Jane, after only a moment's hesitation, obediently tells her husband, "I know that I made many mistakes when I was a law to myself. You are my law now, Bruce," she seems to have been flattened by melodramatic formula (731). But Davis immediately reveals the dramatic irony of this dialogue, enabling the reader to see through Jane's obeisance while Bruce accepts its sincerity.

Jane's interior resistance is revealed by the way she immediately compromises her first dutiful response. Throughout the story Jane has never regretted destroying the legal but immoral will that deprived her father of his inheritance. After she marries and all antagonists have been foiled, Bruce urges her to give the money to charity. He seeks not just agreement with his plan but recognition of it as proper "reparation." This Jane will not grant him. When he asks her whether she is "satisfied that it was right to give back the money," she responds, "Of course! The money was unlucky! It made you uncomfortable too. . . . But," she adds in a low voice, "the money was mine. I was quite right when I burned the will" (731).

The closing passage of this novel focuses on neither character nor plot; it is the narrator's direct explanation of the protagonist's interior passive resistance: "Neckart laughed good-humoredly, and touched the horses with his whip. There is no man living who loves his wife more tenderly; and Jane is the most simple and prosaic of women. Yet there are times when she seems, even to him, a woman whose acquaintance he has scarcely made, and whom he can never hope to know better" (731).

If a critic for the *Nation* is any indication, Davis's fifth published novel was well received. This review, which also discusses Davis's fiction in general, warrants attention because it accurately assesses the strengths in most of her work:

> Mrs. Rebecca Harding Davis writes stories which can hardly be called pleasant, and which frequently, as in "A Law unto Herself," deal with most unpleasant persons, but there is an undercurrent of recognized rectitude and a capacity for calling a spade a spade . . . but though she shows bad taste in various ways, or perhaps because of this, she succeeds in giving a truer impression of American conditions than any writer we know except Mr. Howells. . . . Somehow she contrives to get the American atmosphere, its vague excitement, its strife of effort, its varying possibilities. Add to this a certain intensity, a veiled indignation at prosperity, and doubt of the honesty of success, and we get qualities which make Mrs. Davis's books individual and interesting if not agreeable.[11]

Travel

Fictionalized Travelogues

While family vacations were at the shore, Davis's favorite getaway was always back home to the mountains. She used travel there as the opportunity to gather regional material. Seeing herself as a southerner and a westerner who through print could speak to the northeastern establishment, she felt compelled to mediate the perceived differences that still fragmented the postwar nation. In the 1880s the Davises also made several trips to the deep South, where Rebecca had been born. Henry Grady and other promoters of the New South actively sought the support of Clarke Davis, the editor of a large northeastern daily. These trips, too, provided her with new material.

In the 1880s Davis wrote two multi-installment travel narratives for *Harper's.*[12] Both are episodic fictions with very little plot. Primarily, they record a group of tourists' exposure to the local characters, families, geography, sites, lore, and legends of the areas they visit. The episodes do not focus on the travelers; like the narrators in her frame tales, these characters serve as the vehicles for Davis's cultural mediation. They demonstrate that experience in a region corrects the perceptions of it held by people from another region.

The sightseers in Davis's "By-Paths in the Mountains" (1880) are members of an exploring party, organized by a Mrs. Mulock, who have decided to spend the summer camping in the Alleghenies rather than going to Europe or to any of the fashionable spas. Mrs. Mulock is presented as someone gifted with Davis's imaginative perception: "She had observant, quick, imaginative eyes. She was a person who could find more strange bits of human history, more suggestions of adventure, in a morning's ride in the horse-cars, than [most] would do in a tour through all Europe" (169). In the second installment, the campers spend the next summer experiencing the local color of Appalachia: the old plantation homesteads, the mills, the cottages of artisan weavers, the rude cabins of trappers, the trading villages on the edge of the wilderness, the Cherokee communities, the mountain clans that never communicate with outsiders. The visitors are impressed with the degree to which Appalachia, in the heart of America, has remained a land apart.

In 1885 the Davises toured the Gulf states of the deep South, which provided material for several articles, particularly "Here and There in the South" (1887). In this serialized travelogue, Davis again leads her readers vicariously through locales that might seem foreign. Like the previous regional tour, this one seems intent on dispelling falsehood with truth. In this case, however, she reveals the reality of the New South. Her tourists this time are the Reverend James Ely and his wife, Sarah, from western New York. Mr. Ely's congregation has financed his first, much needed vacation. Instead of their suggested European tour, Mr. Ely has decided to go to the South, where he had been once 40 years ago, before the war. Then he had been entranced by "the leisure and quiet, the laziness" of the region (236).

While enlightening, the trip causes Mr. Ely no little chagrin as he adjusts his misconceptions. "If he had found a decayed, mouldering aristocracy, passively wasting away in their ruined homes," Davis tells the readers, "it would have been in mournful keeping with his recollection" (238). But Davis's project is the realistic revision of myth. The first installment, "Old and New," takes the Elys to Atlanta. The New South that Mr. Ely discovers there is not interested in perpetuating its romantic image. It has learned the power of manufacturing. Major Pogue of Atlanta corrects many myths about the South for his visitors, among them the myth of the frail belle. As Margaret Mitchell would dramatize in *Gone with the Wind,* Davis's host explains that it was the southern women, who, though often perceived as frail and helpless, "were the first to stagger to their feet [after the war]. In every household it was invariably the woman who first faced the inevitable and tried to make the best of it" (238).

The couple travel by train on a course that resembles the present Southern Crescent railroad line. Beginning in New York, they travel first to Washington, D.C., then to Atlanta. From there the Elys travel to Mobile, then Biloxi, and finally to New Orleans. All along the way the protagonists' narrow preconceptions are altered by understanding. The unique qualities of place and race are drawn in detail, but, more important, everywhere they go they find industrial progress and modernization improving the quality of southern life.

These fictional travelogues were very popular. Harper's showcased all the installments of both pieces with numerous detailed illustrations. In 1882 Davis wrote a children's version of "By-Paths" for *Youth's Companion* titled "Vacation Sketches in the Alleghenies." Though she was not writing for the *Atlantic* much at this time, that journal also published a piece inspired by her trip through the Gulf states.[13]

"Some Testimony in the Case" (1885), reflecting her experience touring the deep South, is not a travelogue, it is an essay on the "Negro problem," which she had foreseen in *Waiting for the Verdict.* In it, she argues that the struggle between the races "will certainly affect permanently their domestic relations, their commercial prosperity, and the place which the South will hereafter hold in the scale of civilized peoples" (603). Her purpose is education. By citing the opinions of various southerners – wealthy and poor, male and female, educated and ignorant, white and black – she exposes generalizations as dangerous fallacies: "The character and the claims of the colored man differ with each individual precisely as do those of the white" (607).

Local Color

During the late 1870s and 1880s Davis also wrote a number of local color sketches. This popular magazine genre provided Davis with another opportunity to mediate difference, exposing her readers vicariously to people and places unknown to them. It also allowed her the opportunity to use her travel experiences as material. While she depicts many southern regions, the most frequently used setting at this time was North Carolina. Like her travelogues, her local color sketches usually feature an outsider experiencing the people and situations indigenous to a locale. The outsider, though not a narrator, is the story's privileged consciousness, allowing description of a region, perceptions informed by another region, and the mediation of both. This technique occurs in several stories. "The Yares of the Black Mountains," written for *Lippincott's* in 1875, is an interesting one; it demonstrates the strain of idealism frequently present in Davis's fiction.[14]

The outsider through whose consciousness the reader experiences "The Yares of the Black Mountains" is Mrs. Denby, a young widow. She is journeying into the unknown to save the life of her frail baby son, who the doctors have said will benefit from the balsamic air around Mt. Pisgah. The story begins with the announcement that "civilization stops here" as Mrs. Denby's train reaches the end of its run, 30 miles short of Asheville, North Carolina. There she experiences a feeling of spiritual homecoming to a people and a place she has never known. Mrs. Denby's affinity for the place is emphasized by the juxtaposition of another outsider, Miss Cook, a writer from New York. Miss Cook, who is collecting data for her book, *Causes of the Decadence of the South,* condescends to the locals: "These mountaineers were all originally either French Huguenots or Germans. It would be picturesque, dirt and all, under a Norman peasant's coif and red umbrella, but in a dirty calico wrapper – bah!" (37). She is disappointed in the scenery; "it lacks the element of grandeur." Mrs. Denby, on the other hand, knows only that her baby "has slept every night since we came on to high land" (36).

The distraught mother finds the rural setting restorative. Later, after she has left Miss Cook on the last leg of her journey to the Yares' mountain cabin, Mrs. Denby herself becomes aware of the transcendent potential of the place: "It was as though she had come unbidden into Nature's household and interrupted the inmates talking together." The mountains with their balsams are physically restorative to her son, but they are spiritually restorative to her: "It was as if God had taken her into one of the secret places where He dwelt apart" (42).

The Yares themselves are idealized in their natural state. Against all advice Mrs. Denby has arranged to board at the Yare cabin for the summer. Her hosts, she is told by the Asheville locals, have "lived in the wilderness for three generations, and, by all accounts, like the beasts" (41). But when Jonathan Yare, who is taking her to the cabin, stops along the trail, milks a cow, and returns with fresh warm milk for the baby, she realizes that her urban view of a "beast" – "visions of the Ku-Klux and the Lowery gang" – needs adjustment: "one of the Lowery gang would hardly go to milking cows" (42).

The living conditions of these Appalachian mountaineers, which Davis had seen firsthand, is not idealized, however. When Mrs. Denby finally arrives at the "low log house built into a ledge of the mountain," she is at first shocked at the squalor: "A room on either side opened into a passage, through which a wagon might be driven, and where the rain and wind swept unchecked. An old woman stood in it looking up the stream. Her gray hair hung about her sallow face, her dress was a dirty calico, her feet were bare. Behind her was the kitchen, a large forlorn space scarcely enclosed by the log and mud walls. A pig ran unnoticed past her into it" (42).

As Mrs. Denby lives with this family of mountaineers, she discovers a value to them that a cursory look – of the kind Miss Cook might give – would never reveal, for "nature does not always ennoble her familiars" (43). Though ragged, unclean, poor, illiterate, and not very articulate, this family has a natural purity. As the summer progresses, baby Charley and his mother are "adopted into the family," and they become privy to the truth about what gossips in Asheville had referred to as "the terrible history of the Yares" (43). They discover that the primary cause for the Yares' outcast status is that they were "fur the Union" during the war. At first Mrs. Denby, an abolitionist, makes the mistake of assuming their disagreement was related to slavery. It was not. It was solely the issue of union. Here, too, Davis draws from her intimate knowledge of such people in the hills of her own West Virginia.

The Yares' faith in organic unity also reinforced the idealistic tone of the story. As natural people, they consider their place as individuals within the greater scheme to be a primal law that mandates cooperation. During the war they had refused to fight for destruction of the Union, yet they had also refused to fight their neighbors. Instead, the five Yare sons hid in the mountains and conducted their own mountain version of an underground railroad for runaway Confederate soldiers and escaped Union prisoners. And the Yare home, with mother and sister Nancy, was the central station.

When the summer ends and baby Charley is fat and strong, Mrs. Denby prepares to leave the Yares' rustic home on Black Mountain. No longer outsiders, Mrs. Denby and her son, Charley, leave not only physically and spiritually healed by the Yares but also wiser. They understand that the human being is part of a greater natural unity.

Everything Davis found on her travels into the remote Blue Ridge Mountains was not idyllic, though. Much like "The Yares," "The Man in the Cage" (1877) is set in a "drowsy hamlet in North Carolina, lying literally above the clouds, on one of the mountains of the great Balsam range."[15] In this story, however, she tells of John Matlock's brutal incarceration. In a "low cage, with bars as thick as [one's] wrist," he has been "chained to the floor" for a year (79).

The story focuses on the response of two outsiders – the honeymooning Reverend Mr. Edward Britton and his wife, Phoebe – to "the barbarous custom of this State," in which they treat a "criminal as a brute – chain him by leg and arm to the floor, inside of just such a cage as is used for wild beasts" (81). The two are horrified not just by the man in the cage but by the apparent inhumanity of the warm, friendly inhabitants who condone this practice.

In this story Davis again explores the grounds for civil disobedience when laws are unjust. The prisoner, John Matlock, whom the couple turn out to know, is accused of a murder of which they believe he is innocent. Rev. Britton, like Rev. Imlay in "Across the Gulf," is too bound by propriety to follow his instincts. His wife, Phoebe, a "plump, pink-cheeked dot of a woman" (79), however, cannot ignore the wrong. Unable to prove his innocence, she successfully engineers Matlock's escape by smuggling him a watch-spring saw. When another convict makes a deathbed confession four years later, her rebellion is vindicated.

"At the Station" (1888) is a different sort of North Carolina tale.[16] Set in the lowlands and told by an effaced omniscient narrator, it is primarily a character sketch of Miss Dilly, a "pudgy old woman of sixty" (688). In the spirit of regionalism realism, Davis emphasizes the ordinary nature of the place and of the character who has been shaped by it: "Nothing could well be more commonplace or ignoble than the corner of the world in which Miss Dilly now spent her life. . . . Nothing, too, could have been more commonplace or ignoble than Miss Dilly herself" (687). While not softening the milieu as a determinant of her character's destiny, Davis focuses on Miss Dilly's ability to endure her dependent position and to find fulfillment in her situation.

Here Davis again depicts a passive, waiting woman like the pathetic Knocky-luft of her childhood. Suffering from neuralgia, she has been in "pain only since she [has] lived in the lowland" of North Carolina, where her younger brother, James, moved her and arranged for her support at the Sevier Station Inn, before leaving for the West after the death of their parents. That was 20 years ago, when she was 40. Since then, Miss Dilly has lived in emotional and physical pain, waiting for her brother to return, though "nobody ever heard a groan from Miss Dilly when the attacks of pain came on." She and James are originally from the mountains, and she privately lives on dreams that when James returns, if they "would go back to them[,] she would be cured" (687).

Miss Dilly is not pathetic, though, nor is her life at the tiny railway station village unpleasant. "The jokingest and most agreeable of her sex in this part of Cahliny" (688), she enjoys sympathy and primacy in the little community. Not insensible to her pain, her friends often offer to help her return to her Black Mountain home. Though, as they tell her, "the whole clarin' [would be] powerful interrupted while you all was gone." The occasions of these offers comprise "the happiest moments of Miss Dilly's happy life" (688). Dilly accepts her passive role, just as she accepts her dependency. But she also finds reward in her significance to the community, which appreciates her cheerfulness and fortitude.

Two other noteworthy stories of this period were inspired by Davis's trips through the South. "Walhalla" (1880) is set in mountainous northwestern South Carolina, where German and Swiss farmers actually established a little village and named it for their mythic hall of spirits.[17] The foreign visitor in this story is a young English artist named Reid. Davis manages to satirize Reid's bigotry while depicting the local color of this colony of "German houses and German customs, dropped down right into the midst of Carolina snuff-rubbers, and Georgian clay-eaters" (139). Though the tone and point of view are handled well in this story, the plot itself is uninspired.

More interesting is "Silhouette" (1883), which takes place in southern Virginia and North Carolina.[18] The foreigner in this story is young Lucy Coyt from Fairview, Pennsylvania, who is traveling on her own for the first time to teach in Otoga, North Carolina. Lucy's provincialism is gently ridiculed: "[S]he had gone to Fairview Female Seminary, and had read Carlyle, and the Autocrat in the *Atlantic* . . . and so felt herself an expert in human nature, and quite fitted to criticize any new types which the South might offer her" (624). But she has an openness to her new experiences that retains the reader's sympathy. Through her consciousness, the reader vicariously confronts the horror of a feud, that families "went to bed, sat down to eat, with Death as their perpetual companion, dumb, waiting to strike" (628). More disconcerting is her discovery that there can be likable, even admirable people on both sides of a struggle. Davis's mediating perspective does not necessarily make life easier.

Regional Supernaturalism

Davis was always attracted to tales of the inexplicable in regional lore. She had used such material as the basis for a story as early as 1866, when she published "The Captain's Story" in *Galaxy*.[19] The popularity of regional material, however, coupled with an expansion of realism's scope to include the less comprehensible in human experience, increased both Davis's and, more important, readers' interest in tales of supernatural phenomena. Davis's tales all explore a connection between the spirit world of the dead and the material world of the living.

Her opening to "A Strange Story from the Coast" (1879) shows how realism ironically provided a narrative posture that strengthened Gothic tales: "I can only give you the facts, and very probably your shrewd common sense will readily find a rational explanation of them. I confess honestly, however, that I have never been able to account for them to myself on any ordinary basis of reasoning."[20]

For this story, which is one of her best, Davis again draws from the lore of remote fishing villages on the Jersey shore, where the natives are known for their longevity. For health reasons the narrator and a friend rent the old Whynne farmhouse during the winter and discover from Captain Jeremiah Holdcomb, "a wiry, withered youth of seventy-six," the story of Abner and Priscilla Whynne. Jeremiah takes the guests to meet Priscilla, who at 92 is the last living Whynne. Strangely, she does not live in her childhood home, even though the local belief is that "a man's hold upon life was stronger in the house in which he was born" because "thar is where the yerth first got a grip on him, thar's the last place it'll be loosened" (678).

Amid a setting carefully developed to create a mood of eerie desolation, the guests are haunted by many unanswered questions about the place and its inhabitants, like the "queer squares of brick at the end of the garden . . . almost covered with sand. To certain queries Jeremiah simply says, "Never dig deep into a rotten ma'ash" (679). What they can learn of Priscilla's story is intriguing. As a young woman, her father Abner's favorite, she had left the village for New York City. There she was said to have married a Captain John Salterre, a handsome seaman of "a high family." Abner was proud of her good fortune, but missed her. After several years Abner died, at the age of 104. Following a premonition, Priscilla came to him, but arrived too late; he had already been laid out on his bed for burial. Ordering everyone out of the room, she brought him back from the dead by the force of her will. Sitting up, he asked why he had been brought back from rest. She explained her need to confess that she had never been married to Salterre. On this admission, Abner, a narrow, righteous man, parted from his daughter, ordering her to "Begone" from the house, saying, "you are no da'ater of mine" (684). After Priscilla left, the family found Abner dead as before, but now sitting up. Further tragedy occurred when Salterre, who loved Priscilla even if he had not married her because of class difference, died in a shipwreck off the coast as he was sailing to retrieve her.

All this happened 60 years ago. Priscilla has obeyed her father's dying commandment. Though she salvaged her respectability by marrying Josiah Perot, a villager she did not love, she has never returned to the Whynne home. As a widow she remains across the marsh in Perot's house. In the aged Priscilla, a "nightmare of a woman," Davis again reveals insight into an interior personality. Age has "ravaged and gnawed her away mercilessly" (679). But what really haunts the narrator is Priscilla's strange eyes, through which a young woman looks out: "Old Priscilla Perot, in the isolation of her thirty years of deafness, had grown vulgar and bitter in her speech, but back of that was another creature, who was not vulgar, who never spoke. . . . I wondered idly when this creature in her had ever lived, and what had killed it" (680).

Several weeks after meeting Priscilla, the guests are surprised one night at about 11 o'clock, during a raging nor'easter, by "a small dark figure" who is "crossing the beach, coming toward the house." It is Priscilla; she has changed, though: "The weight of age [has] dropped away," revealing the lost woman, "young, passionate." Entering the house, she flings out her arms with "a vehement gesture of triumph." As the guests follow her, she disappears in front of some "mysterious heaps of brick" (685). The next day they discover that Priscilla died the previous evening at 10 o'clock. They also discover that the mysterious bricks mark the grave where John Salterre was buried after washing ashore.

In 1886, 25 years after "Iron-Mills" first appeared in the *Atlantic Monthly,* Davis published for the last time in that journal. In subject, tone, and style, "Mademoiselle Joan," another story of the supernatural, is a far cry from the doctrinaire realism of Davis's and the *Atlantic*'s earlier years.[21] As sophisticated realist Henry James demonstrated conclusively, however, both in his own fiction and in his critical analysis of Nathaniel Hawthorne's, realism, when exploring human psychology, in many ways validates its antithesis, romance.[22] Davis's tale can be seen as an allegory of the conflict between good and evil within the human spirit.

Set in the obscure French Canadian hamlet of St. Robideaux, the opening of "Mademoiselle Joan" is rich with local color and satiric humor. The narrator, an American forced for medical reasons to abandon the hectic world of business, recounts his sojourn with the idle natives of this backwater community. The old curé Père Drouôt and the physician Olave Demy, who pride themselves on being the only "two live people in St. Robideaux," eagerly befriend another "philosopher" with whom they can discuss literature and affairs, which they glean from "an occasional two months old copy of the London Times" (329).

This story has three levels. The narrator's remembrance provides an outer frame. The story of Père Drouôt and Demy about the strange and tragic events that befall Georges Labadie provides an internal frame. The mystery itself involves the widower Labadie, a poor but honest honey farmer, who barely supports his two surviving daughters, Rose and Josephine. Theirs is an amazing story of the power to will someone's death and to seek vindication from the grave.

One stormy night when the wind blows "suddenly through the gorge with a shrill cry," the men are reminded of a similar night six years earlier. Then, La Veuve Badleigh, "an unpleasant white woman, with puffy fair skin which looked as if water was below it, light gray eyes, [and] faded yellow hair," had arrived in town (331). Though her appearance was disconcerting, she soon ingratiated herself with the entire village, particularly the innocent Labadie. While devoted to the memory of his wife, the farmer worried about his daughters growing up without a mother's care. Soon he married the woman and "presto! all is changed!" (32). Next, Paul Badleigh, "a vulgar fellow, [a] lean, pimpled, loud-talking" drunk, arrived. The mother and son seemed bent on driving Labadie to ruin. During a storm, however, with the wind shrieking, another strange woman appeared in St. Robideaux. A "dark, lean little body," Mademoiselle Joan, as she was known, was just the opposite of La Veuve, her sister. An "honest, right-minded woman," with "the obstinacy, the determination" to inspire respect, Mademoiselle Joan, with "her thin, bloodless arms," was mysterious (333). At this point the two sisters assume psychologically allegorical values: La Veuve, being the will to evil, and Joan, being the will to good. With the power of conscience, Joan tried desperately to control her sister as soon as she arrived, saying, "I have not much time left to control her." But she was undermined by her sister's attempts to kill her.

Mademoiselle Joan went alone to the Labadie farm to do battle with her sister. A week later, the physician and the priest were called to the house to discover Joan fading into death with Veuve and her son "watching every breath of the dying woman with ill-suppressed triumph." Though "a small, insignificant woman, " Joan's departing soul was "inexorable" as she died, declaring, "You shall not hurt those children. You shall come with me" (334).

Just two weeks later, on a still night, the wind suddenly began keening through the gorge. Paul Badleigh, in a drunken stupor and hearing words others could not make out, left the inn, never to be seen alive again. His body was found the next morning. Four days after Paul's death, Le Veuve abducted Rose and Josephine; the entire village caught her by nightfall. The curé recalls how, from outside on that clear night, he was quietly observing Veuve, then exposed as a felon, when something passed him; "it had a rushing force like the wind, but it was not the wind." Demy, who was inside, remembers, "It was a sound that we heard, like a cry, and then there were three sharp strokes on the window and a voice. But no one understood the words but the Veuve Badleigh" (335). In the morning she was found dead from an overdose of opium. Mademoiselle Joan, with her amazing will, "could thrust her hand out of the grave and drag those two creatures after" (335).

Fictional Tensions

Responding in part to the demand for regional writing, Davis pursued her objective of cultural mediation in most everything she wrote during this period. Much of the most interesting writing from her child-rearing years, however, also reveals her need to mediate a continuing ambivalence toward the woman's domestic sphere. In the discrepancy between the choices Davis made in her own life at this time and the treatment of similar choices made by protagonists in her fiction of the period, Davis demonstrates the increasing tension in her life between her two vocations. She seems to move from feelings of guilt about wanting to write to feelings of frustration about compromising her writing.[23]

"Marcia"

"Marcia" (1876) is one of Davis's darkest tales of the tension between autonomy and womanhood.[24] Like Hetty of "The Wife's Story," Marcia Barr, a would-be writer from Yazoo, Mississippi, sacrifices her ambition to fulfill her destiny as a wife, but unlike the earlier tale, this one is ambivalent to the end. Refusing to compromise her dream of being a professional writer, Marcia has rejected a protected life in marriage to Zack Biron, her father's overseer, who, like her father, "thinks women are like mares – only useful to bring forth children" (925). While Marcia's courage is admirable, Davis, the realist, does not make her supremely gifted. Her talent is average, and she is tragically innocent: "The popular belief in the wings of genius, which can carry it over hard work and all such obstacles as ignorance of grammar or even the spelling-book, found in her a marked example" (926).

Marcia struggles to find work writing, suffering from hunger and also frustration because she has "something to say, if people only would hear it" (927). After several years, when she has become a ragged, gaunt writer of social and commercial puffs for the papers, Zack Biron comes to claim her and take her home. He is "an ignorant, small-minded man" (926), but he is genuinely horrified by Marcia's straits and determined that she be cared for "like a lady" (928). In the description of the leave-taking of the new Marcia, "magnificent in plumes, the costliest that her owner's [husband's] money could buy," the narrator of this story voices both sadness at Marcia's failure and horror at her exploitation. Defeat is total as Marcia hands the narrator her unpublished manuscripts, asking, "Will you burn them for me? All: do not leave a line, a word" (928).

"A Day with Doctor Sarah"

While Davis argued in her essays against the notion that the male and female spheres are mutually exclusive, her fiction realistically depicts women torn by that belief. In "A Day with Doctor Sarah" (1878), the protagonist, Sarah Coyt, is a single, middle-aged physician and a feminist: "She had fought her way into her profession, and out of the Christian Church, and now she clinched with Law, Religion, and Society in a hand-to-hand fight because of their treatment of women."[25]

Though committed to her position as an "advanced woman," she suffers from being anomalous. Speaking at a New York City woman's club, she feels keenly the anguish of her difference: "Why should these people look at her as though she were the woman with the iron jaw, or some other such monster?" Yet she does the same, in return: "She felt, as she often did, that the cause was hopeless. These frothy creatures to comprehend its great principles! Even suppose they had suffrage, what would they know of politics, of their fellow-men outside of a ball-room, or even of the money which they squandered?" (612)

Sarah Coyt's error is that in retaliating against derision with derision, her feminism is divisive instead of cohesive. She separates herself from those other women who, in accepting their situation within the received domestic sphere, have, to her mind, perpetuated its oppression. But in doing so, she weakens herself. In her cautionary treatment of this self-destructive tendency inherent in the feminist movement, Davis's story could have been written in the context of 1978 instead of 1878.

Sarah, who has given up her medical practice to devote herself to the cause of suffrage, feels herself betrayed on all sides. As she bemoans the fact that "there's not another woman in the field who gives more than half her time and energy to the cause," she ironically foreshadows her own eventual change of heart. "There's always an obstacle," she complains: "This one must make her living by writing slipshod novels or lecturing, that one has a baby, another a dead lover to mope over" (613). When an old lover dies, leaving three orphans in need of a mother, Sarah discovers that, even for her, there can be something bigger than her ideological cause: motherhood.

Another aspect of this story that seems modern is that spousal love has no part in it. Unlike most of Davis's female characters, Sarah Coyt has no husband, wants no husband, and finds no husband. She realizes that she wants children, and she ultimately receives them. This is a story about maternal love and about a 40-year-old professional woman's becoming conscious of her maternal desire.

The action of the story centers on Sarah's accidental reunion with an old lover who is now an impoverished clergyman, the Reverend Matthew Niles. But this is not a story of rekindled romance. A weak man, Matthew is intimidated by Sarah: "What if she should propose to him? There was nothing which these unsexed women would not do" (615). Having "cast the man off as her inferior when she was a girl," Sarah is now no more attracted to him than he with her. But he does have something she wants: " 'Matthew's daughter? She might have been my child,' thought Doctor Sarah. . . . As Sarah held the child closer to [her breast] she remembered how hard it was, as became the mongrel creature which the newspapers called an Advanced Female" (614). Explaining that "Doctor Sarah, with her thin lips and broad forehead, had very few of the qualities which go to make a happy marriage; but she was a born mother" (615), Davis takes a radical position for 1878: she suggests maternity should not necessarily be linked with matrimony.

Though marriage is not the issue, this story still assumes an inherent incompatibility between the private sphere of motherhood and the public sphere of profession and politics. When Matthew is killed, Sarah does not hesitate long before abandoning "the cause to which she had given her life" to mother the children (617).

"A Wayside Episode"

In "A Wayside Episode" (1883), a story that mediates between the individual and society, Davis draws one of her most intriguing characters: Emily Wootton, a discontent socialite wife.[26] Like so many of Davis's females, she seems on the surface to be quite unremarkable. As one of her group remembers, "Emily Souders at seventeen set out to be eccentric, – an Advanced Female!" She enrolled in a Methodist Female College instead of "the convent where all the girls were who were to be debutantes," but discovered "she was a dunce" (179). She tried to be an artist in Italy, but "it took her a year to find out she was fit for nothing at that." So her "mother took her in hand and married her to little Neddy Wootton" (180). Married, she is an unhappy, lonely wife.

In this story of one woman's quest for selfhood, the shallow materialistic forces of polite society are antagonistic. Emily's attempt to explain social oppression to a group of young girls who are eager to enter this realm reveals her own recalcitrant position:

> "As for society, as you call it, when I think of it here it reminds me of one of those glass boxes which you see in an apothecary's window, in which a few gold-fishes and minnows swim round and round, eying each other year in and year out, and bumping their noses against the sides."
>
> "You speak as if it were a sort of jail!" cried Dora indignantly.
>
> Mrs. Wootton answered only with that pretty set smile which they thought so charming.
>
> It seems to me the most desirable place in the world," persisted the girl, "I mean, of course," smiling, "the glass case where only the gold-fish swim."
>
> "Yes. You probably will never bump against the sides," said the lady carelessly. (181)

Emily's silent rebellion against living in a fish-bowl prison is to hide within herself. While wearing a mask of contentment, she fantasizes about living a free life, as "a squirrel, or fox, or wolf, – some wild creature that could go up that path into the woods and stay there" (182). While on a party caravan through the southern Appalachians, she encounters a mountain man who shows her that her interiority is really a form of self-deceit.

The sight of this strange, natural man at first fills her with such "a horrible thirst" to escape the "little world of society, of gossip, of insignificant ideas," "to run wild like a stag or satyr," that she discards her protective interiority. She no longer even cares "what Neddy would think if he should find out the real wife under the charming leader of society he knew" (183). Her fantasies, which she usually has held "in check, even beyond her own knowledge," gain intensity; "her thoughts [rush] out beyond her control" (183). She is obsessed with the desire "to be alone, to climb mountains, plunge into the rivers, to be man, beast, anything that [is] free to gratify its own instincts and passions, good or bad!" (183).

We see in Emily Wootton the author's sensitivity to alienated individuals and her fascination with psychological interiority. Unlike later realists, however, Davis does not allow the character's personality to dictate the story line. Her unconventional protagonist ultimately serves a rather conventional plot. The eventual transformation of Emily to a woman of domestic contentment lies in her discovery of a subtle, but fundamental, error. For Davis and her readers, the protagonist's discontent with society is valid; her discontent with marriage is not.

The story's resolution suggests that individual autonomy can be enhanced by a spouse who also rejects society's false values. With much less ambiguity, this story also advocates an agrarian way of life over capitalistic materialism. At the psychological point of no return, when Emily has fully confronted the depth of her own desires, a reversal of fortune turns the Wootton's married life around. Ned is financially ruined; they will be rejected by society, and Ned will need Emily's help as a productive partner.

The story has other dimensions, but essentially she and Ned live happily ever after. They go to California, start a seed-farm, and work together as "comrades." As for Emily, a few years after the story's action, an eastern visitor to the Wootton farm clarifies her significance to the story's theme: "She has what she needed, – work and children. A woman at a certain age wants a baby to nurse and something to do. That is nature. It is women that have neither who go groping about for congenial souls or female suffrage, or try some other devilment to fill up the gap in their lives" (189). Though the conclusion upholds the sanctity of the domestic sphere, the story's tensions suggest Davis's ambivalence toward the traditional role of women. She has developed her rebellious protagonist with such sympathy and psychological insight that the character's recantation is unconvincing.

"Tirar y Soult"

"Tirar y Soult" (1887), one of the stories most often anthologized during Davis's life, is a regional tale that does not depict her usual Appalachian or Atlantic coastal locale.[27] Most of this story is set on the Louisiana rice plantation of Lit de Fleurs, the home of Mr. de Fourgon. Robert Knight, a young civil engineer from New England, has been hired by de Fourgon and others from the Gulf parishes to bring progress in the form of draining their marshlands. Parts of the story, however, take place in Throop, Massachusetts, where Robert's mother and his "confidential friend," Emma Cramer, receive letters.

This is a story of mediated difference, of prejudice transformed through understanding, and of universality conformed by particularity. Its development of two regional perspectives is characteristic of Davis's own particular style. Knight's first letter to Emma articulates the theme of cultural mediation. The first part of the letter comforts Emma with its confirmation of their expectations that the change would be "great and sudden": "from Boston to the Bed of Flowers, from the Concord School of Philosophy to the companionship of ex-slave-holders, from Emerson to Gayarré" (564). As the letter progresses, however, Emma, at home in New England, is disconcerted by many of the facts of Robert's new experience, which seem to contradict expectation with their normality: "I expected to find the plantation a vast exhibit of fertility, disorder, and dirt; the men illiterate fire-eaters; the women, houris such as our fathers used to read of in Tom Moore. Instead, I find the farm, huge, it is true, but orderly. . . . Madame de Fourgon is a fat, commonplace little woman. There are other women – the house swarms with guests – but not an houri among them" (564).

Through the privileged consciousness of Robert, the new place is constantly evaluated in terms of his own home. Since his is a male consciousness, both places are evaluated in terms of the females who embody, in his mind, the values of each place. In his polarization of the southern belle, Lucretia Venn, and Emma, he reveals his deeper evaluation of the larger differences represented by the two. Lucretia, with her "soft, loose masses of reddish hair, and the large, calm, blue eyes," is "the very embodiment of the lavish life of this place" (566). For Robert, "whose brain had long been rasped by Emma's prickly ideas," even Lucretia's "dulness [*sic*] was a downy bed of ideas." Having known only rigorous stimulation in the environment and the people of his New England home, Robert is entranced by the gentle ease of this new place and its people: "In Throop, too, there was much hard prejudice between the neighbors, to be clever was to have a sharp acerbity of wit: Emma's sarcasms cut like a thong. But these people were born kind; they were friendly at all the world, while in Lucretia there was a warm affluence of nature which made her the centre of all this warm, pleasant life" (566-67).

Robert is most fascinated with Lucretia's guardian, the aging dandy José Tirar y Soult. Left a pauper aristocrat after the war, the charming Tirar lives an ideal life of dependence on his friends. Robert cannot understand Tirar; he is irritated by, yet attracted to, the incomprehensible culture that Tirar embodies: "To live without work on those rich, prodigal prairies, never to think of to-morrow, to give without stint, even to lazy parasites – there was something royal about that" (566).

Davis's development of Tirar not as a type but as an embodiment of the ideological forces that define a region suggests an increased sensitivity to the value of regional fiction. Tirar's world is the old, genteel South, not the "New South" of de Fourgon's land-reclaiming syndicate. He is appreciated as a "*petit gourmand*" who has "many secrets of crabs and soups"; his voice is "famous throughout the Gulf parishes" (565).

"Knight at first took him for an overgrown boy," Davis says; "but on coming close to him, he perceived streaks of gray in the close-cut hair and beard" (565). Like the culture that has created him, he is described in images of impotence and decadence: "The little fop was dazzling in white linen, diamond solitaires blazing on his breast and wrists" (567). Tirar is old and fat, but it is not until the young, energetic Robert Knight arrives to rival his suit for Lucretia that Tirar becomes aware of his own ludicrousness. "I grow old," he confides to a friend. "I dress no more as a young man. I accommodate myself to the age – the wrinkles" (568).

But the old, fat little fop, as Davis has created him, is also a man of breeding; he is charming and, in the end, suavely heroic. He risks his own life to save that of Knight when a spring tide floods the bayou. His grace under pressure reminds both those of the New South and those of the North that, along with the benefits of progress, certain desirable qualities are also being threatened in the loss of the old South: "The Tirars and Soults had been men of courage and honor for generations. Their blood was quickening in his fat little body" (571).

Davis's story is not simply of José Tirar y Soult, though, or of Robert Knight's experience with him and Lucretia in Louisiana. It is also of Emma Cramer, the woman who waits to devour his letters as the "cold twilight [settles] down over the rocky fields, with their thin crops of hay" (564). As Robert Knight's exposure to difference teaches him knowledge of himself and of the world, Emma Cramer waits. Without the broadening experience of travel, it is hard for her to believe that "the night air that [is] so thin and chilly in Throop [blows] over the Lit de Fleurs wet and heavy with the scents, good and bad, of the Gulf marshes" (565).

There are moments during her wait for Robert's return when jealousy of his free life causes her to curse her own: "Now he had laid his hand on the world's neck and conquered it! North and West and that great tropical South, with its flowers and houris – all were open to him! She looked around the circle of barren fields. He had gone out of doors, and she was shut in!" (565). Davis's placement of this story in the domestic setting of two very different regions makes three points: first, that travel provides both an understanding of obvious difference and an appreciation of similarity beneath difference; second, that women at home are denied much if denied the experiences of difference afforded by travel; third, that regional writing can provide these learning experiences vicariously.

"Anne"

In 1889, when Rebecca Harding Davis was 58 and her children ranged between 17 and 25 years of age, she wrote "Anne," a story of midlife crisis.[28] More than any other, this story demonstrates the mediation of tension within Davis's own psyche at this time of her life.

Illumination of Anne's interior state of mind dramatizes a tragic disparity between sense of herself and her family's sense of her. Throughout, there are two Annes. The external Mrs. Anne Palmer, "a stout woman of fifty with grizzled hair and a big nose," tries to sing, but produces only a "discordant yawp." Always, however, "something within her" cries out, "*I* am her – Anne! I am beautiful and young. If this old throat were different my voice would ring through earth and heaven" (227).

At the crux of Anne's midlife crisis is the crushing discovery that her life lacks fulfillment in all aspects. She is a "woman of masculine intellect," whose prudent management of the family peach farm since her husband's death and shrewd stock investments have considerably improved the family estate. But she is bored with her life. Increasingly her mind wanders to her first love, George Forbes, now a famous author. Unknown to either of her two overly solicitous children, the Anne within is racked with discontent, crying out, "I should have had my true life" (232). The Anne within finally even convinces Mrs. Anne Palmer, the wife and mother, to run away: "She would go away. Why should she not go away? She had done her full duty to husband, children and property. Why should she not begin somewhere else, live out her own life? Why should she not have her chance for the few years left? Music and art and the companionship of thinkers and scholars, Mrs. Palmer's face grew pale as she named these things so long forbidden to her" (234). She does run away. but eventually, like Hetty Manning of "The Wife's Story" and many other of Davis's men and women, she is led by events to realize that life is best and values are truest at home.

Once again, though, Davis's commitment to her "it's-a-wonderful-life" theme seems to compromise the integrity of her character. Davis herself seems quite ambivalent about this story's resolution. The comfortable conclusion, in which Anne, who has been welcomed back home, enjoys a "quiet, luxurious, happy life," is jeopardized by a reassertion of her interiority and discontent:

> Yet sometimes in the midst of all this comfort and sunshine a chance note of music or the sound of the restless wind will bring an expression into her eyes which her children do not understand, as if some creature unknown to them looked out of them.
>
> At such times Mrs. Palmer will say to herself, "Poor Anne!" (242)

The constantly recurring motif of female frustration during these years of her apparent domestic contentment leads one to wonder whether some inner part of Davis did not occasionally think back to "Iron-Mills" and sigh, "Poor Rebecca."

Chapter Six

Revival (1890-1910)

New Energies in the 1890s

Though in her 60s in the 1890s, Davis was far from slowing down. In a burst of creative energy she produced four books in five years and wrote much of her strongest prose. With her children grown and her husband's career secure as the editor of the *Philadelphia Public Ledger*, one of the nation's leading papers, Davis apparently found the needed time and stamina for more ambitious projects than she had pursued in the previous decade.

These years also brought Davis great joy as a mother, taking pride in the success of her firstborn. In 1890 Richard Harding Davis published "Gallagher," which catapulted him to literary fame. He also became emblemized as the paragon of his age when popular illustrator Charles Dana Gibson made him the "Gibson man." In both his life and his writing he came to epitomize the American ideals of adventure and honor at the turn of the century. Of her three children, Richard seems to have enjoyed a particularly close relationship with his mother, perhaps because they were both writers, perhaps because he was the eldest. Any favoritism that existed does not seem to have bothered the others, though; everyone in this mutually adoring family seems to have favored him.

Rebecca was unabashedly proud of her famous son, and her delight in Richard was reciprocated. As Gerald Langford has documented, no matter where he was around the world, Richard wrote almost daily to Rebecca, and he always submitted his manuscripts to her for approval. In one of her letters praising Richard for his ability to dramatize character through action, Davis revealed what she saw as her greatest weakness as a writer: "You take a man at the crisis of his life and show how he is dragged one way & the other by god & the devil by *what he does*. I always had to set down his thoughts. Yours is the stronger just as much as dramatic action is stronger that soliloquy" (UVA [1892], Langford 110).

It was not just Richard who was carrying on his mother's literary tradition. Charles also began writing fiction and drama in the 1890s, though he did not experience the success of his brother. Shaeffer (271) notes that in volume 94 of *Harper's* Rebecca Harding Davis and both sons had stories: Richard's "The Coronation" in February, Charles's "La Gommeuse" in March, and Rebecca's "The Education of Bob" in May.[1] After a brief career as a diplomat, Charles went into publishing. Only Nora, apparently a quiet, unassuming young woman, seems to have had no literary aspirations.

Journalism

In 1889 Davis severed her long association with the *New York Tribune* in protest of censorship. She had written numerous editorials criticizing several northern industrial concerns for hoarding certain chemicals needed in medicines to treat disease in the South. When pressure from advertisers forced the *Tribune* to attempt to silence her on the subject, Davis resigned (Shaeffer, 271).

All of Davis's writing for the *Tribune* had been unsigned. While her work there was well known in the profession, it was as a regular contributor to the *New York Independent*, beginning in 1889, and later with the *Saturday Evening Post* that she made her reputation as an essayist.[2] Her prose was both respected and popular. As publication of "Some Testimony in the Case" in the *Atlantic* attests, Davis was appreciated for her research and insight as well as her writing style. *Encyclopedia Britannica* was not the only case in which her journalism was solicited for its authority. In 1899 her *North American Review* essay "The Curse of Education," which argues for prison reform that offers practical educational opportunities, was incorporated into that year's U.S. Congressional Report on Education and Crime.[3]

In her essays Davis mediates the same dialectic of values as in her fiction. She promotes a sentimental theology, but she argues for the realistic confrontation of social ills; she affirms spiritual mystery and divine design, but she adheres to a practical, commonsense philosophy; always she champions spiritual integrity against the forces of materialistic relativism and urges a return to the agrarian familial communities of preindustrial society. Davis's journalism also mediates genres, blurring the line between fiction and nonfiction. As a realist, she often wrote absolutely factual stories; as an essayist, she frequently wrote narrative essays that were morality fables. A brief survey of her essays in the *New York Independent* over two decades offers a sampling of representative concerns.[4]

Davis's essays often assert sentimental Christianity as a social principle. In "Leebsmall" (39: 1887) she reports on a bit of Pennsylvania local color: a Moravian community "love feast." The ritual consists primarily of the entire community serving bread and coffee to one another, then eating together. These communions of "brotherhood and equality in Christ" are, for Davis, the perfect emblem of loving community (966). In addition to using contemporary events like the Moravian love feast, Davis often frames her essays with historic facts from which she can inductively derive her point. In "On the Jersey Coast" (52: 1900), Davis offers the story of Thomas Potter and John Murray, the founders of the Universalist Church in America, as another example of love and humble acceptance in true Christianity. Though Episcopalian herself, for Davis any firmly held sectarian faith was a form of apostasy. In "On Trial" (44: 1892), she praises the feminine values implicit in European Catholicism. She discusses the "Marie" prayers as being specifically those that request nurture and refuge. Then she offers Queen Matilda, wife of William the Conqueror of Normandy, as the embodiment of this nurturing Catholicism in action. Matilda established the first hospital, l'Hotel Dieu, as "a refuge for the sick and poor" (1685).

Davis's dissenting voice joins many others as she criticizes nineteenth-century progress. In "The Disease of Money-Getting" (54: 1902), she warns against materialism infecting American values. "The ruling Power in this country now," she cries, "is not the love of liberty or patriotism or God, but – the Dollar" (1459). In "The Passing of Niagara" (49: 1897), she premises her essay on a dystopian vision in which utilitarian values that foster only what is profitable have allowed beauty to vanish from America.

In terms other than money, Davis also questions the economics of nineteenth-century advancements, asking what is being given for what is being gained. Her 1903 essay "Lost" (55) bemoans the cost of progress, even when aspects of it have been good. She wonders if advances have been worth the loss of a "personal" flavor in American life, of domestic values, of Christian values, of a work ethic. "What will become of the American nation at the end of another century," she asks, "if there are in it no home-loving mother, no baby in the cradle, and – no Christ?" (1507). By 1908, in "One or Two Plain Questions" (65), she is more ready to recognize that "humanity and womanity are advancing upward" (945). Referring to zealots who destroy the beauty of art and books in their quest for right, however, Davis asks women, in particular, "Is there any danger that we, in our suicidal zeal to be rich and busy in the work of the world, may leave the errand on which God sent us into life forever undone?" (946).

Her fear that women had ceased pursuing their spiritually redemptive role and begun ascribing to the false values of a materialistic society advanced with the century. "The Newly Discovered Woman" (45: 1893) is typical of many essays. It was triggered by the self-congratulatory tone of the Women's Exposition at the 1893 Chicago World's Fair, which Davis criticized: "There is too much sex consciousness in it, and a great deal too much boasting" (1601). The essay admonishes women not to cut themselves off from the history of their foremothers and not to assume so readily that the older ways are wrong.

Davis, as a social critic, found much room for complaint in the institutions of her society. In areas such as education, health, religion, welfare, labor, and politics, she criticized the incapacity of institutions to serve people's real needs and to perpetuate true values.

She argued repeatedly in favor of vocational education for African Americans, for women, for immigrants, maintaining that its absence was a covert strategy for oppression. In "Low Wages for Women" (40: 1888) she asserts that pity and charity are equally as pernicious as the evils they address: they salve the symptom, but do not remedy the cause. She demands reformation of economically closed classes through job training: "Is sympathy what these unsuccessful women-workers need? Shall we stand and weep with the lines of hungry seamstresses waiting for the gingham shirts or inquire into the reason why they are there? Is there no better-paid work? Why is it not given to them?" (1425).

The institution Davis found most dangerously misguided was the church. In "An Unlighted Lamp" (53: 1901) she examines the many ways that churches had been perverted by the shallow materialism of the age. Citing the Saturday newspaper section on religious services, she exposes church advertising tactics as offering the allure of entertainment, not salvation. "I do not mean to say that great music is not helpful to the soul – in its place," she explains. But does it "help the overworked man or drunken boy or silly girl find God?" (1904).

This same essay demonstrates that in Davis's mind established religion had not merely become shallow; it had also gradually become misguided in its primary work: charity. The essay exposes turn-of-the-century church practices as perversions of true Christian ideals. It laments the loss of the humanitarian impulse that had fueled the original evangelical fervor of post-Puritan Americans, when "the feeling of brotherhood which Christ came to teach us never has had a purer development" (1905). Davis frequently criticizes contemporary church philanthropy as she does here. She attacks efforts to improve the quality of life in the impoverished classes as superficial, in their attention to aesthetics like art, music, even libraries. She urges instead remedying the more profound problems – economically, through job training, and spiritually, through God's word. The pernicious result of contemporary church religiosity for Davis was that it also perpetuated rather than reformed the status quo: "There are and always must be, widely differing occupations for men and women. We cannot all be millionaires or *grandes dames*. There must be plowmen and mechanics, cooks and seamstresses. The mistake we make is in thinking that the ease and luxuries of one condition make it more honorable than the other" (1908).

Much of Davis's dissatisfaction with social institutions was that they threatened domestic primacy. "The Trained Nurse" (63: 1907) responds to the appropriation of nursing education by male physicians in their efforts to upgrade and formalize the medical profession. She was concerned that specialized training, while perhaps producing better trained nurses, had led to the perception that nursing was strictly a hospital-trained profession, instead of part of every woman's domestic sphere of responsibility: "You must remember that since the world began the care of children and of the sick and wounded have been in the hands of woman" (814). She mourns the devaluation of "the real Wise Woman," as the result of nineteenth-century progress: "Every village had its matron, neither drunk nor imbecile, but wise, from long practice, in symptoms and in remedies, and skilled in the handling of the sick. . . . I remember the old mulattoes in Southern neighborhoods, in their gay turbans and huge, white aprons, and the Quaker mid-wives of Pennsylvania towns, gray robed and placid" (814-15). After surveying the curriculum in several female college catalogues, Davis concludes, "There are not ten minutes of these school years given to teaching the future wife and mother how to spread a plaster for a sick child" (816). To guard against the loss of practical nursing knowledge as part of every girl's home training, she urges the inclusion of nursing in the vocational training that would be part of every girl's education.

In many essays Davis took on misguided philanthropic projects. While charity was not necessarily the missionary arm of a church, it was the human enactment of Christian principle. For Davis, this fact required that charity also be personal and humble. "At Our Gates" (41: 1889) asks readers to question the motives behind organized social welfare that demonstrates Christianity "by united efforts, rather than by individual action." The purpose of organized welfare, Davis writes, "is the protection of well-to-do people from impostors, rather than the help of the poor. . . . [It] is not the work which Christ exacted from you and me, and which he never intended we should hand over any agent. . . . We must visit, feed, help the sick, the poor, the prisoner, in person, *not* by agents" (451).

In another instance, specifically an essay on the Johnstown flood, Davis criticizes charity in response to disasters as a means of glossing over the political or economic corruption that causes them. In "Some Significant Facts" (41: 1889), after citing a few other catastrophes in trains, mills, and theaters, she asks why wealthy managers and manufacturers do not receive punishment for allowing the conditions rather than receiving gratitude for their charity afterward. Her criticism is of both the corrupt and the complacent: "The iniquity is perpetrated and the money made by a few corrupt politicians – bosses, whom [the ordinary American] despises, morally and socially. But he is too lazy and good-humored to vote them out of office" (753).

Fame, another of the nineteenth century's false gods, was also one of Davis's concerns, for it, too, caused misdirected humanitarian efforts. In "Two Methods" (45: 1893), Davis contrasts the accounts of "two little histories" of women who devoted their lives to the care of lepers. Her purpose is to illustrate the superiority of the older mode of care, which is performed at home, personally and quietly, to the modern one, which is public and grand. In the essay, Davis is responding to a contemporary book written by a Kate Marsden.[5] Having studied leprosy in Europe, Marsden desired to minister to a Russian leper colony in Siberia. Before leaving for the other side of the globe, however, she toured America, promoting her effort. Davis compares this misguided project to an account from some 40 years earlier of a young woman whose name was never recorded. When an old woman in her Louisiana parish developed leprosy and was abandoned by her neighbors and her husband, this young woman nursed her for five years, until the old woman died. Afterward, "she purified herself and returned home, receiving no payment of any kind. The only reason she gave for her act was that she 'was sorry for her old neighbor' " (416).

In a classed society that celebrated self-reliance, Davis recognized the necessity for communal responsibility that attended to the economic and spiritual welfare of all. "The Recovery of American Life" (59: 1905) responds to contemporary concerns that the loss of the servant class to industry was threatening the stability of the family unit. To this Davis asserts two simple truths: first, that "there is no nation in the world in which caste is more important than in ours, altho [*sic*] we profess to have no such thing" (674); next, that in America, at least, pay is the social determinant of job dignity. Her solution is simply the assurance of job dignity by giving "necessary work and good pay" (675).

Earlier, Davis had written an essay called "The Mistress and the Maid" (44: 1892), which offers "a bit of domestic history" as possibly instructive to the modern American housewife in reference to "her own household and its foreign inmates" (533). The history is of Deborah Peyton, a housewife of a large Pennsylvania homestead in 1800, who "thrust her autocratic little hand" into the management of her home, her children, and her servants. Her servants were young European indentured girls for whom Deborah accepted moral as well as economic responsibility; she trained each to be American, and also "to be a wife and mother" (533). Davis posits maternalism as the basis for a symbiotic and responsible social system, much as other nineteenth-century critics of democracy and capitalism urged a return to medieval paternalism.

Davis strove always to diminish the mutual reduction of oppressor and oppressed, inherent to a degree in any hierarchy. She also battled continually against what she perceived as the most destructive force in a mutually aggrandizing society: greed. As she had exposed it in slavery, in labor abuses, in popular materialism, in political corruption, she also exposed it in imperialism. In "Lord Kitchener's Methods" (53: 1901) Davis responds to the British imperialistic atrocities of the Boer War. Her horror at Kitchener's genocide – "the wholesale destruction of food, the blazing homesteads, the women and children flying from soldiery" – is paralleled by her shock at the condoning silence of the British people.

America, Davis was quick to point out, was not innocent of the evil of imperialism. "The Disease of Money-Getting" (54: 1902) points to American involvement in the Philippines as imperialistic in motive and evil in effect. In this article she supports her accusations by clarifying the connection between imperialism and greed: "The popular policy of Imperialism is, stripped of verbiage, merely the seizing of territory and subjection of foreign peoples with whom we have no quarrel, by force, in order to increase the national wealth" (1459). Linked with the greed of imperialism is its oppressing ethnocentrism. In "The Work before Us" (51: 1899) Davis takes both Britons and Americans to task for their chauvinism, "the complacent self-conceit of the English race. . . . We are always right: hence all other races must be more or less wrong. . . . We hold that they are inferior, as a matter of course. When, therefore, we set out to raise and better them, we naturally try to turn them into a poor copy of ourselves. . . . [Racial arrogance] blinds us, too, to the possibilities in other races, and unfits us to deal with them intelligently" (178).

Interestingly, Davis remained moderate and surprisingly silent in her prose on the two biggest issues of the day, temperance and suffrage. Her restraint in the national debate over suffrage suggests an uncomfortable ambivalence.[6] In both these controversies Davis struggled to find a middle ground of common sense. Thomas Beer relates an anecdote that typifies Davis's pragmatic approach to temperance issues. In the 1890s a young son of family friends landed in jail after a drunken night in a brothel. When his own parents disowned him, he went to Rebecca, whose response was, "Go up and take a bath while I get you some breakfast, you silly child!" After this, she sent him to New York with connections for a job, her solution to irresponsibility.[7]

Davis's prominence as a social commentator did not diminish her reputation as a writer of fiction. In 1891 the *New York Independent* ran a series of articles on "The Enlargement of the Woman's Sphere" (43) by a number of "Distinguished Progressive Women." In company with Julia Ward Howe, Mary A. Livermore, Frances E. Willard, and Lucy Stone was Rebecca Harding Davis.[8] Davis's essay, "Women in Literature," recognizes the value of regional realism to the development of a national literature and notes that "it is a significant fact that so many of these distinctively American portraits and landscapes are the work of women." She urges women writers to continue in their course as regionalists, creating "genre pictures of individual characters in our national drama, each with his own scene and framing" (662).

Davis expressed optimism about the growing number of serious, trained women writers: "There can surely be little doubt that women will occupy a much wider space in American literature during the next thirty years than they have done hitherto. Chatauquan circles, University Extension lectures, the innumerable literary, scientific, religious and charitable classes and clubs which young women are forming from Murray Hill to Montana ranches, are all doing a quickening work" (661-62). In this essay she also offers several contemporary female regionalists as models:

> Marion Harland preserved for us the old Virginia plantation with its men and women. Miss Murfree has made the mountaineer of Tennessee as immortal as his mountains, Mary Dean painted pictures of rural New York with a touch as fine and strong as Meissonier's own, Mrs. Catherwood and Mary Halleck Foote have sketched picturesque poses of the Western man. Miss Woolson on her larger canvas inserts marvelous portraits of gentle, lazy, shrewd Southern women, and while Elizabeth Phelps draws the educated Puritan woman from the life, Sara Jewett [*sic*] and Miss Wilkins give us pictures of the race in its decadence, the New England villager, hungry in soul and body, with a fidelity equal to any other photographs of dying man.[9]

In addition to urging women to write regional fiction, Davis encourages them in another direction in "Women in Literature," which she sees guided by the same principles. That is the personal history – "the Memoir, the Journal and the Autobiography" – validating both female experience and a female perspective: "There are, as yet, very few such books to illustrate our own history. Even the Revolutionary and Civil Wars, with their infinite phases of individual tragedy and comedy, did not bring them out. Our people had not had time to keep journals, and our history is so short that we do not even yet understand how invaluable its details will be to our descendants" (662). Asserting the power of art, she admonishes reform-conscious women writers "to leave something more permanent behind them than Reports of Sanitary or Archeological clubs." And she asks them to "paint as they only can do, for the next generation, the inner life and history of their time with a power which shall make that time alive for the future ages" (662).

The *Independent*'s choice of Davis to write the essay on "Women in Literature" is understandable. Davis's long career as a prolific female writer of critical, reformative fiction and essays caused many aspiring women writers to admire her. Prior to her publication of *A Century of Dishonor*, for instance, Helen Hunt Jackson wrote personally to Davis, requesting her "help to circulate the real knowledge of the Indian" by "getting it [her book] well noticed."[10]

In 1895 Davis wrote an influential exposé for *Century*, titled "In the Gray Cabins of New England." It elaborates on a concern that recurs throughout her fiction and prose: the powerless position of middle-class women.[11] In this case she directs attention to the "surplus of unattached women," living "starved, coffined lives at home" in rural New England in the latter part of the nineteenth century (623). These women, possessing as much native energy and intelligence as their brothers, were left behind when most free young men followed their fortunes westward. The essay argues that the lives of these young women – unable to be wives and mothers in a land without men and unable to use their intelligence and energy for any self-sustaining productive end – are being wasted. "Nervous prostration is an almost universal ailment among them," Davis explains, "following, as it always does, long self-repression" (622). She concludes with two solutions that follow as common sense from her argument: "First, they should have remunerative work. Establish industries among them. . . . [Next] Let them follow their brothers. . . . From every town and camp and ranch in the west comes the demand for house-servants, nurses, teachers, and – wives" (623).

Beer relates an intriguing anecdote regarding a public falling-out between Davis and Frances Willard that resulted from Davis's "Gray Cabins" essay. Although Davis admired Willard's "power which lies in the purely feminine quality" and her courage in undertaking "to stamp out a universal evil [drunkenness]" (*Bits*, 228-29), she did not advocate the narrow vision necessary for such zeal. Davis had offered what she saw as practical solutions to the tragedy of "undedicated nuns" of New England villages. Willard, leader of the temperance movement, argued that "membership in the greatest spiritual movement since our savior's time should be enough" fulfillment for these women. This, to Davis, was nonsense, and she apparently said so (Beer, 114).

Awareness of the realities of women's lives often led Davis to paint images of rural limitation in other parts of the country as well. She again treats the plight of unfulfilled women in homes that have no husband, no children, no meaningful work in "Country Girls in Town" (54: 1902). Observing the phenomenon of single women, "poor and unprotected, who rush into [eastern cities] from the West and South with the hope of making their fortune, or at least a living," she argues: "Nobody can blame them for coming. On most Western ranches the woman is overworked, and the loneliness of her life is intolerable; while in the smaller Southern towns the monotony, the pettiness of events in the slow-going hours and days and years stifle and kill an active brain, just as the creeping gray moss smothers a living plant" (1691).

On the whole, Davis's prose is thematically consistent with her fiction. She tried to meld the mundane and the spiritual in both forms. In every aspect of human relations – from the way human beings relate to their God, to the way housewives relate to their servants, to the way nations relate to each other – Davis asserted her vision of spiritual reform. Her essays and fables give concrete form and specific instance to what she saw as undeniable, if abstract, truths. In more than one instance Davis expounds on the "value of symbols" to communicate "the facts on which the Christian faith is based" ("Old Lamps for New" [44: 1892; 113]). Another essay, "A Great Object Lesson" (55: 1903), illuminates much concerning Davis's mediation of idealism and realism. Hers was still that attention to the concrete as an inductive approach to the abstract that marks the transition between romanticism and realism.

Responding to the death of Pope Leo, she advises her readers to be sensible to people and events as "God's object lessons." If we would ponder these facts, she says, "many dark questions would grow clearer" (1780). But beyond all else, Davis always argued for common sense.

As a realist, Davis was always demythologizing her culture. In "Some Hobgoblins in Literature," written for the *Book Buyer* (1897), she claims that Americans are ingenuously in awe of genius, seeing the artist as either a "demigod or a devil."[12] The truth, as always for Davis, is somewhere in between. To illustrate, she contrasts fiction and fact in the lives of Margaret Fuller, Walt Whitman, and Edgar Allan Poe. According to Davis, Fuller, seen by some as "a female Buddha who once made an avatar in Boston," was quite mortal. She reports that, according to an unnamed Quaker associate, Fuller was "the vainest and most voluble human being," but she had "insight into ideas and men as keen as divination" (229). Whitman, Davis says, was thought by some to be the "bard of the century" and "the chief Patriot and Friend of his age, the universal brother of us all," while by others he was considered "a sort of devil," a "monster of vice," writing "heaps of filth and corruption." She contends that in reality he was a "huge, uncouth fellow" with "the eye and tongue of the seer. . . . while the light burning within may have been divine, the outer case of the lamp was assuredly cheap and mean" (230). The greatest "hobgoblin in American literature," according to Davis, is Poe, whose myth arose from the malicious fabrications of Rufus Griswold.[13] According to friends and professional associates, however, Poe was "a gentle gentleman, always courteous, kindly and honorable. He had one common failing [drinking] and was ashamed of it. His character was in no way unnatural or abnormal" (231). The facts of these three lives, Davis argues, deflate the romantic notion of superhuman genius. Though "the light of genius may burn" in someone, that person "will be in no sense a god or a fiend, but remain a very ordinary fellow" (231).

Juvenile Fiction – *Kent Hampden*

By 1890 Davis was apparently becoming concerned that her pursuit of a journalistic career had gradually drawn her away from more ambitious writing. Instrumental in pointing out this fact before it was too late were her two sons, Richard and Charles, who were both launching their own literary careers. During the summer of 1890, she began seeking a publisher for what would become *Kent Hampden*, her first novel in over a decade. In a letter to Richard Watson Gilder, the editor of *Century*, she explains: "Are you open as to treaty of a long serial? My boys have been anxious for a long time that I should write one. And to please them I gave up newspaper work [the *Tribune*] two years ago and rested before doing it."[14]

The story, an adolescent mystery, was ultimately serialized in the *Youth's Companion* and then published as a novel by Scribners.[15] Set in her home town, Wheeling, at the time of her own youth, the story features the Hampden family, who in many ways resemble the Hardings. Ralph Hampden is a businessman and civic leader. Though well respected, he withholds a secret past from everyone, even his wife. During the course of the novel, this secret causes the community to distrust him. His 15-year-old son, Kent, is also a leader of his peers. He is president of the Order of Wild Beasts, a secret hunting society, and he is being considered for nomination to West Point.

The novel is well written and suspenseful, if somewhat melodramatic. When Ralph Hampden loses $10,000 that has been entrusted to him, he is brought to shame and financial ruin. Through courage and cunning, Kent eventually discovers the real thief and recovers the money. Several mysteries create the suspense. First is the stolen money, which Ralph Hampden, while on a business trip to Philadelphia, is supposed to deliver as a favor to several other Wheeling businessmen. Though he carries the parcel with him always, at the bank he unwraps it to find that, somehow, blank papers have been switched for the notes. A more serious mystery is Ralph's past. For most of the town, "the mystery in which he chose to shroud his past life was almost proof of his guilt" (59). Several other mysteries also implicate Kent. The essential threat to the Hampdens is not financial loss; it is loss of honor, which in practical terms will ruin the father's mayoral bid and the son's candidacy to West Point.

In addition to being a mystery, the novel is essentially an adolescent rescue fantasy. Kent resolves to prove his father's innocence with "a man's spirit, not a lad's" (64). Retracing Ralph's journey to solve the mystery of the money, he eventually discovers that his father has been framed by Mr. Jarrett, the banker who had asked him to deliver the money. Si Jarrett, his son, exchanged blank notes for the real ones before Hampden ever left on the trip. Indirectly, Kent also brings to light his father's honorable past that no longer needs to be secret. Like Laidley, in *A Law unto Herself*, Ralph had been made the beneficiary of a will unfairly, except Ralph had done the honorable thing. Subverting the ignoble will, he had assumed a new identity so a female relative who was the rightful heir could inherit. When it is discovered that she too has died, the truth can be known. Kent Hampden's precocious heroism is not unappreciated. His father publicly recognizes his gratitude for being able to hold up his head once again: "I owe it to my son that I can do it; to my son, and – to God [in that order]" (151).

This novel draws more on Davis's talents as a writer of sensational fiction than of realism. For the most part the characters are simple, melodramatic types. The villainous Mr. Jarrett and his son, Si, lack any clear motivation other than rivalry for the West Point nomination and perhaps political difference with Ralph Hampden, who is a Whig party leader. Ralph Hampden, "a Quixotic fool, but . . . an honorable man," is a typical Davis ideal (58). Occasionally, however, her realism enriches the narrative, as it does in depicting Ralph Hampden's reaction to the stress of public ostracism: "He shut himself up in the house, neglected his business, and tormented his wife, his children, and the servants with his querulous ill-temper" (59).

With *Kent Hampden* being prepared for postserial book publication, Davis embarked on a cruise to Europe with 19-year-old Nora. This was Davis's first European tour, but several more trips were to follow. Charles was the American Consul in Florence, Italy, at this time, and Richard's reporting assignments sent him all over the globe. Many of the concerns in Davis's journalism resulted from her European travels, as did the plot for her last novel, *Frances Waldeaux*.

In addition to their transatlantic travels, the Davises made other changes in the vacation routine. Urged by his close friend and fishing companion President Grover Cleveland, Clarke moved the family summer place to Marion, on the coast of Massachusetts. It was at Marion that Davis developed her sensitivity to the plight of New England spinsters.

Short Fiction

Silhouettes of American Life

Following on the heels of *Kent Hampden* was the publication of *Silhouettes of American Life* in 1892. This volume, which is Davis's only collection of stories, includes much of her best regional fiction from the *Atlantic*, *Scribner's*, *Lippincott's*, and *Harper's*, most of which have been previously discussed.[16] The latest story in the collection, "An Ignoble Martyr" (1890), depicts an undedicated nun in a gray cabin in New England.[17] The ignoble martyr is Jane Pettit, a spinster who chooses to remain unmarried in sterile, impoverished New England to care for her mother. Unlike her prose treatment of the subject, however, here Davis mediates between a naturalistic and a sentimental perspective. While not softening the harshness of Jane's circumstance, Davis focuses on her protagonist's ability to salvage a life of dignity and meaning out of her narrow existence. She does this by emphasizing the comfort Jane receives from the knowledge that "of her own will" she has renounced the possibility of a fuller life (60).

This is a disturbing story, striking for its anticipation of Wharton's *Ethan Frome* and O'Neill's *Desire under the Elms* in its treatment of the effect of a repressive environment on the human spirit. It begins at the death of Jane's father, "who had tried to live for ten years with half of his body dead from paralysis" (607). The Pettits, like all their neighbors, "were poor, and they had reduced economy to an art so hard and cruel that it dominated them now in body and soul" (605). Jane, who, though 30, is "as submissive and timid as when she was six" (59), supports her mother by sewing "men's seersucker coats for a factory in Boston." She is "paid sixty cents for a dozen" (605). Her brother, Bowles, an unskilled "helper," can find no work.

In this story Davis emphasizes a variety of subtle ways that women like Jane Pettit are victimized by their society. Most obvious is the fact that they are unable to live fulfilled lives as wives and mothers. More subtle is a wrong suffered by many young women, according to Davis; they are denied the opportunity to make choices about their own lives. Jane is given both these opportunities. When Mr. Rameaux, a visitor from Louisiana, proposes to Jane, she is given the chance she never thought she would have to direct her own life.

But, unlike her brother, who leaves without a backward glance, Jane chooses to stay to care for her aged mother, who refuses to leave. Her lover leaves, never to return; her brother leaves, to find profit and plenty in the Southwest. Though her life afterward may seem as stark as before, for Jane it is not:

> For thirty years she had done her dull duty faithfully, because, in fact, there was nothing else to do.
>
> Then, as it seemed to her, the gates were opened, the kingdoms of the world were laid at her feet.
>
> Of her own will she had given them up.
>
> God only knew what the sacrifice cost her, but after it she was a different and alive creature. She was like a woman who has given birth to a child. She had struck her note in life, and it was not a mean one. She now looked out on the world with authoritative, understanding eyes; even her step became firm and decided. (609)

This story, however, is not without a tone of irony as it closes with Jane nourishing herself on fantasies of the life she sacrificed. Davis makes it difficult to feel as good about Jane's choice as the protagonist herself seems to when the narrator closes by reporting that, as years went by, memory of Rameaux "began to take on the graces and charms of the heroes of romance." The reader is even more disconcerted by reading that, when Jane "saw mothers caress their children, she fancied she felt Lola's head [Rameaux's daughter] again on her breast" (609). In Davis's healthy world of living passions, these are disturbing signs of repression.

Psychological insights into complex characters shaped by and reacting to their particular environments make this collection memorable. In its review of *Silhouettes of American Life*, *The Nation* noted this quality, praising Davis's regional sketches for containing more than local color: "Mrs. Davis is always ready to place her mountains and her woods in due prominence, and is evidently a lover of the out-door world, but it is the human interest, after all, which is first with her and which gives the best value to her work."[18]

"An Old-Time Love Story"

In her later years Davis continued to mine the Philadelphia archives for story material. Records of early Swedish colonists in the mid-Atlantic region, whom William Penn found already in residence, were her source for "An Old-Time Love Story" (1908).[19] This story tells of the Swedish botanist Peter Kalm, who discovered the American mountain laurel that bears his name, *Kalmia Latifolia*.

Davis's love story, however, dwells not on Kalm or his discovery but on Aggie Kyn, the woman who loved him. Though she is in love with Kalm, her family and community pressure her to marry Dr. Snorr, a minister going to the Swedish colony in America, so that her village can be represented in the great experiment. She obediently marries him and goes, but she never stops loving Kalm. Aggie is a good frontier wife; "being, in fact stronger than he," she helps Snorr dig their first home in the new world, a cave (220). But in the first winter a fever kills her husband and her new baby. Alone, she is left to continue her life in this foreign land. After several years, when Kalm happens to come to America on an expedition, the two lovers are reunited and Aggie begins a happier life. Professor Kalm stayed in America working for several years, Davis reports, and "he was always accompanied by his wife" (221).

"The Coming of Night"

Written when Davis was 78, her last adult story, "The Coming of Night" (1909), is about old age.[20] It is also about two ways of treating the aged: institutionalized philanthropy versus individual involvement. Mrs. Cross, a native New Englander and "one of those women who expect to give the world a big boost upward," has landed in the midwestern village of Oakford as a result of her husband's business. She adopts as her pet project the modernization of this provincial community through the development of a "Home for Aged Men" (58). To ensure its success, she attempts to convince one of the town's leading senior citizens, Dr. Paull, a retired college professor, to commit himself, since old age "makes every old man and woman a dead weight in the community" (61).

Mrs. Cross's manipulation and coercion finally fail, though, when Dr. Paull's sons and daughter-in-law discover her plot. They retrieve him from the institution and bring him back to their home where "all nest together" (58). In its final scene of Dr. Paull, "settled back in his chair with the children at his feet," the story reaffirms the family as the truest model of God's plan (67). Home again, "[t]he world seemed to [Dr. Paull] only a big friendly home, and the world beyond death, which he had feared so much, just another, more friendly and more real" (68). While this is a very sentimental story,

Davis's depiction of Mrs. Cross, the selfish and insensitive reformer, demonstrates her satiric voice, which actually became stronger in these later years.

Novels

The most noteworthy projects of this energetic period were two serialized novels that appeared in close succession: *Doctor Warrick's Daughter* in 1895 and *Frances Waldeaux* in 1896. With these Davis again expanded her journal affiliation. Harper and Brothers publishers had long been associated with Davis and her family, having printed 14 of her stories in *Harper's New Monthly Magazine* and employing Richard as editor of *Harper's Weekly* for two years. Before printing her new novels as books, however, Harper serialized them in their women's fashion magazine *Harper's Bazaar*. Publication in this journal indicates a slight change, perhaps, in Davis's contemporary reception at the close of the century, or at least, in Davis's perception of her target audience.

Doctor Warrick's Daughters

As one contemporary reviewer stated, *Doctor Warrick's Daughters* is about the seductive danger of "the great god Mammon, which is made very repulsive, while yet his worshippers are seen to be sometimes men of like passions with ourselves."[21] It is also about the false god Ego, about whose temptations Davis was always particularly sensitive.

Doctor Warrick's daughters, the novel's protagonists, are two very complicated characters. Mildred – the older, beautiful one – is basically an unattractive personality, though she has strengths, and we sympathize with her to a degree. Anne – the younger, homelier one – is much more admirable, but she too has faults. Surrounding these characters, primarily in the form of relatives and lovers, are less complicated, but still fully rounded, characters. The story traces the Warrick daughters and those who love them from youth to maturity, showing their errors and successes in courtship, in marriage, and in childbearing.

The novel opens at the close of the Civil War. It is set in Luxborough, once a sleepy hamlet, now becoming an affluent suburb of Philadelphia. Amid joy at Lee's surrender and grief over Lincoln's assassination, Sarah Warrick, who has been preparing for her husband's return, discovers that she is dying of an incurable disease. Though Sarah is an infinitely capable woman, she is humbly unaware of her talents, feeling dull and common compared with her genteel husband. Both Mildred and Anne adore their mother and each other, but they are very different girls. Anne is outspoken, rebellious, and uncompromising; but she is also honest. Appearing demure and passive, Mildred is deceptive. Her malleable exterior hides an inner self that is aggressively ambitious. Anne is an idealist, Mildred a pragmatist. In addition to being loved by her daughters, Sarah is loved by two young men in town: Brooke Calhoun, a distant cousin who plays with Anne, and David Plunkett, a fat, awkward, sensitive boy who has a crush on Mildred.

At Sarah's funeral, her loved ones discuss the precariousness of the girls' futures, left to their father's rearing. A dilettante of both the arts and the sciences, Dr. Samuel Warrick is focused on his own interests; furthermore, he has little desire to reestablish his medical practice and less ability to make it pay. Julia Dane and Paul Franciscus, concerned relatives, try in vain to explain to him that in postwar society, where "money . . . is now the dominant power, . . . the future lives of your daughters will largely depend on your income" (31). Out of sincere concern for Mildred and Anne, these two representatives of Luxborough society and all its false values assume the financial responsibility for the girls' success. Though Sarah Warrick had not prepared her daughters for this world, she had at least tried to give them defenses. Without her, they are at the mercy of these various undesirable influences.

The story then jumps eight years. Mildred, the pragmatist, is fully committed to wealth as the key to prestige. Through diligent frugality and desperate creativity she has managed to participate in the town's very exclusive social set. She has also devoted herself to the care of an ancient, wealthy relative, Eliza Joyce, in the silent hope of becoming her heir. Anne is just returning from five years away at school. Because both looks and personality discourage Anne's success on the society marriage market, her relatives have given her an education. She longs to do some great good in the world, praying nightly, "Here am I. What wilt thou have me to do?" (79). In her search for a worthy mission, Anne disparages the humble ambitions of Brooke Calhoun, now a farmer and small-town attorney, who has loved her since childhood.

The majority of the novel covers a trip into the deep South that Dr. Warrick and his daughters take in company with the philanthropist and reformer John Mears. Since Mears is trying to gain support for his project to reform "New York toughs and Chicago anarchists" by relocating them on dairy and chicken farms in the South, he also invites Calhoun as an agricultural advisor. Anne becomes enthralled with Mears's project, seeing him as another St. Augustine; and, although much older than Anne, he becomes enthralled with her. She continues to misunderstand her frustrated, passionate feelings toward Calhoun as dislike, although the reader knows otherwise. First in Mobile and then in New Orleans, Mildred is pursued by an impoverished aristocrat named John Soudé, whose courtship is rivaled by David Plunkett, now an oil tycoon. Plunkett, whom Mildred describes as a "huge tobacco-worm set on end," does not stand a chance; she truly loves Soudé.

For all her self-sacrificing machinations, nothing goes right for Mildred. She is left a mere $500 out of Mrs. Joyce's fortune, and she discovers that Soudé will inherit nothing but debts. Deeply in love, she agrees to marry him anyway, abandoning her ambitions. But, back home, on the eve of her wedding, she is seduced by Plunkett's millions to marry him instead and flees to Europe. Bound for life to a man who disgusts her, she throws herself, heart and soul, into acquisition, damning herself further in the process. Ironically, she fails to see the true value of David Plunkett, who loves her. While pregnant, she begins playing the stock market, becoming obsessed with amassing a fortune that will be her own. When she loses all as the dupe of a professional swindler, it is her final disappointment. She has a breakdown, which eventually leads to her death after the birth of a son. The novel ends with Plunkett and his son living with old Dr. Warrick on the old family homestead. Nearby live Anne and Brooke, who have finally realized their love. Anne has abandoned her ambitions for improving the world in order to run the family dairy farm.

John Soudé makes a brief appearance at the end when, as a nationally renowned orator speaking at a Democratic caucus in Philadelphia, he and his wife visit the Calhouns. The story of the Soudés is a rich and complicated tale of southern honor and decadence. It is, however, arguably too large and unrelated to the story of Dr. Warrick's daughters to be considered a well-crafted subplot.

As the title indicates, the novel's main concern is the two daughters. As a character, Anne exemplifies Davis's ideal young woman. One of those people "who are born without the outer cuticle," she "gets more out of life" than others (39). A bright, energetic woman, restrained by nineteenth-century rules of decorum, her "crazy longing to do – something," her rebellious declaration that "If [she] were are boy, [she'd] run away to sea" are entirely sympathetic (84). Fresh from school and eager to participate in "the great struggles going on in the world. . . . to win fame, to help humanity," Anne's only error is to see Brooke, "a plowman, content with his turnips and pigs," as "ignoble" and "utterly unworthy" (61, 78). Eventually, however, she recants the error of her ways. Anne may be the story's ideal, but, as usual, Davis seems less intrigued by her positive exemplar than by her negative one. Much more of the novel is devoted to Mildred's self-motivated downfall than to Anne's well-learned lesson.

By far the most fascinating character, psychologically, is Mildred Warrick, whose interiority is absolute: "No human being ever had guessed what Milly thought of Milly" or of anything else (113). To all she appears docile, meek, and selfless, when she is really ruthlessly practical and aggressively focused on her goal – wealth. When Anne confronts her with the pretense of being a "butterfly" while she really "work[s] like a grub" to "carry the whole family," Mildred responds, "you do not understand men. They want to manage – to be at the head" (81). Most of the men in the novel prove her right. If this were the extent of her deception, she would be far less harmful than she is. Mildred's commitment and drive are in many ways admirable, but her goal of wealth is unworthy, as are "the little envies and rages of her life against richer women" (85).

Mildred's rejection of love is all the more tragic because it alone has the power to redeem her: "She suddenly loathed this eternal plotting and managing! She felt strangely alone and neglected. Some women did not need to work, or plan, or think of social success or money. They simply sat tranquil, and were – loved" (99-100). Still, even though "a fierce contempt for herself sometimes [comes] over her" when deceiving John Soudé, she continues to weave her trap of deception (185).

Mildred Warrick replicates the drama of the individual conscience that obsessed Davis throughout her career. As early as *Margret Howth* Davis had proclaimed her theme: the "great warfare" waged against the "enemy, Self," in which some are victorious but more are worsted (7). Although Davis's protagonists often meet the test, many do not. As a matter of fact, Davis's own sensibility, unaltered by public sentiment, seems more attuned to those who fail. When Hugh Wolfe, succumbing to the attraction of a comfortable life, fails to return the stolen money, we are told, "The trial-day of this man's life was over, and he had lost the victory" ("Iron-Mills," 50). Though less noble, Mildred similarly fails her test. Contrasting life with Soudé ("the dusty cabin in Camp Street, and the beggarly gowns") to life with Plunkett ("one of the four richest men in America"), she damns herself, telling the "huge creature standing there, with his great, obese body and round unmeaning face," whom she has always "loathed," "I love you, David" (245, 247). She throws away her love for John Soudé and essentially sells herself to David Plunkett to buy material wealth, but much worse than her betrayal of either man is the self-betrayal of her own affections. Mildred is not merely a shallow, materialistic conniver; she is a tragically ambivalent personality. Her true love for Soudé is great, but her insecure need for wealth is greater.

The title, *Dr. Warrick's Daughters*, is also somewhat ironic. The plot is unified not by the influence of their father, who is frequently referred to as another child, but of their strong yet silent, competent yet insecure mother. Although she is self-effacing in life and absent during most of her daughters' lives, at the end of this novel it is Mrs. Warrick whose legacy is emphasized. As a family friend notes: "Sarah Warrick was a dull, commonplace woman! but she has left her mark, deep, on all of her descendants" (299). It is clear that both girls are truly Sarah Warrick's daughters.

Mildred's tragic end demonstrates the hazard of abandoning her mother's agrarian values. Her course of error begins when, as a young woman, she decides that perhaps there were things in the world "which even mamma did not know" (34). As an adult, Mildred senses that the influence of her mother is the best part of her. As she explains enigmatically to her lover Soudé, "She seems to be with us.

On your side" (227). Ironically, it is the capitalist, David Plunkett, who, realizing that "it's a mean world," returns his son to Mrs. Warrick's traditional values (142).

In abandoning her aspirations to a larger sphere of influence by marrying Brooke Calhoun, Anne stays true to her mother's code. Some women complain, "It is women like Anne who block our wheels." They think she "neglect[s] her public duties. . . . Her farm, Brooke, the children, two or three friends, and her work people – there is her one-acre lot in the world!" (299). This passage from the last chapter echoes one from the first, in which Mrs. Warrick "ignored the town. . . . Her children, her garden, the cook, the turkeys – here was the world" (4). The Calhouns reject the materialistic, competitive values of provincial Luxborough just as Sarah Warrick had done.

Though Davis narrows the scope of female ambition in this novel, she does not disparage it altogether. She contends that women, like men, need meaningful work. Anne does not merely help on the family dairy; she runs it while Brooke practices law. Her unabashed pride in her own abilities is presented positively. When Soudé's wife interrupts Anne's "little lecture on the different grades of milk," asking, "Do you really know so much?" Anne's response is filled with a dignity that, for Davis, comes only from having meaningful work: "Certainly; it's my business. I am the farmer" (295). The Calhouns' farm offers another agrarian model of community, in which women's roles that have been marginalized, if not trivialized, in industrial society are corrected. Even misguided Mildred is sympathetic as she sets out to conquer the stock market, proclaiming, "I want to make a capable women of myself" (272). Her error is selecting an unworthy goal, wanting "to learn the value of things" (272). Money and ego are the false gods of this novel, but the need for everyone to find work worthy of his or her energy and intelligence is upheld.

Davis's satiric voice, which she had begun developing in the 1870s, is full blown in this late novel. The primary targets of her derision are the snobbery and materialism of Americans, the vanity of men, and the excessiveness of feminists. The people of Luxborough, inspired most likely by the real Roxborough, a suburb of Philadelphia, see their community as "the final result of the creation. For it Columbus had sailed, and Washington fought" (1). There, rigorously exclusive bastions of old blood like the Monthly Whist Club (est. A.D. 1767) struggle valiantly against the polluting influence of new money: "The mill-owners beat in vain at its closed doors. They jeered at the sandwiches and tea which were its fixed features, but their hearts were sore with envy" (2). But as David Plunkett points out, after tearing up his invitation to join, when the gilded cow is large enough, all doors open. Mrs. Dane and Mr. Franciscus are untiring in their efforts to assure Mildred and Anne of the "enduring good things" in life: "marriages into old Luxborough families, incomes that would warrant a pair of horses and a man-servant; and a membership for themselves and their descendants in the Monthly Thursday Club" (136).

Davis casts her satiric eye at both men and women in this novel. While all the men are flattered by Mildred's adoration, John Soudé most demonstrates this foible. When his writing evokes her tears, he is thrilled: "[I]t was his own genius that had drawn these from the child. Child – yes! But what an intellect she had! What unerring perception!" (108). Throughout the novel Davis takes female reformers to task for disparaging the private domestic sphere of influence. She also mocks the excessive feminism of women who argue that the "world has been misgoverned by men long enough. For the most part they are brutes or fools. If the human experiment is to be run through to the end successfully, our sagacity and purity must take command" (298). This late novel shows that Davis, with her keen awareness of human frailty, was able to write social satire for late nineteenth-century audiences just as she had pleased earlier audiences with her reform fiction.

Frances Waldeaux

A courtship story of Americans in Europe, *Frances Waldeaux* has great satiric potential, but this, Davis's last novel, is weak.[22] Perhaps the problem lies in the fact that she rushed it out just months after *Doctor Warrick's Daughters*. Perhaps her erring protagonist, an aging female hack who has a "queer attachment" to her son, was too close for Davis to see objectively. Whatever the reason, this novel lacks the interesting tension that Davis's successful mediation of polar perspectives and sensibilities produced in much of her writing. *Frances Waldeaux* is worthy of attention, however, because it clearly illustrates the incongruity that sometimes weakens her fiction.

Here, as elsewhere, she has created characters who are compelling in their complexity and has offered provocative psychological insight as well as disturbing social critique; but at the end she has compromised her characters and her themes by forcing the characters to play formulaic parts in a melodramatic plot with a sentimental ending.

The most intriguing aspect of this novel is the characterization of Frances Waldeaux. Typically, Davis's protagonist is not heroic; she is strong and resourceful, but tragically in error. Widowed at a young age by an irresponsible wastrel, she has supported her son, George, well as a fruit farmer and as a writer. Under the pseudonym "Quigg," she writes "comical squibs" that are "not vulgar but coarse and biting" for a New York newspaper (14). All this is positive, but Frances has also been deceptive – always a failing, for Davis, even when it is done for noble reasons. She maintains anonymity in the press so that she can delude her son into thinking that his support comes from his father's well-planned trust. Her self-sacrifice has also been misguided because it has been motivated by dependency. Her needy love undermines George's development as well as her own. During an early conversation with him, she reveals the unhealthy extent to which she has submerged her own identity in his:

> I never think of you as my son, or a man, or anything outside of me – not at all. You are just *me*, doing the things I should have done if I had not been a woman. . . . When I was a girl it seemed as if there was something in me that I must say, so I tried to write poems. . . . I've been dumb, as you might say, for years. But when I read your article, George – do you know if I had written it I should have used just the phrases you did? . . . I am dumb, but you speak for me now. It is because we are just one. (9)

When he falls in love, she discovers that they indeed are not one. Forcing George to choose between her and Lisa, his bride, Frances finds herself left alone. Much of the plot develops around Frances's gradual and troubled acceptance of George's right to an individual existence – his choice of career, his wife, and his home. Eventually, Frances reclaims her own life, though not without causing great pain to George and Lisa. By the end she has done a complete reversal, sounding much like the protagonist of Davis's earlier story "Anne," as she proclaims, "Even out in that other world I shall not be only a mother. I shall be me. *Me*!" (204).

Frances's dependent affection for her son bears a disconcerting resemblance to Davis's attachment to Richard, particularly in her final years, after Clarke's death. In her latter years Davis's letters to Richard are filled with expressions of maudlin neediness of which the following is just one example: "I can't do anything but think how you look and how hungry I am for the sight of you and the touch of your dear arms round me. . . . Oh Dick I wonder if you will ever guess what you are to me" (UVA [c. 1908]).

In this novel Davis also raises issues of female sexuality in late Victorian society, which do not seem to have any autobiographical relevance, when she implies that Frances's rather Freudian attachment to her son is related in some way to her having been victimized by an abusive husband. Explaining to a friend why she has never considered marrying again even though she is still a relatively young woman, Frances explains that Robert Waldeaux "killed in me the capacity for that kind of love. It is not in me." Her subsequent confidence, "I have but one feeling, and that is for my boy," signals trouble (19).

In addition to probing the implications of an all-consuming affection for one's grown son, Davis, who was then 65, explores the anxiety of aging in her characterization of Frances. As she had done in "Anne," Davis tries to communicate the pain of being considered less by others because of physical deterioration while still feeling vibrant inside. Frances explains, "It is only my eyes and ears that are wearing out. *I* am not deaf nor blind. *I* am not old" (202).

Of greater thematic significance than her destructive dependency on her son is Frances's sanctimonious belief that some people, like Lisa's mother, the notorious Pauline Felix, are "born vicious," while others like herself are pure (26). "No woman," she maintains, "could fall as [Pauline] did, who was not rotten to the core" (26). As hatred for Lisa consumes her, Frances realizes that "there is some brutal passion hiding in every human soul, waiting its chance" (76). But before she finally recants her hypocrisy, she further compounds her sin by seeking righteous vengeance, praying to God "that Lisa might soon be put off this earth" (154). When the opportunity presents itself, Frances is ready to commit murder; she attempts to poison her daughter-in-law. Fortunately, she is unsuccessful, and the extremity of her crime shocks her into contrition. Conveniently, Lisa soon dies on her own. Frances is given back her son and a new grandson, but she has also been given the insight that she, too, is capable of evil.

Also traveling in Europe are two wealthy young women and their chaperon, Clara Vance, who is Frances Waldeaux's friend. The adventures of these ingénues comprise the novel's American-versus-European theme. Davis's satiric coverage of the titles-for-dollars international marriage market is sound, if not original. Eventually, the beautiful and demure Lucy Dunbar comes home to become George's second wife, with his mother's blessing. The less lovely and more outspoken Jean Hassard ends up marrying a German prince whom Lucy has rejected and using her money to gloss an American veneer on his crumbling castle.

Jean Hassard, one of Davis's rare positive images of the "New Woman," is a delightful creation. While shocking to her associates, her candid exuberance disarms the reader: "I'm going to paint a great picture some day that all the world shall go mad about. Of Eve. I'll put all the power of all women into her. But in the meantime I'd like to see one man turn pale and pant before me as the fat little prince does when Lucy snubs him" (86). There is not a shred of hypocrisy in her: "Of course we Americans are bound to say that rank and royalty are dead things. But if I had them, I'd galvanize the corpses! If they are useful as shows, I'd make the show worth seeing" (102). The last we hear of Jean she is in Munich, rebuilding the prince's Schloss, holding American tea every Wednesday, and "fighting her way up among the Herrschaft" (182).

While not as free-spirited as Jean, Lucy, who is more important to the plot, is also an independent woman. Regrettably, to achieve a conventionally sentimental conclusion, this character is compromised to a degree that undermines the novel's integrity. While Davis's females often disavow fame in public life for love in a private one, they do not abandon their individual autonomy without censure as Lucy does. This novel, which has traced the disaster of submerging oneself in another, ends with Lucy doing just that. Earlier in the story much is made of the fact that as an orphan she has total control of all her own assets. The Americans are shocked by the European assumption that she will hand over her wealth to her husband. But the novel concludes with Lucy assuring the penniless George, who is disconcerted by her wealth, of just that. "My husband, I believe, is a rich man," she tells him, "and I shall have what he gives me" (206). So ends Davis's last novel.

Looking Backward

The twentieth century brought both personal and professional changes to Davis, now in her 70s. Several were happy changes. Richard married Cecil Clark, and the couple set up house in Marion, Massachusetts, where Davis made long and frequent visits. Charles returned to the States and began a career in publishing in nearby New York. Most of the changes, however, were sad. On 14 December 1904, Davis suffered the most tragic loss of her life when Clarke Davis, her husband for 41 years, died of heart disease. She was also suffering the loss of her eyesight, so necessary to her professionally. Her frustration is apparent from letters, like this one from 1905, in which she apologizes to a cousin: "I cannot write to you at length for my eyes are giving me much trouble and I am only allowed to use them a short time each day" (Shaeffer, 333).

During the last years of her life, Davis was also concerned for her daughter's health. Throughout the decade Nora, in her 30s, the unmarried companion of her widowed mother, suffered from a series of nervous illnesses. Ironically, Davis might have contributed unwittingly to her daughter's problem. While there is very little written record of Nora Davis, there are suggestions that the relationship between mother and daughter, while close and loving, was fraught with certain tensions not present in Davis's relationship with her two more outgoing sons. This is not surprising. In a letter to Richard, written while on board a ship taking them to Italy for Nora's health in 1906, Rebecca reveals one of the few notes of discord in the harmony of the Davis family. She is recounting an incident that occurred in the ship's salon:

> The woman who was managing – there always is one – came to Nora & said "Wont you play for us?" "Thank you I dont play" Noll [Nora] said. "Then you sing?" "No I dont sing." "Perhaps you recite?" "Oh then you will tell a story." "No I dont tell stories." "And yet," said the woman turning to the listening room, "and yet she is Richard Harding Davis's sister!" Then everyone talked & said how they had read every word you wrote.

Even though the critical tone detectable in this passage is softened as Davis goes on – "Noll came down laughing at them. But I saw she was very much pleased" – the letter does seem to reveal a disturbing insensitivity (UVA, 1 May [1906]). Harris argues that the letter shows, beyond all else, that Davis and her daughter were in total agreement that Nora would not " 'market' herself for the entertainment of strangers" (298). Whatever the spirit of this one letter might have been, Davis was sincerely concerned about her daughter; and Nora, like Richard and Charles, was sincerely attached to her mother. Mother and daughter seem to have been constant companions during Davis's last years.[23]

While Davis, suffering from failing eyesight and personal grief, could not sustain the tremendous productivity of the 1890s, she continued to write and publish both fiction and essays until her death. In addition to her weekly articles for the *Saturday Evening Post*, her work appeared in numerous and varied journals: lesser-known or short-lived ones, like the *Congregationalist*, *Smart Set*, *Outlook*, *Success*, and *Metropolitan Magazine*; nineteenth-century leaders, like *Scribner's*, *Harper's*, and *Century*; and some still popular today, like *Ladies Home Journal*, *Harper's Bazaar*, and *Good Housekeeping*.

Saturday Evening Post

While Davis continued to publish in the *Independent*, she switched her primary affiliation to the *Saturday Evening Post* in 1902. During the next five years she wrote over 70 articles, fiction and prose, for the *Post*, as well as a recurring feature: "Literary Folk – Their Ways and Their Work."[24] With her shift from the *Independent* to the *Post*, Davis's work altered in matter and tone. While some of the *Post* articles have the exposé quality of her *Independent* work, most are personal reminiscences. The move seems to mark Davis's becoming an elderly author.

Of special interest, perhaps, is one of her "Literary Folk" pieces on Emile Zola. Though Zola's scientific determinism and Davis's Christianity ultimately make their writing very different, Davis's essay demonstrates the affinity of their styles: "Long afterward came Zola, who sent a sudden flood of words into the world. There was panting, breathless ambition in them; there were delicate, pure fancies, holy family love, filthy passions, and, behind all, shrewd calculation of gain. . . . the original Gaul spoke through him" (176 [4 Jul 1903]: 20).

In another column, a few years later, she reveals her aversion to the subtle convolutions of Henry James's later work in a discussion of "hammock fiction," her tongue-in-cheek recommendation of good summer books to fall asleep by. First recognizing the power of earlier novels like *The Americans* and *The Portrait of a Lady*, she laments the direction marked by *The Golden Bowl*: "There is much pretty filigree work of phrasing in this book which will delight the class of critics whose one idea of literature is bounded by split or whole infinitives. For the rest, Mr. James gives us his usual international *dramatis personae* . . . they still talk in the Jamesonian dialect and wrap the simplest meaning in an involved jumble of words until we lay down the book in despair of ever finding out what any of them mean at any time" (178 [29 July 1905]: 16). Though a pioneer of realistic sensibility and technique, the elderly Davis was clearly disassociated from the ultimate direction of realism.

Bits of Gossip

In October 1904, just months before Clarke's death, Davis saw publication of her last book. *Bits of Gossip*, published by Houghton Mifflin, is a collection of reminiscences, many of which appeared as essays in the *Saturday Evening Post*. The first three chapters contain most of the autobiographical background on Davis, which is discussed in the early chapters of this volume. Chapter 1 tells of her childhood. But more than that it paints a detailed, colorful picture of village life on the expanding frontier of pre-Civil War America. Wheeling, West Virginia, sat literally at a great crossroads, where the National Road carried stages and wagons north and south and the Ohio River opened the West to them. Chapter 2 records her memorable trip to Boston and Concord and her recollection of the literary giants she met there as a feted young author. She remembers with clarity her admiration for Nathaniel Hawthorne, with whom she felt affinity, her frustration with his aggressive sister-in-law, Elizabeth Peabody, her respect for Oliver Wendell Holmes, her sympathy for Louisa May Alcott, her disgust with the author's transcendentalist father, Bronson Alcott, her ambivalent awe of Ralph Waldo Emerson, and her grateful affection for James T. Fields and his wife, Annie. The trip having taken place in 1862, she also recounts the contrast between northern abolitionist perspectives on the Civil War and what she had experienced as a southerner in a border state. In chapter 3 Davis recalls her very early years in the deep South. Mixed with her own memories are family stories of harsh, primitive life in Alabama that belie the myth of a genteel South.

The fourth chapter discusses people of the middle states, who reflect the Scotch-Irish Protestant, middle-class values that she sees as having shaped America. To this heritage she credits the American's common sense, frugality, and family values. She contrasts these with the New England Puritan, to whom she credits intelligence, and the Virginian Cavalier, to whom she credits courage. Chapter 5 returns the memoir to autobiography, focusing on the Civil War, as it was experienced by herself and others on the border that became West Virginia. It contains poignant accounts of lives that were reduced to wretchedness, if not ruined, by the conflict.

In the last three chapters Davis discusses memorable groups of people. In chapter 6 she recalls what she describes as "the shipwrecked crew": female writers and journalists she has known who lived slightly outside the boundaries of respectability. She also discusses the need to separate an artist's work from the artist. Chapter 7 reviews the abolitionists whom she has known well or briefly: statesmen like F. Julius Le Moyne, John C. Frémont, and Charles Sumner; public spokesmen like Horace Greeley, Henry Ward Beecher, and Wendell Phillips; poets like James Russell Lowell and John Greenleaf Whittier; the radical John Brown; African-American abolitionists like William Still and Frances Harper; and most of all Quaker women like Eliza Randolf Turner, Mary Grew, Margaret Burleigh, and their unofficial leader, Lucretia Mott.

Davis concludes her memoir with a chapter on people she has known who she feels have shaped their age in some way, but who have not been covered in any of the previous chapters. These include Henry Clay, the hero of her childhood, and her cousin James G. Blaine in politics; Walt Whitman and Edgar Allan Poe in literature; and two women – the southerner Jessie Benton Frémont and the northerner Frances Willard.

Each chapter of *Bits of Gossip* is more than a reminiscence of Davis's life. It is a thoughtful portrait of life as she found it throughout the United States in the nineteenth century. The northeasterner's faith in progress, the New Englander's urge toward self-development, the southerner's code of honor, the common sense of the Scotch-Irish, the ambivalence of those on the borders are all recorded, as are the contributions made by farmers, merchants, homemakers, journalists, abolitionists, adventurers, reformers, writers, and statesmen. *Bits of Gossip* illuminates the extent to which her sensitive response to the facts of her experience bore fruit in her fiction.

In 1910 Davis suffered a slight stroke, but she recovered and by summer was able to visit her old retreat at Point Pleasant with Nora. From there they went to visit Richard at Crossroads, his country estate at Mt. Kisco, New York. While with Richard, she suffered another stroke. Rebecca Harding Davis died two days later on 29 September 1910. Her cremated remains are interred in the same grave with her husband's in Leverington Cemetery, Roxborough, Pennsylvania. Her humility and her desire to keep her private self separate from her public voice are demonstrated by the inscription on their tombstone. Far below the original inscription – "L. CLARKE DAVIS, 1834-1904" – she had requested the simple addition: "AND HIS WIFE."

No better conclusion to Davis's life in writing can be found than her own introduction to *Bits of Gossip:*

> It has always seemed to me that each human being, before going out into the silence, should leave behind him, not the story of his own life, but of the time in which he lived, – as he saw it, – its creed, its purpose, its queer habits, and the work which it did or left undone in the world.
>
> Taken singly, these accounts might be weak and trivial, but together they would make history live and breathe.

In an immense corpus exceeding 500 pieces of fiction and prose published over 49 years, Rebecca Harding Davis left behind the story of her time, 1831-1910.

Chapter Seven

Conclusion

Rebecca Harding Davis would probably have been pleased with her obituary in the *New York Times,* which paid tribute to her "stern but artistic realism" and "power not unlike Zola's" only after recognizing her roles as wife and mother.[1] The article first credits her with being the "widow of the late L. Clarke Davis, at one time editor of The Philadelphia Public Ledger," then with being the "mother of Richard Harding Davis, the novelist and dramatist," and finally with being "herself a novelist and editorial writer of power." For better or worse, Davis chose to subordinate being a writer of power to being a wife and mother.

She also chose to live as quiet a private life as possible. In its entry on Rebecca Harding Davis, the 1898 *National Cyclopedia of American Biography* quotes the author, then in her late 60s, as summarizing her life in the following way: "I never belonged to a club nor any kind of society; never made a speech and never wanted to do it."[2] Though sincere, Davis's reticence and humility reflect a lack of self-awareness about the self-assertion inherent in her vocation. She says nothing about her life in writing: nearly 50 years as a critical realist, writing fiction on such subjects as immigrant, child, and female labor abuses; post-Civil War racial hatred, mistrust, and guilt; child prostitution; abuses in the insanity laws; the legal restriction of women's freedom; and political corruption. Nor does she mention her 40 years as a journalist, known for her essays exposing injustice and urging humane social reform on subjects that varied from the need to educate prisoners in penitentiaries and care for lepers in the bayous of Louisiana to the need to train woman in skilled trades for economic independence. Yet, obviously, Davis did want her voice to be heard. In an undated letter to Annie Fields she admitted, "It is a necessity for me to write – well or ill. . . . every animal has speech and that is mine" (UVA). This disparity between the facts of Davis's life and her self-image suggests an ambivalence toward her role as a literary woman.

Davis resolved her ambivalence by writing in service to humanity. Richard Harding Davis apparently understood this; on his mother's seventieth birthday in 1901, he praised her, saying, "[Y]ou were always year after year making the ways straighter, lifting up people, making them happier and better. No woman ever did better for her time than you and no shrieking suffragette will ever understand the influence you wielded, greater than hundreds of thousands of women's votes" (*Letters*, 293).

The tensions that shape Davis's writing arise out of her identity as a nineteenth-century Christian woman. The author's enterprise of egoistic self-assertion conflicted with her belief in altruistic self-denial. Writing moral reform fiction with a didactic tone, she could resolve the tension. Her ambivalence toward the vocation of writing and her resolution of it were shared by many women in the nineteenth century. Though Davis's synthesis of these various impulses perhaps makes her writing less accessible to modern readers, it is intriguing historically, sociologically, and psychologically.

In the vanguard of writers implementing an inchoate realistic aesthetic, Davis also mediated other polarities in her fiction. She views the material present with the cynical eye of a satirist, yet she maintains the faith in everlasting spiritual truth of a meliorist. At times her deterministic emphasis seems to qualify as naturalism, but her eventual affirmation of spiritual transcendence shows her sensibility to be more akin to romanticism. Many other early female realists, such as Davis's associates Harriet Beecher Stowe and Louisa May Alcott, evidence similar tensions in their fiction. Because Davis's realistic vision can be startlingly bold, however, her mediation of it with other perspectives may seem more pronounced than theirs. Though sometimes unreconciled tensions seem to fragment the unity of her narratives, more often various perspectives are successfully integrated.

Added to these fundamental tensions is yet another that undermined the potential power of Davis's writing: her decision to write for money. Though motivated by the desire to accommodate maternal responsibilities, Davis's decision to write as much as she could as fast as she could for the highest paying periodicals compromised the quality of her writing. It sometimes led to formulaic plots, indistinct characters, or trite themes. Davis was well aware of what her choice cost her career. In 1890 she wrote a letter to Richard urging him to resist the temptation that she had not: "For one thing, you will lose prestige writing for ––––'s paper. For another, I dread beyond everything your beginning to do hack work for money. It is the beginning of decadence both in work and reputation for you. I know by my own and a thousand other people. Begin to write because it 'is a lot of money' and you stop doing your best work. . . . do only your best work – even if you starve doing it" (*Letters*, 55). Though a great deal of Davis's writing is compelling and insightful, many pieces were simply potboilers, and she knew it.

But Davis wrote much that is indeed powerful. In 1890, critic Helen Gray Cone included Davis in her essay, "Women in American Literature."[3] There she praises Davis's "Browning-like insistence on the rare test-moments of life," arguing that "the hopeless heart-hunger of the poor has seldom been so passionately pictured" as in her fiction. Throughout Davis's long career as a magazine writer, a novelist, and a journalist, she garnered respect for these qualities.

The reception of Davis's novels has always been mixed to some degree. In her day, she was a respected writer, and, as such, her work was seriously reviewed in the *Nation*, *Atlantic*, *Harper's*, *Dial*, *Critic*, and others. Reviews of her work are generally positive, praising most her characters and themes, though at times lamenting her tendency toward didacticism and morbidity. As one would expect, Davis's novels, with their somber tone and commonplace subjects, were never best sellers. Regardless, she was consistently published by reputable presses – Ticknor and Fields, Scribner's Sons, Harper and Brothers, Houghton Mifflin – over 40 years.

Most literary historians recognize Davis's significance as "one of the boldest pioneers of American realistic fiction," whose story "Life in the Iron-Mills," "a bit of Realism as depressed as anything ever produced by the Russian school," is often credited as the first appearance of the genre. With the exception of Arthur Hobson Quinn's *American Fiction*, however, most literary histories do little examination her subsequent texts.[4] The *Literary History of the United States* is typical in its assessment of Davis's writing according to contemporary aesthetics, saying "Unfortunately the faults of melodrama and didacticism mar even her best work" (1: 881). Most critics agree that Davis's work, while interesting, does not achieve its early promise.

Recent shifts in critical focus that have manifested themselves in the movement toward revision of the American literary canon have affected the reception of Davis. These shifts are concerned with learning from attention to the writer's imaginative response to his or her social and ideological context, as well as assessing the writer's value according to current literary aesthetics. The recent *Columbia Literary History of the United States*, for instance, credits Davis not just with "uncanny industrial romances," but with influencing later regionalists like Mary E. Wilkin Freeman through her concern with how time and place affects "the family and the lives of women."[5] This new approach to Davis began with Tillie Olsen's first edition of *Life in the Iron Mills* for the Feminist Press in 1972. There Olsen proved that sensitivity to the pressures shaping the artist does not handicap one's critical judgment: noting sparks of "power, beauty, comprehension – genius" in Davis's early work, yet regretting the "woeful deterioration" into "botched art" evident in subsequent writing (159, 155).

More recently, Sharon M. Harris has employed this approach in *Rebecca Harding Davis and American Literary Realism*. Harris convincingly argues that, far from being an anomaly among American realists, Davis represents a little recognized but highly influential strain in the early development of realism, whose practitioners she terms "metarealists." Davis and other metarealists, "synthesize several modes (romanticism, sentimentalism, regionalism), but realism remains their most explicit focus, and the incorporation of realism into their writings is a conscious effort to transform literature from the mystical or other-worldly realm of romanticism into an art form that represents quotidian experience" (19).

As critics from Olsen to Harris have demonstrated, the most productive reading of Rebecca Harding Davis requires sympathetic attention to the tensions within her texts, the ideological forces that caused them, and her imaginative mediation of them. Davis's faith in the imminence of a benign if inscrutable God separates her most from the realistic tradition she helped develop, but not from the tradition of early metarealists or from the tradition of women writers in the nineteenth century. Her significance should not be ignored. As Hawthorne recognized in 1861, she pointed the way to the future, even if it eventually passed her. Davis's mediation of realistic and idealistic impulses may be problematic, but it is also interesting. The ambiguity that handicaps her successful reception also provokes fruitful analysis of the genre.

Furthermore, Davis has inspired many would-be authors through the years, particularly aspiring female writers. Nineteenth-century authors like Louisa May Alcott, Elizabeth Stuart Phelps, and Helen Hunt Jackson all realized their debt to her. Almost a century later, Tillie Olsen describes her discovery of an anonymous story called "Life in the Iron-Mills" in an old torn volume of the *Atlantic* found in an Omaha junk shop. She spent years wanting desperately to know "the author of this work which meant increasingly more to me over the years, saying 'Literature can be made out of the lives of despised people,' and 'You, too, must write' " (158). The intelligence, sincerity, and courage of Davis's best writing continues to influence readers today.

Rebecca Harding Davis's entire corpus is instructive. It stands as an artifact of a pioneer critical realist who was also a typical nineteenth-century American women.

Notes and References

Preface

1. Several forthcoming reprint editions will make Davis's writing much more accessible. Jean Pfaelzer has collected and edited fiction and topical essays in *A Rebecca Harding Davis Reader* (Pittsburgh University Press, 1993), and I have edited a reprint of Davis's collection, *Silhouettes of American Life* (North Carolina University Press, 1994).

2. In his forthcoming *A Casebook on Rebecca Harding Davis's "Life in the Iron-Mills"* (Rutgers University Press, 1994), Paul Lauter demonstrates the richness of Davis's most studied text in his collection of various critical approaches.

Chapter One

1. "Men's Rights," *Putnam's* n.s., 3 (1869): 212; hereafter cited in the text as "Men's Rights."

2. Davis's private family history, last held by Hope Davis Kehrig, the daughter of Richard Harding Davis, is lost; references to this record are from Gerald Langford's *The Richard Harding Davis Years* (New York: Holt, Rinehart and Winston, 1961); hereafter cited in the text as Langford.

3. *Bits of Gossip* (Boston: Houghton Mifflin, 1904), 6; hereafter cited in the text as *Bits*.

4. *Bits*, 29; along with John Bunyan, author of *Pilgrim's Progress*, and Sir Walter Raleigh is Maria Edgeworth (1767-1849), an early novelist of rural domestic life in Ireland and a proponent of female education.

5. *Louisa May Alcott: Her Life, Letters, and Journals* (Boston: Roberts, 1892), 131.

6. Davis's school years are documented by Helen Woodward Shaeffer, "Rebecca Harding Davis: Pioneer Realist" (Ph.D. diss., University of Pennsylvania, 1947), 31; hereafter cited in the text as Shaeffer.

7. First published as "A Story of To-day," *Atlantic* 8-9 (October 1861-March 1862): 471-86, 582-97, 707-18, 40-51, 202-13, 282-98; and with no substantive changes as *Margret Howth* (Boston: Houghton, Mifflin, 1862; reprint, Upper Saddle River, N.J.: Gregg, 1970); hereafter cited in the text as *Margret Howth*.

8. Sharon M. Harris, *Rebecca Harding Davis and American Realism* (Philadelphia: University of Pennsylvania Press, 1991), 25, documents the significance of Davis's apprenticeship at the *Intelligencer*, as well as her

close friendship with its editor, Archibald W. Campbell; hereafter cited in the text as Harris.

9. Letters, Huntington Library, San Marino, California, FI 1165-68; hereafter cited in the text as Huntington.

10. Gordon S. Haight, "Realism Defined: William Dean Howells," *Literary History of the United States*, ed. Robert E. Spiller et al., 3d. ed. (New York: Macmillan, 1946), 1:881; hereafter cited in the text as Haight.

11. Charles Belmont Davis, ed., *Adventures and Letters of Richard Harding Davis* (New York: Scribners, 1917), 40; hereafter cited in the text as *Letters*.

12. For serious analysis of midcentury popular fiction by what Hawthorne described as that "d – – – –d mob of scribbling women," see Nina Baym, *Woman's Fiction: A Guide to Novels by and about Women in America, 1820-1870* (Ithaca, N.Y.: Cornell University Press, 1978).

13. Vernon Louis Parrington, *The Beginning of Critical Realism*, vol. 3 of *Main Currents in American Thought* (New York: Harcourt Brace, 1930).

14. George Eliot, "Silly Novels by Lady Novelists," *Westminster Review* 66 (1856): 252.

15. Frank Norris, "Zola as a Romantic Writer," *Wave*, 27 June 1896; reprint, *Frank Norris: Novels and Essays* (New York: Library of America, 1986), 1106-8.

Chapter Two

1. "Life in the Iron-Mills," *Atlantic Monthly* 7 (April 1861): 430-51; reprint, *Life in the Iron Mills and Other Stories*, ed. Tillie Olsen (1972; reprint, Old Westbury, N.Y.: Feminist Press, 1985), 11; hereafter cited in the text as "Iron-Mills."

2. Elizabeth Stuart Phelps, "Stories that Stay," *Century* 81 (1910): 118-24; hereafter cited in the text. The fiction of Phelps, who is sometimes catalogued under her married name, Ward, has attracted increased interest in recent years; her most famous novel is *The Story of Avis*.

3. For aesthetic genre analysis, see James C. Austin, "Success and Failure of Rebecca Harding Davis," *Midcontinent American Studies Journal* 3 (1962): 44-46; John Conran, "Assailant Landscapes and the Man of Feeling: Rebecca Harding Davis's *Life in the Iron Mills*," *Journal of American Culture* 3 (1980): 487-500; Sharon M. Harris, "Rebecca Harding Davis: From Romanticism to Realism," *American Literary Realism* 21, no. 2 (Winter 1989): 4-20; and Walter Hesford, "Literary Contexts of 'Life in the Iron-Mills,' " *American Literature* 49 (1977-78): 70-85. For feminist analysis, see Charlotte Goodman, "Portraits of the *Artiste Manqué* by Three Women Novelists," *Frontiers* 5, no. 3 (1981): 57-59; Maribel W. Molyneaux, "Sculpture in the Iron Mills: Rebecca Harding Davis's Korl Woman," *Women's Studies* 17 (1991): 152-72; Tillie Olsen, "Biographical Interpreta-

tion," *Life in the Iron Mills and Other Stories,* (1972; reprint, Old Westbury, N.Y.: Feminist Press, 1985); Jean Pfaelzer, "Rebecca Harding Davis: Domesticity, Social Order, and the Industrial Novel," *International Journal of Women's Studies* 4 (1981): 234-44; Jane Atteridge Rose, "The Artist Manqué in the Fiction of Rebecca Harding Davis," in *Writing the Woman Artist*, ed. Suzanne Jones (Philadelphia: University of Pennsylvania Press, 1991) 155-74; and Rose, "Reading 'Life in the Iron-Mills' Contextually: A Key to Rebecca Harding Davis's Fiction," in *Conversations: Contemporary Critical Theory and the Teaching of Literature*, ed. Charles Moran and Elizabeth Penfield (Urbana, Ill.: NCTE, 1990) 187-99. *A Casebook on Rebecca Harding Davis's "Life in the Iron-Mills,"* ed. Paul Lauter (New Brunswick, N.J.: Rutgers University Press, forthcoming 1994), presents a variety of critical approaches.

4. A cotton-mill picker threw a shuttle across a loom in the weaving process; an iron-mill puddler stirred molten pig-iron as part of the smelting process.

5. Since "Iron-Mills" was published anonymously, readers would not have assumed the narrator to be female like its author. Quite to the contrary, since well-bred young women in the nineteenth century would have no knowledge of crime and death in urban slums, readers would probably assume the narrator to be the persona of a male author. Furthermore, this narrator assumes to be addressing a male reader, referring at one point to the reader's wife (40).

6. Letter dated 26 January, probably 1861; the unpublished Fields-Davis correspondence comprises the majority of Rebecca Harding Davis's papers in the Richard Harding Davis Collection (#6109), Clifton Waller Barrett Library, Manuscript Division, Special Collections Department, University of Virginia Library; hereafter cited as UVA and dated in the text. Some of Davis's correspondence is undated; bracketed dates are suppositions founded on textual evidence by Langford, by Harris, and by William Frazer Grayburn, "The Major Fiction of Rebecca Harding Davis," (Ph.D. diss., Pennsylvania State University, 1965); hereafter cited in the text as Grayburn.

7. UVA, 11 April 1861; neither the manuscript of "The Deaf and the Dumb" nor Fields's letter exists, as Davis did not save personal papers. Facts are pieced out of her subsequent letters.

8. Huntington, 1167; Johann Gottlieb Fichte (1762-1814) was a German romantic philosopher whose ideas about self-development were similar to Hegel's.

9. For further discussion, see Jean Fagan Yellin, "The 'Feminization' of Rebecca Harding Davis," *American Literary History* 2, no. 2 (1990): 203-19.

10. See Louise Duus, "Neither Saint nor Sinner: Women in Late Nineteenth-Century Fiction," *American Literary Realism* 7 (1974): 276-78.

11. *Bits*, 32-33; Davis's term "Areopagites" alludes to the prestigious body of legislators who ruled ancient Athens.

Chapter Three

1. Grayburn (151) notes the April review in *Knickerbocker* 59 (1862): 320.

2. *Petersons's* 43 (January-June 1863): 350. For magazine circulation see Frank Luther Mott, *A History of American Magazines* (Cambridge, Mass.: Harvard University Press, 1938), 2:306-311.

3. *Peterson's* 48 (July-December 1865): 291.

4. "The Murder of Glen Ross," *Peterson's* 40 (November-December 1861): 347.

5. "The Second Life," *Peterson's* 43 (January-June 1863): 33-39, 121-30, 204-11, 293-300, 348-53, 420-30; hereafter cited in the text.

6. "The Promise of Dawn," *Atlantic* 11 (January 1863): 10-25; hereafter cited in the text.

7. "Paul Blecker," *Atlantic* 11-12 (May-July 1863): 580-98, 677-91, 52-69; hereafter cited in the text.

8. Elizabeth Stuart Phelps, "At Bay," *Harper's* 34 (1867): 780.

9. "Blind Tom," *All the Year Round* 8 (October 1862): 126-29, and *Atlantic* 10 (November 1862): 580-85; hereafter cited in the text.

10. "Ellen," *Peterson's* 44 (July 1863): 38-48, and *Atlantic* 16 (July 1865): 22-34; hereafter cited in the text.

11. "The Harmonists," *Atlantic* 17 (May 1866): 529-38; hereafter cited in the text. The Harmony Society, founded in 1803 by German religious reformer George Rapp, established Economy, Pennsylania, its third community based on communism and celibacy, in 1825. For discussion Davis's critique of patriarchal modes of thinking, see Jean Pfaelzer, "The Sentimental Promise and the Utopian Myth: Rebecca Harding Davis's 'The Harmonists' and Louisa May Alcott's 'Transcendental Wild Oats,' " *American Transcendental Quarterly* n.s., 3, no. 1 (March 1989): 85-99.

12. "John Lamar," *Atlantic* 9 (April 1862): 411-23; hereafter cited in the text. This story has been reprinted for the first time in *Kaleidoscope: Stories of the American Experience,* ed. Barbara Perkins and George Perkins (New York: Oxford University Press, 1993), 249-65.

13. See Jan Cohn, "The Negro Character in Northern Magazine Fiction of the 1860's," *New England Quarterly* 43 (1970): 572-92.

14. "David Gaunt," *Atlantic* 10 (September-October 1862): 259-71, 403-21; hereafter cited in the text.

15. UVA [late 1863]; many letters during this period of Davis's illness are not dated.

16. UVA [late 1863-early 1864]; references in Davis's letters from this period suggest that writer/physician S. Weir Mitchell, whose prohibition of Charlotte Perkins Gilman's reading and writing inspired "The Yellow Wall-Paper," also treated Davis for the same mysterious "hysteria." Mitchell was a

close family friend of the Davises in Philadelphia and at Point Pleasant. Several years after her trouble, Davis wrote to Annie Fields on the occasion of Mitchell's first publication in the *Atlantic*, praising Mitchell as a physician and a friend: "I owe much to him – life – and what is better than life" (UVA [1866]); for more on this subject, see Jane Atteridge Rose, "Images of Self: The Example of Rebecca Harding Davis and Charlotte Perkins Gilman," *ELN* 29, no. 4 (1992): 70-78.

17. "The Wife's Story," *Atlantic* 14 (July 1864): 1-19; reprint, Olsen, 177-222; hereafter cited in the text.

18. For further discussion of Hetty's dream as an arena for psychic conflict, see Margaret M. Culley, "Vain Dreams: The Dream Convention in Nineteenth-Century American Women's Fiction," *Frontiers* 1, no. 3 (1976): 94-102.

19. Although she never met transcendentalist, author, and activist Margaret Fuller, who had died in 1850, Davis seems haunted by her image, as if she saw in Fuller aspects of her own personality she wished to deny.

20. Rosa Bonheur (1822-99) was a French painter, famous for her realistic depiction of animals.

21. "Out of the Sea," *Atlantic* 15 (May 1865): 533-49; hereafter cited in the text.

Chapter Four

1. Remnants of Davis's journal, containing sporadic entries from 1865 to 1879, are included in the Richard Harding Davis Collection (#6109), Clifton Waller Barrett Library, Manuscripts Division, Special Collections Department, University of Virginia Library.

2. *Waiting for the Verdict, Galaxy* 3-4 (February 1867-December 1867): 341-64, 435-74, 581-605, 693-716, 805-34, 5-29, 197-225, 325-359, 445-75, 574-608; and New York: Sheldon, 1867; reprint Upper Saddle River, N.J.: Gregg, 1968; hereafter cited in the text.

3. "In the Market," *Peterson's* 53 (January 1868): 49-57; hereafter cited in the text; reprint, *LEGACY* 8 (1991): 22-32; for criticism, see Sharon M. Harris's "Redefining the Feminine: Women and Work in Rebecca Harding Davis's 'In the Market,' " *LEGACY* 8 (1991): 118-21.

4. "Put Out of the Way," *Peterson's* 57-58 (May-August 1870): 355-67, 431-43, 30-41, 109-18; hereafter cited in the text.

5. Clarke Davis, "A Modern Lettre de Cachet," *Atlantic* 21 (1868): 588-602.

6. *John Andross, Hearth and Home* 5-6 (December 1873-May 1874): 797-99, 813-14, 828-29, 9-11, 25-26, 41-43, 57-59, 73-75, 89-90, 105-7, 121-22, 137-39, 153-55, 169-71, 185-87, 201-3, 217-18, 233-34, 249-51, 265-67, 281-82; and New York: Orange Judd, 1874; hereafter cited in the text from the 1874 Orange Judd book.

7. Grayburn (283-91) discusses the *Public Ledger* editorial "The Brooks Assassination" (8 September 1869) and Brooks's *Whiskey Drops* (W. B. Evans, Philadelphia, 1873).

8. *Dallas Galbraith, Lippincott's Magazine* 1-2 (Jan 1868-October 1869): 373; and Philadelphia: Lippincott: 1869; hereafter cited in the text.

9. Grayburn (261n13) documents James's authorship of the particular *Nation* review (7 [22 October 1868]: 331) through Daniel C. Haskell, *The Nation, Index of Titles and Contributors* (1951), 1:15, 2:256, and Leon Edel and Dan H. Lawrence, *A Bibliography of Henry James* (London: Hart-Davis, 1957): 287.

10. "A Pearl of Great Price," *Lippincott's Magazine* 2-3 (December 1868-January 1869): 606-17, 74-88; hereafter cited in the text.

11. *New York Daily Tribune*, 13 July 1870, 6; for more explanation of this misattribution, see Philip Eppard, "Rebecca Harding Davis: A Misattribution," *PBSA* 69 (1975): 265-67; Sharon M. Harris, "Rebecca Harding Davis: A Continuing Misattribution," *LEGACY* 5, no. 1 (1988): 33-34; and Harris, *Davis and American Realism*, 2-4.

12. "A Faded Leaf of History," *Atlantic Monthly* 31 (January 1873): 44; hereafter cited in the text.

13. "A Hundred Years Ago," *Riverside* 4 (June-July 1870): 279-83, 323-25; "Naylor o' the Bowl," *St. Nicholas* 1 (December 1873): 65-69; "Hard Tack," *Youth's Companion* 44 (January 1871): 46-54; "The Paw Paw Hunt," *Youth's Companion* 44 (November 1871): 353-54; "Two Brave Boys," *St. Nicholas* 37 (July 1910): 835.

14. "Pepper-Pot Woman," *Scribner's Monthly* 8 (September 1874): 541-43; hereafter cited in the text.

15. "Dolly," *Scribner's Monthly* 9 (November 1874): 89-92; hereafter cited in the text.

16. "The Poetess of Clap City," *Scribner's Monthly* 9 (March 1875): 612; hereafter cited in the text.

17. "The Middle-Aged Woman," *Scribner's Monthly* 10 (July 1875): 345; hereafter cited in the text.

18. *Natasqua, Scribner's Monthly* 1 (November 1870-January 1871): 58-69, 159-69, 283-90; hereafter cited in the text; and New York: Cassell-Rainbow, 1886.

19. "Ballachi Brothers," *Lippincott's* 10 (July 1872): 66-75; reprint, *Kitty's Choice, or Berrytown and Other Stories* (Philadelphia: Lippincott, 1873), and *Stories by American Authors* (New York: Scribners, 1884).

20. *Kitty's Choice, or Berrytown, Lippincott's* 11-12 (April-July 1873): 400-11, 579-87, 697-707, 35-48; reprint, *Kitty's Choice, or Berrytown and Other Stories* (Philadelphia: Lippincott, 1873), and *Stories by American Authors* (New York: Scribners, 1884); hereafter cited in the text.

21. Many communities practicing alternative religious, political, social, and economic systems were established in nineteenth-century America. Two of the better known are New Harmony, founded by George Rapp and Developed by British socialist Robert Owen and which Davis satirized in "The Harmonites," and Brook Farm, which followed French socialist Charles Fourier and attracted Concord Transcendentalists. Davis agreed with their social criticism but argued with their idealism, especially their rejection of the nuclear family.

22. "Earthen Pitchers," *Scribner's Monthly* 7 (November 1873-April 1874): 73-81, 199-207, 74-81, 490-94, 595-600, 714-211; hereafter cited in the text.

Chapter Five

1. Lemuel Clarke Davis, *A Stranded Ship* (New York: Putnam, 1869; reprint, 1881).

2. Langford (77) tells of Richard Harding Davis discovering boxes of the 25-cent paperback in the attic years later.

3. Harris also notes that the Women's Pavilion, allowed but not financed as other exhibits were, was highly controversial, with vocal feminist opponents as well as proponents (193-95). More than likely, Davis's silence on the issue reflects ambivalence more than lack of interest.

4. "Old Philadelphia," *Harper's* 53 (April-May 1876): 705-21, 868-82; hereafter cited in the text; "Old Landmarks in Philadelphia," *Scribner's Monthly* 12 (June 1876): 145-66; hereafter cited in the text; and "A Glimpse of Philadelphia, in July, 1776," *Lippincott's* 18 (July 1876): 27-38; hereafter cited in the text.

5. "How the 'Gull' Went Down," *St. Nicholas* 1 (June 1874): 441-44; "The Shipwreck," *Youth's Companion* 49 (February 1876): 51-52.

6. "The House on the Beach," *Lippincott's* 17 (January 1876): 72-80; hereafter cited in the text; "Life-Saving Stations," *Lippincott's* 17 (March 1876): 301-10; hereafter cited in the text.

7. *Encyclopedia Britannica*, 9th ed., supplement, s.v. "Life-Saving Service, U.S."

8. "Across the Gulf," *Lippincott's* 28 (July 1881): 59-71; hereafter cited in the text.

9. *A Law unto Herself, Lippincott's* 2 (July-December 1877): 39-49, 167-82, 292-302, 464-78, 614-28, 719-31; hereafter cited in the text; and Philadelphia: Lippincott, 1878.

10. Grayburn argues that "how much this belief in comfort affected her own literary career may be more important than how often it is embodied in her fiction" (281).

11. Review of *A Law unto Herself, Nation* 26 (7 March 1878): 176.

12. "By-Paths in the Mountains," *Harper's* 61 (July-September 1880): 167-85, 353-69, 532-47; hereafter cited in the text; "Here and There in the South," *Harper's* 75 (July-November 1887): 235-46, 431-43, 593-606, 747-60, 914-25; hereafter cited in the text.

13. "Vacation Sketches among the Alleghenies," *Youth's Companion* 55 (June 1882): 243; "Some Testimony in the Case," *Atlantic* 56 (November 1885): 602-8; hereafter cited in the text.

14. "The Yares of Black Mountain," *Lippincott's* 16 (July 1875): 35-47; hereafter cited in the text; reprint, *Silhouettes of American Life* (New York: Scribners, 1982); hereafter cited in the text as *Silhouettes.*

15. "The Man in the Cage," *Harper's* 56 (December 1877): 79-84; hereafter cited in the text.

16. "At the Station," *Scribner's Monthly* 4 (December 1888): 687-96; hereafter cited in the text; reprint, *Silhouettes*.

17. "Walhalla," *Scribner's Monthly* 20 (May 1880): 139-45; hereafter cited in the text; reprint, *Silhouettes*.

18. "Silhouette," *Harper's* 67 (September 1883): 622-31; hereafter cited in the text; reprint, "The End of the Vendetta," in *Silhouettes*.

19. "The Captain's Story," *Galaxy* 2 (December 1866): 725-34.

20. "A Strange Story from the Coast," *Lippincott's* 23 (January 1879): 677-85; hereafter cited in the text.

21. "Mademoiselle Joan," *Atlantic* 58 (September 1886): 328-36; hereafter cited in the text; reprint, *Silhouettes*.

22. See James's supernatural novella *A Turn of the Screw* (1898), as well as critical analysis in his biography of Nataniel Hawthorne (English Men of Letters Series, 1879) and his preface to *The Aspern Papers* (New York Edition, 1907), collected in *The Art of the Novel* (New York: Charles Scribner's Sons, 1934).

23. For more thorough development of this idea in all of Davis's female artist figures, see Rose, "The Artist Manqué."

24. "Marcia," *Harper's* 53 (November 1876): 925-28; hereafter cited in the text; reprint, *Silhouettes* and *LEGACY* 4, no. 1 (1987): 6-10; for criticism on "Marcia," see Jean Pfaelzer's introduction to the story in *LEGACY* 4, no. 1 (1987): 3-5.

25. "A Day with Doctor Sarah," *Harper's* 57 (September 1878): 611; story on pp. 611-17.

26. "A Wayside Episode," *Lippincott's* 31 (February 1883): 179-90; hereafter cited in the text; reprint, *Silhouettes*.

27. "Tirar y Soult," *Scribner's Magazine* 2 (November 1887): 563-72; hereafter cited in the text; reprint, *Silhouettes* and *Stories of the South* (New York: Scribners, 1893).

28. "Anne," *Harper's* 78 (April 1889): 744-50; reprint, *Silhouettes* and Olsen, 225-42; hereafter cited in the text.

Chapter Six

1. Richard Harding Davis, "The Coronation," *Harper's* 94 (February 1897): 335-52; Charles Belmont Davis, "La Gommeuse," *Harper's* 94 (March 1897): 372-79; Rebecca Harding Davis, "The Education of Bob" *Harper's* 94 (May 1897): 934-40.

2. Davis had begun writing children's pieces for the *Independent* in 1882 and had written occasional adult articles since 1886; from 1902 to 1906, when she became a regular contributor to the *Post*, she continued as an occasional contributor to the *Independent*; her last piece in the liberal New York weekly appeared two years before her death.

3. "Education and Crime," Report of the United States Department of the Interior-Education, 1899, vol. 2, House Document, vol. 31, 56th Congress, 1st Session, 1899-1900.

4. The 22 articles following appeared between 1887 and 1908 in volumes 39 through 65 of the *Independent;* hereafter individual titles will be cited in the text by volume and year, with passages cited by page number.

5. See Kate Marsden's *On Sledge and Horseback to the Outcast Siberian Lepers* (New York: Record, 1891).

6. For a subtle and sensitive analysis of Davis's feminism in the context of nineteenth-century ideology and the suffrage movement, see Harris.

7. Thomas Beer, *The Mauve Decade: American Life at the End of the Nineteenth Century* (New York: Knopf, 1926), 113; hereafter cited in the text.

8. Julia Ward Howe (1819-1910), author of "Battle Hymn of the Republic," was an essayist and lecturer for women's suffrage; Mary A. Livermore (1821-1905), founder of the *Woman's Journal*, was a suffrage and temperance activist; Frances E. Willard (1839-1898), founder of the Women's Christian Temperance Union, was a suffrage and temperance activist; Lucy Stone (1818-1893) editor of the *Woman's Journal* for 20 years, was an abolitionist and a suffragist.

9. Quote from p. 662; Marion Harland [Mary Terhune] (1830-1922) wrote sentimental fiction set in the South; Mary Noailles Murfree (1850-1922) wrote local-color sketches of Tennessee under the name of Charles Egbert Craddock; Mary Hartwell Catherwood (1847-1920) wrote historical fiction set in the the Midwest and Great Lakes regions; Mary Halleck Foote (1847-1938), who was also an illustrator, wrote stories of the California and Colorado mining regions; Constance Fenimore Woolson (1840-94), like Davis, wrote fiction set in many different regions that was always marked by interest in locale; Elizabeth Stuart Phelps [Ward] (1844-1911) wrote stories and novels about educated New England women who felt restricted by

their society; Sarah Orne Jewett (1849-1909), the finest nineteenth-century regionalist, wrote novels and stories of the Maine coast that define the clash of new urban and old rural ways as also a clash of masculine and feminine values; Mary E. Wilkins [Freeman] (1852-1930), the most realistic of these regionalists, wrote stories that show the stoic endurance and occasional rebellion of usually impoverished New England women. I have not been able to identify Mary Dean.

10. UVA, 30 December 1880; Jackson's ground-breaking exposé of the dispossession and genocide of Native Americans remains significant today. See *A Century of Dishonor* (New York: Harper, 1881).

11. "In the Gray Cabins of New England," *Century* 49 [n.s., 29] (February 1895): 620-23; hereafter cited in the text.

12. "Some Hobgoblins in Literature," *Book Buyer*, 3d ser., 14 (April 1897): 229-31.

13. She is referring, of course, to the slanderous lies spread by Griswold in the *New York Tribune* and the *International Monthly Magazine* immediately after Poe's death, and again in his 1850 edition of Poe's work.

14. Shaeffer (261) cites the *Century* Collection Manuscripts New York Library.

15. Kent Hampden, *Youth's Companion* 64 (January-February 1891): 3-4, 21-22, 33-34, 45-46, 57-58, 71-71, 89-90; and New York: Scribners, 1892; hereafter cited in the text.

16. A reprint edition of *Silhouettes of American Life* (New York: Scribners, 1892) is forthcoming from the North Carolina University Press in 1994. This collection provides a more complete sense of Davis's mature writing than any of the stories or novels now available. Its contents include the following: from *Atlantic*, "A Faded Leaf of History" (1873) and "Mademoiselle Joan" (1886); from *Lippincott's*, "The Yares of the Black Mountains" (1875), "Across the Gulf" (1881), and "A Wayside Episode" (1883); from *Scribner's Monthly*, "The Doctor's Wife" (1874) and "Walhalla" (1880); from *Scribner's Magazine*, "Tirar y Soult" (1887) and "At the Station" (1888); and from *Harper's*, "Marcia" (1876), "The End of the Vendetta" (1883), "Anne" (1889), and "An Ignoble Martyr" (1890).

17. "An Undedicated Nun," *Harper's* 80 (March 1890): 604-10; hereafter cited in the text; reprint, *Silhouettes*.

18. Review of *Silhouettes of American Life*, *Nation* 55 (October 1892): 262.

19. "An Old-Time Love Story," *Century* 77 (December 1908): 219-21; hereafter cited in the text.

20. "The Coming of Night," *Scribner's Magazine* 45 (January 1909): 58-68; hereafter cited in the text.

21. Review of *Doctor Warrick's Daughters* in the *Nation* 62 (June 1996): 459. *Doctor Warrick's Daughters* published in *Harper's Bazaar* 28 (July-

November 1859): 541-43, 561-63, 578-79, 601-2, 618-19, 641-42, 661-62, 681-82, 705-6, 725-26, 746-47, 765-66, 785-86, 805-6, 822-23, 855-57, 866, 885-86, 921-23, 953-55; and New York: Harper, 1896; hereafter cited in the text from the 1896 Harper edition.

22. *Frances Waldeaux, Harper's Bazaar* 29 (October-December 1896): 841, 846-47, 870, 889-90, 910-11, 925-26, 950-51, 969-70, 994, 1017-19; and New York: Harper, 1897; hereafter cited in the text from the 1897 Harper edition.

23. According to Langford (277), a few months after her mother's death, Nora married Percival Farrar, an Englishman she had known for some years. He had been her father's secretary in Philadelphia before becoming an Anglican priest. Richard also finally officially separated from his wife, Cecil, only after Davis's death.

24. Grayburn first documented all of Davis's *Post* articles; "Literary Folk: Their Ways and Their Work," her irregularly recurring feature on past and current writers, ran from 1903 through 1905; as the subtitle indicates, she discusses the writers' personalities and personal background as well as their work.

Chapter Seven

1. "Rebecca Harding Davis Dies," *New York Times*, 9 September 1910, 13.

2. *National Cyclopedia of American Biography*, 78 vols. to date (New York: White, 1891-), 8:177.

3. *Helen Gray Cone*, "Women in American Literature," *Century* 40 (October 1890): 927.

4. Fred Lewis Pattee, *Development of the American Short Story* (1932; reprint, New York: Biblo, 1966), 141; Arthur Hobson Quinn, *American Fiction* (New York: Appleton, 1936); Gordon S. Haight, "Realism Defined," *Literary History of the United States*, ed. Robert E. Spiller, 2 vols., 3d. ed. (New York: Macmillan, 1946).

5. Martha Banta, "Realism and Regionalism," *Columbia Literary History of the United States*, ed. Emory Elliott (New York: Columbia University Press, 1988), 510.

Selected Bibliography

PRIMARY WORKS

Books

Bits of Gossip. Boston: Houghton Mifflin, 1904.

Dallas Galbraith. Philadelphia: Lippincott, 1868.

Doctor Warrick's Daughters. New York: Harper, 1896.

Frances Waldeaux. New York: Harper, 1897.

John Andross. New York: Orange, 1874.

Kent Hampden. New York: Scribners, 1892.

Kitty's Choice, or Berrytown and Other Stories. Philadelphia: Lippincott, 1873.

A Law unto Herself. Philadelphia: Lippincott, 1878.

Life in the Iron Mills and Other Stories. 1972. Old Westbury, N.Y.: Feminist, 1985.

Margret Howth. 1862. Upper Saddle River, N.J.: Gregg, 1970.

Natasqua. New York: Cassell-Rainbow, 1886.

Silhouettes of American Life. New York: Scribners, 1892.

Waiting for the Verdict. 1867. Upper Saddle River, N.J.: Gregg, 1968.

Selected Uncollected Fiction

"David Gaunt." *Atlantic* 10 (1862): 259-71, 403-21.

"A Day with Doctor Sarah." *Harper's* 57 (1878): 611-17.

"Earthen Pitchers." *Scribner's Monthly* 7 (1873-74): 73-81, 199-207, 274-81, 490-94, 595-600, 714-21.

"Ellen." *Atlantic* 16 (1865): 22-34.

"The Harmonists." *Atlantic* 17 (1866): 529-38.

"Here and There in the South." *Harper's* 75 (1887): 235-46, 431-43, 593-606, 747-60, 914-25.

"In the Market." *Peterson's* 53 (1868): 49-57; reprint, *LEGACY* 8 (1991): 22-32.

"John Lamar." *Atlantic* 9 (1862): 411-23.

"Marcia." *Harper's* 53 (1876): 925-28; reprint, *LEGACY* 4, no. 1 (1987): 6-10.

"Paul Blecker." *Atlantic* 11 (1863): 52-69.

"A Pearl of Great Price." *Lippincott's* 2 (1868): 606-17; 3 (1869): 74-88.

"Put Out of the Way." *Independent* 57 (1870): 355-67, 413-43, 58 (1870): 30-41, 109-18.

Selected Uncollected Essays

"The Disease of Money-Getting." *Independent* 54 (1902): 1457-60.

"In the Gray Cabins of New England." *Century* 49 [n.s., 29] (1895): 620-23.

"Men's Rights." *Putnam's*, n.s., 3 (1869): 212-24.

"Some Testimony in the Case." *Atlantic* 56 (1885): 602-8.

"Women in Literature." *Independent* 43 (1891): 6612.

Unpublished Letters and Manuscripts

The Richard Harding Davis Collection, Clifton Waller Barrett Library of American Literature, University of Virginia's Alderman Libarary.

SECONDARY WORKS

Books and Parts of Books

Beer, Thomas. *The Mauve Decade: American Life at the End of the Nineteenth Century*. New York: Knopf, 1926. The source of several anecdotes on Davis, which are often treated as facts in subsequent scholarship.

Davis, Charles Belmont. *The Adventure and Letters of Richard Harding Davis*, 1-36. New York: Scribners, 1917. Peripheral references to Davis's family life in this biography of her son, Richard, written by her other son and based on Richard's family correspondence, primarily to his mother.

Haight, Gordon S. "Realism Defined: William Dean Howells." In *Literary History of the United States*, edited by Robert E. Spiller et al., 880-81. 2 vols. 3d. ed. New York: Macmillan, 1946. Briefly discusses "Iron-Mills," *Margret Howth*, *Waiting for the Verdict*, "John Lamar," and *John Andross*, illustrating Davis's "realism mingled with sentiment."

Harris, Sharon M. *Rebecca Harding Davis and American Realism*. Philadelphia: University of Pennsylvania Press, 1991. A thorough book-length study of Davis's contribution as a "metarealist" to the development of American literature, analyzing more than 50 pieces of fiction and prose in the context of nineteenth-century thought and the texts of other writers within the tradition. Well documented with correspondence and other primary materials that correct some long-held misconceptions.

Langford, Gerald. "Book I: Rebecca." In *The Richard Harding Davis Years: A Biography for a Mother and Son*, 3-58. New York: Holt, 1961. Contains biographical information on Davis, using information from family records written by Davis for her family that seem no longer extant, as well as other Davis correspondence.

Olsen, Tillie. "A Biographical Interpretation." In *Life in the Iron Mills*, by Rebecca Harding Davis, 69-174. New York: Feminist Press, 1972. Significant not only as the first modern reprinting of "Iron-Mills" but also as the essay that stimulated renewed critical interest in Davis with its feminist analysis. Also mentions "David Gaunt," *Margret Howth*, "Earthen Pitchers," *John Andross*, *A Law unto Herself*, "Ellen," "Anne," and "The Wife's Story."

Pattee, Fred Lewis. *Development of the American Short Story: An Historical Overview*, 169-73. 1923; reprint, New York: Biblo, 1966. Early critical assessment of realism in "Iron-Mills" and *Margret Howth* and of Davis as "pioneer of American fiction."

Quinn, Arthur Hobson. *American Fiction: An Historical Survey*, 180-92. New York: Appleton, 1936. Early critical overview of Davis's work. Briefly discusses 19 texts, including "Iron-Mills," "John Lamar," "David Gaunt," "Paul Blecker," "The Wife's Story," *Waiting for the Verdict*, *Dallas Galbraith*, "Earthen Pitchers," *John Andross*, *Doctor Warrick's Daughters*, and *Frances Waldeaux*.

Rose, Jane Atteridge. "The Artist Manqué in the Fiction of Rebecca Harding Davis." In *Writing the Woman Artist*, edited by Suzanne W. Jones, 155-74. Philadelphia: University of Pennsylvania Press, 1991. Plots Davis's fictional renderings of failed artists alongside her life; reveals Davis's changing attitude toward her own situation as a female artist. Examines "Iron-Mills," "Blind Tom," "The Wife's Story," "Marcia," "The Poetess of Clap City," "Clement Moore's Vocation," "Earthen Pitchers," *A Law unto Herself*, "Anne," and *Frances Waldeaux*.

_____. "Reading 'Life in the Iron-Mills' contextually: A Key to Rebecca Harding Davis' Fiction." In *Conversations: Contemporary Critical Theory and the Teaching of Literature*, edited by Charles Moran and Elizabeth F. Penfield, 187-99. Urbana, Ill.: NCTE, 1990. A reading of "Iron-Mills" as a text informed by domestic ideology that demonstrates Davis's assimilation of certain cultural values and her rejection of others.

Articles

Austin, James C. "Success and Failure of Rebecca Harding Davis." *Midcontinent American Studies Journal* 3 (1962): 44-46. Argues that "Davis was born too early"; flaws in her style can be traced to her unsuccessful attempts at modifying her naturalistic vision to accommodate popular taste. Looks at "Iron-Mills," "David Gaunt," *Waiting for the Verdict*, "Paul Blecker," "Natasqua," *John Andross*, *Doctor Warrick's Daughters*, and *Dallas Galbraith*.

Cohn, Jan. "The Negro Character in Northern Magazine Fiction of the 1860's." *New England Quarterly* 43 (1970): 572-92. Discusses Davis's

"John Lamar" as the first appearance of a black protagonist in American fiction.

Conron, John. "Assailant Landscapes and the Man of Feeling: Rebecca Harding Davis's *Life in the Iron Mills*." *Journal of American Culture* 3 (1980): 487-500. Examines Davis's depiction of industrial landscapes in "Iron-Mills" from a symbolic perspective, noting in her treatment the transition from romantic to realistic perception of the industrial landscape.

Culley, Margaret M. "Vain Dreams: The Dream Convention in Some Nineteenth-Century American Women's Fiction." *Frontiers* 1, no. 3 (1976): 94-102. Observes Davis's use of the dream convention in "The Wife's Story" as a projection of desires that were "not so much vain, as in vain."

Downey, Fairfax. "Portrait of a Pioneer." *Colophon* 12 (1932): n.p. The earliest biographical essay of her life and work; sympathetic and appreciative, but contains inaccuracies.

Duus, Louise. "Neither Saint nor Sinner: Women in Late Nineteenth-Century Fiction." *American Literary Realism* 7 (1974): 276-78. Argues that, though flawed, *Margret Howth* is noteworthy as the earliest example of the way realism would eventually "provide an accurate picture of the commonplace life the American woman."

Eppard, Philip. "Rebecca Harding Davis: A Misattribution." *PBSA* 69 (1975): 265-67. Documents the misattribution of the antisuffrage *Pro Aris et Focis* to Davis.

Goodman, Charlotte. "Portraits of the *Artiste Manqué* by Three Women Novelists." *Frontiers* 5, no. 3 (1981): 57-59. Looking at several female depictions of artistes manqués, among them Davis's Hugh Wolfe in "Iron-Mills," notes the "insurmountable difficulties faced by women artists in a patriarchal society."

Harris, Sharon M. "Rebecca Harding Davis: A Continuing Misattribution." *LEGACY* 5, no. 1 (Spring 1988): 33-34. Reasserts Eppard's argument.

_____. "Rebecca Harding Davis: From Romanticism to Realism." *American Literary Realism* 21, no. 2 (1989): 4-20. Argues that "Iron-Mills" is "pure naturalism," asserting that its romantic and sentimental elements were meant as ironic critiques of prevailing attitudes.

_____. "Redefining the Feminine: Women and Work in Rebecca Harding Davis's 'In the Market.' " *LEGACY* 8 (1991): 118-21. Recovers little-known, strongly feminist story on the need for women to be economically independent.

Hesford, Walter. "Literary Contexts of 'Life in the Iron-Mills.' " *American Literature* 49 (1977-78): 70-85. Asserts that "Iron-Mills" is astonishing not as realism but as a new direction within the romance tradition.

Malpezzi, Frances E. "Sisters in Protest: Rebecca Harding Davis and Tillie Olsen." *RE: Artes Liberales* 12 (1986): 1-9. Compares "Iron-Mills" with *Yonnondio* to show that Davis "inspired theme and style" in Olsen's fiction.

Molyneaux, Maribel W. "Sculpture in the Iron Mills: Rebecca Harding Davis's Korl Woman." *Women's Studies* 17 (1990): 157-77. Demonstrates the thematic function of the korl woman as an image linking art and work for both Hugh Wolfe and Davis.

Pfaelzer, Jean. Introduction to "Marcia." *LEGACY* 4, no. 1 (1987): 3-5. Introduces a reprint of "Marcia," describing it as a "self-reflexive story about writing."

_____. "Rebecca Harding Davis: Domesticity, Social Order, and the Industrial Novel." *International Journal of Women's Studies* 4 (1981): 234-44. Focuses on "Iron-Mills" to demonstrate how Davis "portrayed the changed nature of women's role in industrial family life."

_____. "The Sentimental Promise and the Utopian Myth: Rebecca Harding Davis's 'The Harmonists' and Louisa May Alcott's 'Transcendental Wild Oats.' " *American Transcendental Quarterly*, n.s., 3 (1989): 85-99. Reveals both Davis's and Alcott's texts as female critiques of "patriarchal assumptions within the reformist tendencies of romanticism."

Rose, Jane Atteridge. "Images of Self: The Example of Rebecca Harding Davis and Charlotte Perkins Gilman." *English Language Notes* 29, no. 4 (1992): 70-78. Compares and contrasts autobiographical origins and texts of "The Wife's Story" and "The Yellow Wall-Paper."

Yellin, Jean Fagan. "The 'Feminization' of Rebecca Harding Davis." *American Literary History* 2, no. 2 (1990): 203-19. Analyzes the transformation of *Margret Howth* from its first "despairing" version to its final "affirmative" form, theorizing about the publishing pressures causing Davis to "feminize" her text.

Bibliography

Rose, Jane Atteridge. "A Bibliography of Fiction and Non-Fiction by Rebecca Harding Davis." *American Literary Realism* 22, no. 3 (Spring 1990): 67-86. A complete listing of Davis's writing presented chronologically and classified by genre.

Unpublished Dissertations

Grayburn, William Frazer. "The Major Fiction of Rebecca Harding Davis." Ph.D. dissertation, Pennsylvania State University, 1965. Assesses Davis's contribution to American literature, focusing on her major works, closely examining correspondence, and enlarging her bibliography.

Rose, Jane Atteridge. "The Fiction of Rebecca Harding Davis: A Palimpsest of Domestic Ideology beneath a Surface of Realism." Ph.D. dissertation, University of Georgia, 1988. Examines Davis's entire corpus within its cultural context, noting its mediation of realistic impulses and received domestic values.

Shaeffer, Helen Woodward. "Rebecca Harding Davis: Pioneer Realist." Ph.D. dissertation, University of Pennsylvania, 1947. The earliest scholarly assessment of Davis writing, containing information gathered from interviews with surviving relatives and neighbors in Wheeling and Washington. Also contains, however, some inaccurate suppositions later corrected in Grayburn, Langford, and Harris.

Index

The Author

Since 1989 Jane Atteridge Rose has been an assistant professor of English at Georgia College, where she teaches a variety of courses in American literature. Prior to then she taught at the University of Georgia, where she earned a Ph.D. in English.

Professor Rose has published articles on Rebecca Harding Davis in *American Literary Realism* (Spring 1990), *Conversations: Contemporary Critical Theory and the Teaching of Literature* (1990), *Writing the Female Artist* (1991), and *English Language Notes* (Spring 1992). She has also edited a reprint of Davis's *Silhouettes of American Life* (forthcoming 1993).

Her research interest continues to be the recovery of little-known American women writers. She is currently editing a collection of naturalistic stories by Lillie Chace Wyman, whose work is unknown to most students of American literature. She is also working on a reassessment of the feminist novels of Mary Johnston.